Second Edition

Brain-Based Teaching *With* Adolescent Learning *in Mind*

To Mother

Second Edition

Brain-Based Teaching *With* Adolescent Learning *in Mind*

Glenda Beamon Crawford

CORWIN PRESS
A SAGE Publications Company
Thousand Oaks, CA 91320

For information:

Corwin Press
A Sage Publications Company
2455 Teller Road
Thousand Oaks, California 91320
www.corwinpress.com

SAGE Publications India Pvt Ltd
B 1/I 1 Mohan Cooperative
Industrial Area
Mathura Road, New Delhi
India 110 044

Sage Publications Ltd.
1 Oliver's Yard
55 City Road
London EC1Y 1SP
United Kingdom

SAGE Publications Asia-Pacific Pte Ltd
33 Pekin Street #02-01
Far East Square
Singapore 048763

Printed in the United States of America.

Library of Congress Cataloging-in-Publication Data

Crawford, Glenda Beamon.
Brain-based teaching with adolescent learning in mind / Glenda Crawford. — 2nd ed.
p. cm.
Rev. ed of: Teaching with adolescent learning in mind. 2000.
Includes bibliographical references and index.
ISBN-13: 978-1-4129-5018-3 (cloth)
ISBN-13: 978-1-4129-5019-0 (pbk.)
1. High school teaching. 2. Learning, Psychology of. 3. Adolescent psychology.
I. Crawford, Glenda Beamon. Teaching with adolescent learning in mind. II. Title.

LB1607.B315 2007
373.1102—dc22 2006034137

This book is printed on acid-free paper.

07 08 09 10 11 10 9 8 7 6 5 4 3 2 1

Acquisitions Editor: Jean Ward
Editorial Assistant: Jordan Barbakow
Production Editor: Diane S. Foster
Copy Editor: Karen E. Taylor
Typesetter: C&M Digitals (P) Ltd.
Proofreader: Andrea Martin
Indexer: Molly Hall
Cover Designer: Monique Hahn
Graphic Designer: Karine Hovsepian

Contents

Preface

Much has been written about adolescence as a turbulent period characterized by contradiction and paradox. Normalcy seems far from normal as students' minds and bodies undergo change more rapid and remarkable than during any phase since infancy. Physical development is both pleasing and awkward; peer relationships can be inclusive or exclusive; and emerging intellects bring similar capacities for intense curiosity and abstract thinking, on the one hand, and self-consciousness and worry, on the other. Perhaps most perplexing in this developmental scenario is the unpredictability of adolescents' emotional judgment. Outside of classrooms, students confront pressure to engage, frequently under the duress of strong peer or gang influence, in self-destructive activities including shoplifting, drinking, drug use, self-injury, and physically risky behavior. Current research in the field of neuroscience, however, gives educators a better understanding of the development of the adolescent brain during the teen years, and this new knowledge has implications for classroom teaching.

This book addresses adolescent learning, curriculum design, and research-based instruction in the context of brain development. Written for preservice and practicing teachers of adolescents, and for teacher educators, it profiles adolescents as learners whose intellectual, emotional, and social needs must be at the center of teaching. The book further acknowledges the many differences that new-century adolescents bring to the classroom, including varying cultural backgrounds, levels of English language proficiency, background experiences and prior knowledge, and individual abilities and interests, and it addresses this challenge.

Brain-Based Teaching With Adolescent Learning in Mind introduces early, and develops with ongoing applications, key concepts related to adolescent learning, including metacognition, motivation, social cognition, and self-regulation. The content examples and scenarios focus on the elements of relevance: active learning, content depth, collaboration, inquiry, challenge, student ownership, ongoing assessment, and guided reflection. Consistently important throughout is the role of the teacher in planning for and guiding adolescents' learning, and their social, emotional, and intellectual development.

Teaching adolescents is both rewarding and challenging. An understanding of their brain development as it relates to their social, emotional, and intellectual needs is developed by knowing them as learners and as individual students and by making critical connections between long-standing and current theory and

Your Ideas

its implication for instruction. The book's purpose is to offer, through discussion and example, a conceptual and flexible framework on which daily instructional decisions can be made about content and pedagogy. The Adolescent-Centered Teaching (ACT) Models in each chapter illustrate this framework, and feature specific concepts developed within the chapters.

The format for each ACT Model encapsulates the following research-based instructional components, each of which promotes adolescent learning and metacognitive development.

- Content understanding, which involves an emphasis on the essential understandings of the discipline and pertinent state and national curricular standards
- Strategies for inquiry, which focus on adolescent motivation and challenge through intriguing and authentic events, problems, and questions
- Guided interaction, which promotes the teacher's role as active facilitator as students set up strategies for inquiry, proceed through the learning experiences, and become progressively self-directive
- Metacognitive development and assessment, during which adolescents are involved in evaluation, reflection, and the transfer of learning to comparable and extended experiences

Chapter 1 sets the context for the book through a discussion of the current findings in neuroscience research on the adolescent brain and the implications of these findings for learning and teaching. Adolescent brain development is characterized by emerging intellectual capacity for abstract and reflexive thinking. Less rapid and sophisticated growth in areas of the brain related to emotional regulation is also explained physiologically. Adolescent brain-based premises and developmentally responsive practices are aligned and the ACT Model is introduced.

Chapter 2 portrays adolescents of this generation as having outgrown the practices and boundaries of the traditional classroom. They are an age group connected by instant text and imaging messaging, Web pages, and "blogs"; yet many graduate without content understanding, lacking skills for intellectual engagement and problem solving, and with limited cognitive strategies for self-regulated learning. Getting and keeping adolescents' attention requires an interfacing of classroom experiences and their world of technological advancement.

Chapter 3 describes a brain-compatible, community-based learning environment that is responsive to adolescents' affective, cognitive, and social needs. Sustaining factors in this learning setting are emotional support, teacher and student dispositions, collaboration, learner autonomy and empowerment, and interpersonal connection. Multiple examples illustrate these interacting social, affective, and cognitive dimensions of an environment that is conducive to adolescent learning.

Chapter 4 develops the strategic role of the teacher in structuring thinking and inquiry. Current cognitive, social-cognitive, and social-emotional research informs processes of knowledge construction, mastery of content, thinking development, interpersonal relationships, and social interaction. A central premise is

Your Ideas

that adolescent learning is an active, emotional, and socially shared process of higher order knowledge building for understanding. The teacher becomes less directive as adolescents assume increasing responsibility for personal learning management. Specific instructional strategies that facilitate content integration, inquiry, and problem solving are illustrated, including problem-based learning, Web-based and other technology-enhanced projects and simulations, seminars, and cooperative learning.

Chapter 5 explores adolescent thinking and learning through curriculum design in the subject areas of mathematics, social studies, science, language arts, and the fine arts. Instructional practices that are conducive to learning transfer are examined. The book ends with strategies for promoting student transfer of learning to new contexts and practical guidelines for putting brain-based, adolescent-centered teaching into practice.

This book acknowledges the challenging circumstances in middle and high school classrooms. The pressures and expectations on teachers far exceed the time and energy of the most conscientious. The push for coverage and the direct assessment of information tend to restrain instruction to a mode that maximizes teacher delivery and minimizes student interaction. Many teachers of adolescents, however, persevere. Regardless of external demands and daily responsibilities, they remain undaunted in their efforts to structure developmentally responsive learning experiences. Recognizing adolescents' need for pertinence, they center instruction on relevant issues and reality-based problems. Noting adolescents' propensity to question and explore, they incorporate student-directed inquiry, interpretation, debate, and analysis. Understanding their desire for active and social involvement and technological access, they allow for local and global collaboration. In recognition of adolescents' need for stronger content in a knowledge-driven society, they teach more conceptually.

Brain-Based Teaching With Adolescent Learning in Mind is intended to support educators of adolescents in the practical daily pursuit of their ultimate goal: that their students will complete secondary education and carry with them a strong understanding of content, as well as the social and emotional skills for productivity and lifetime learning, and the intrinsic motivation for intellectual pursuit and societal contribution.

Acknowledgments

I owe deep appreciation to several individuals for supporting me in the publication of this revised edition.

To my students and colleagues who shared many outstanding adolescent-centered learning ideas. I celebrate their belief in the power of the adolescent mind.

To Jean Ward, former senior acquisitions editor at Corwin Press. Her friendship and continuing encouragement of my professional endeavors are sincerely appreciated.

To Karen Taylor, my copy editor at Corwin Press. Her friendliness and sense of humor made the editing stage less tedious.

To my sons, Michael and Brent, and "daughter" Dodi. They are my most spirited and faithful advocates.

To my mother, Polly, whose mind has been so keen, and in memory of my father, Claude. Their love for me has been steadfast.

To Larry, my husband, for his patience and understanding through the long hours of writing. Late night dinners were always served with a smile.

About the Author

Glenda Beamon Crawford's experience with young adolescent learners spans nearly 30 years. She has taught Grades 4 through 12, and currently coordinates the Middle Grades Education Program at Elon University, where she is a professor. She has written three books and published several articles on structuring classrooms for adolescent thinking and learning. Dr. Crawford consults and presents regularly at state, national, and international conferences. She has conducted professional development in Tajikistan and has taught in London and at Southeast University in the People's Republic of China. Her research and teaching honors include the 2002 North Carolina Award for Outstanding Contribution to Gifted Education and the 2004 Award for Outstanding Scholarship in the School of Education at Elon University.

CHAPTER

1

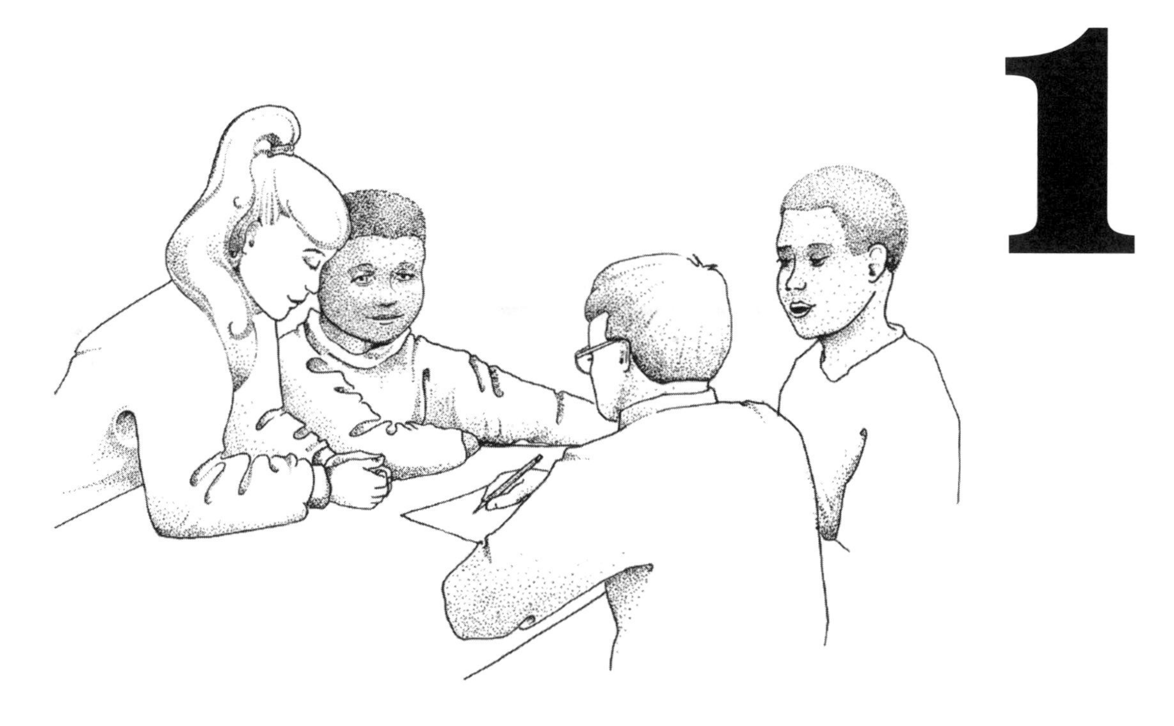

Understanding the Adolescent Learner

The Developing Brain

Danielle is taller than most of the boys in her class, awkward in her lanky frame, and feels certain everyone is looking at her *all of the time.* She loves her lime green flip phone and anything with sparkles and sequins, and has just finished reading *Girls in Pants: The Third Summer of the Sisterhood* (Brashares, 2005). She and her girlfriends consume fashion magazines and Internet celebrity gossip in envy of the slim models with perfect skin and intrigued by the edgy, sexy, life choices of the dangerous and famous. She takes dance lessons, plays goalie for the school soccer team, wishes she could sleep until noon . . . *every* day. Currently, Danielle is grounded for what her mother refers to as "impulsive and reckless behavior." Instead of going to the movies as planned, she and her friends decided to have their belly buttons pierced. It seemed like a sexy thing to do.

Danielle has mixed feelings about school. She enjoys her English class. The teacher puts the students in small groups to discuss books written about

Your Ideas

characters their age. Sometimes they are allowed to choose their own book for literature circle. On one hand, Danielle loves to write, and the teacher has encouraged her to write a short story during writer's workshop. On the other hand, Danielle dreads algebra class and its impersonal regimen. The teacher works through homework problems on the overhead, checks for correct answers, and assigns more. Danielle can work through the steps of a formula but cannot explain how or why it works. With word problems, getting the right response is generally "hit or miss," and she feels like a mathematics failure!

Danielle is the prototype of an adolescent. What she does not realize is that normalcy for this phase in her life is alternately defined by self-consciousness, self-absorption, impulsivity, confusion, worry, and the excitement of friends, fashion, fads, and new-found independence. Developmental changes surpass and override adolescents' ability to process, assimilate, and understand the significance of these changes. It's no wonder that Danielle resonates to the classroom where instruction is personalized, interactive, flexible, relevant, supportive, and adolescent centered.

THE NEED FOR ADOLESCENT-CENTERED TEACHING

Adolescents are likely the most developmentally varied group of learners in the education system. Danielle is a fairly typical middle class student, from a stable and supportive home environment, and yet her personal learning needs are distinctive. She and her diverse peers pose both a collective and differentiated range of issues as their adolescent brains, physiological development, and personal challenges overlap and impinge on their learning needs. Along with Danielle, the adolescent demographic includes the student who has never seen parents read a book; the student who speaks limited English, and whose family is even less fluent; the student whose mathematical acumen exceeds that of peers by three grade levels, yet has difficulty with penmanship; the student whose family does not have a computer, much less Internet access; the student who has to care for siblings in the evenings while both parents work; the student whose parents have predetermined that it's "Ivy League or bust"; the student grappling with racial or gender identity; and the student who lives on the street because teenage boys are not allowed in the homeless shelter where the rest of his family resides.

Adolescents embody an increasingly wide range of school diversity that includes social class, levels of language and literacy proficiency, learning abilities, racial and cultural backgrounds, past and current experiences, and interests. The host of diversity indicators is further confounded by the vast and uneven range of physical, intellectual, social, and emotional immaturities and maturities typical of adolescents (Tomlinson, 2005). While teachers have little control over the magnitude of factors that make adolescents uniquely who they are, they do have the power to make strategic decisions that affect their learning. Figure 1.1 displays a graphic of the personal, intellectual, and social dimensions of adolescent-centered teaching.

Figure 1.1 Adolescent-Centered Teaching

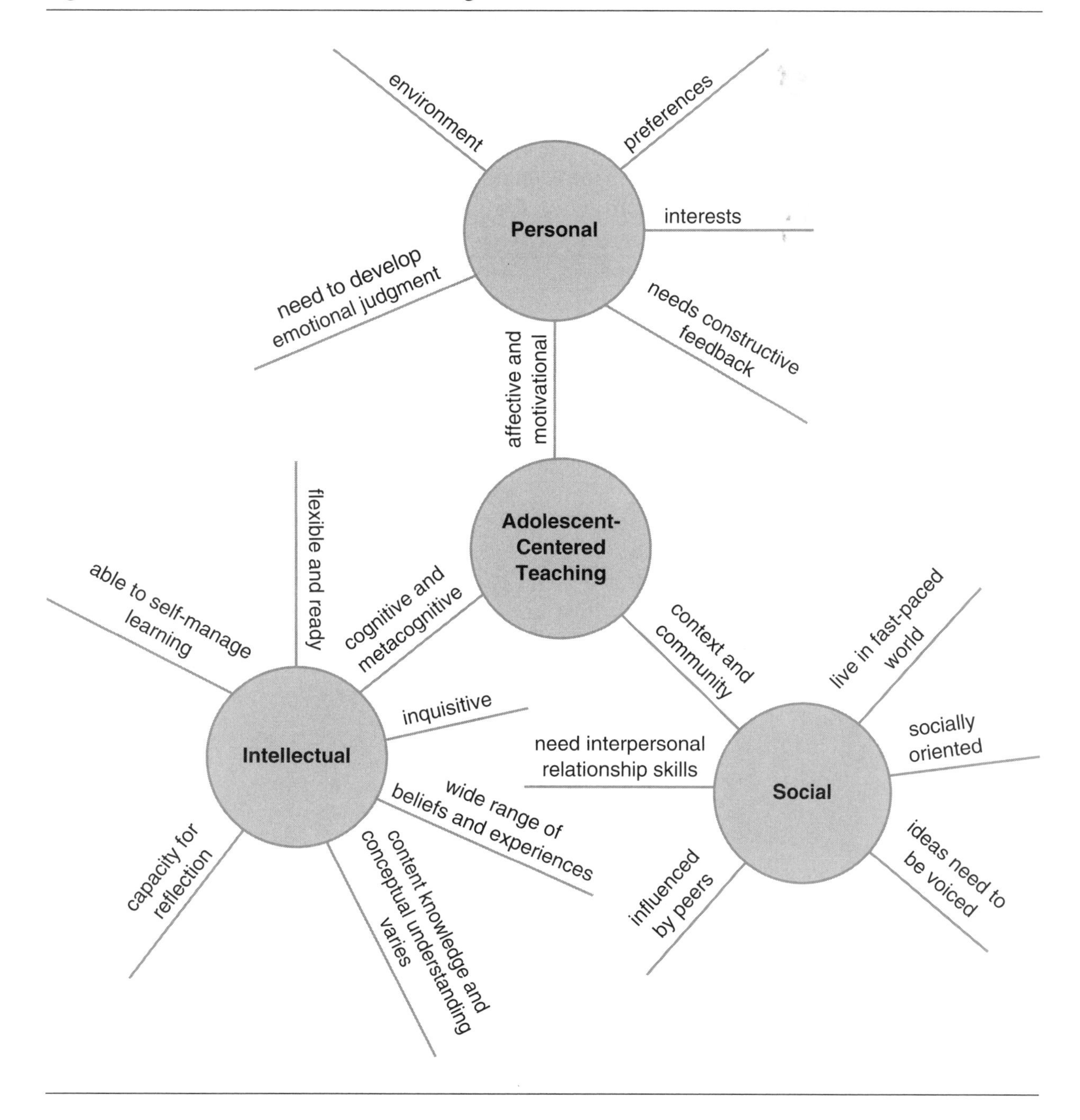

Regardless of the many diverse experiences and needs adolescents bring to the learning environment, they should *all* have the opportunity to learn and achieve. Teachers who teach with adolescent learning in mind do the following:

- Ask students about their personal strengths, preferences, and interests, and incorporate these into planning.
- Ask students about their backgrounds and make academic connections between academic content and their cultures.
- Find out what students know or remember and help them relate to new learning by building connections.

- Look for broad themes in the content to include a wider range of students' ideas.
- Help students make a bridge between subject matter and real life.
- Vary tasks to accommodate individual learning strengths and preferences.
- Structure groups that are flexible to validate interests and a range of learning abilities.
- Give assignments that differentiate for students' varying learning needs.
- Allow students to discuss, explore, wonder, and question.
- Listen, guide, encourage, expect, push, facilitate, and challenge.
- Celebrate adolescents' individuality by letting their thoughts be heard and their creativity flourish.
- Allow students to work, talk, and question together.
- Permit students to delve into and better understand content through direct, meaningful, and relevant involvement.
- Challenge students to use knowledge in a way that makes sense and a difference in their lives and in the lives of others in the community.
- Trust and guide students to make decisions about their learning.
- Respect and value adolescents' differences and help them become more competent and confident in personal learning management.
- Allow students to expand the horizons of learning to tap and interact with resources in the local and global communities.

ADOLESCENT LEARNING

Adolescents need to be understood as complex individuals who bring diverse perspectives to the learning context (McCombs & Whisler, 1997). Varied and random biological and environmental factors have affected how they feel about themselves and how they view school in general. They bring different prior knowledge, experiences, and preconceptions about how the world works (Bransford, Brown, & Cocking, 2000). Though all are capable of learning, none responds uniformly to one style of teaching, one curriculum, one mode of assessment, one cultural perspective, or one language. Sensitivity to their differences validates who they are and what they can contribute as learners. Figure 1.2 represents the varying adolescent perspective.

Understanding the adolescent as learner ultimately means knowing the conditions under which learning best occurs (Beamon, 2001; Lambert & McCombs, 1998). Learning is a natural, ongoing, and active process of constructing meaning from information and experience. It is an intuitive and universal human capacity that enables, from an early age, the mastery of symbolic systems such as language, music, and mathematics (Gardner, 1991). Learning is internally mediated, controlled primarily by the learner, and affected by personal motivation, perceptions, skills, and knowledge. It is an intellectual process highly influenced by social interaction, situational context, personal beliefs, dispositions, and emotions (Bransford et al., 2000; Vygotsky, 1978).

Adolescent learning occurs when students are able to make mental and emotional connections with what they already know, understand, or have personally experienced. Preconditions for adolescent learning are their motivation to put

Figure 1.2 The Adolescent Perspective

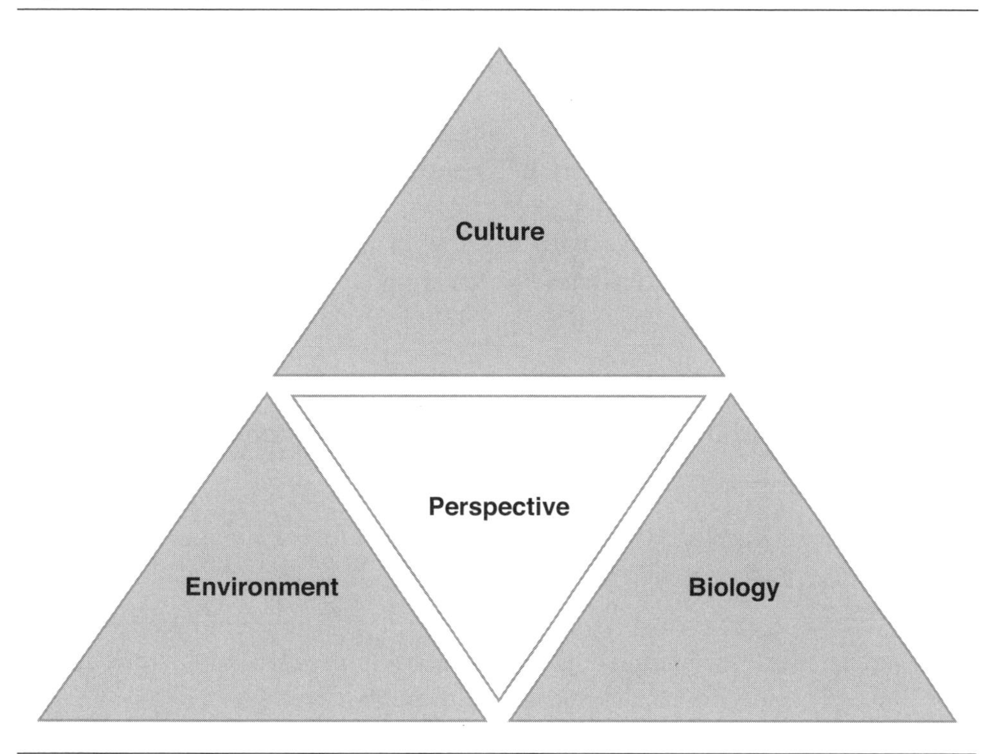

forth the necessary effort and time required and that they have the appropriate readiness level for these connections to happen. Adolescent learning involves active, interactive, purposeful, and meaningful engagement within a supportive context, including the assistance of others (Beamon, 2001; Perkins, 1992; Sizer, 1996; Vygotsky, 1978). It happens best under the following circumstances:

- Adolescents "do something" that makes sense in a larger context, such as confronting real-life issues and problems. For example, the complexity of citizens' rights is better understood when students follow legislative debates over gun control and discuss continuing problems of school violence.
- Their personal initiative and energy are moved into action through meaningful involvement with relevant and current content. For example, health issues take on new meaning when students conduct a research awareness campaign on the life-threatening impact of cigarette smoking and discuss the ethics of juvenile-targeted advertisement.
- Their cognitive and affective capabilities are challenged, such as when connections are made between difficult content and its application to personal experiences. For example, physics gains relevance when adolescents observe the movement of playground equipment at the neighborhood park.
- They can draw upon a variety of resources in the learning environment, including personal experience, the local community, and the Internet. For example, the principles of economics become less mysterious when classes enter into a collaborative enterprise with an area radio station to record and market a CD.

Your Ideas

- Their knowledge and understanding are substantively broadened or deepened. For example, neuroscience becomes less abstract when students use digital imagery to view the workings of the human brain.

Adolescent learning is a complex endeavor, yet current research is clear about the conditions that support it (Beamon, 2001; Bransford, Brown, & Cocking, 2000; Lambert & McCombs, 1998; McCombs & Whisler, 1997; Resnick, 1987, 1991, 1999). The box below provides a summary of several broad premises that facilitate adolescent learning.

Conditions That Support Adolescent Learning

Adolescents learn better when they . . .

- Encounter learning that is appropriate to their developmental level and is presented in multiple ways and in an enjoyable and interesting manner
- Are intellectually intrigued by tasks that are "authentic" and perceived as challenging, novel, and relevant to their own lives
- Receive teaching that is differentiated and culturally responsive
- Are allowed to share and discuss ideas and to work together on tasks, projects, and problems
- Are afforded multiple strategies to acquire, integrate, and interpret knowledge meaningfully; to demonstrate understanding; and to apply knowledge to new situations
- Are provided opportunities to develop and use strategic thinking skills, such as reasoning and problem solving
- Are given guidance and feedback about their work, yet are permitted to monitor personal progress and understanding
- Are in a safe, supportive environment where value is given to personal ideas and where negative emotions, such as fear of punishment and embarrassment, are minimized

ADOLESCENT LEARNING AND DEVELOPMENTAL TENDENCIES

Adolescence is a developmental period when students' minds and bodies undergo changes more rapid and remarkable than during any phase since infancy (Beamon, 1997). Bone structures grow and ossify as skin and muscles stretch to accommodate expanding body frames. A new social game has begun, and figuring out the rules determines who can play. Interaction within this new social arena becomes more enticing as sexual awareness and physical attraction escalate. Personal identity is precarious and tentative, a negotiation between perceptions of self-worth, peer acceptance, and competence. Emerging intellectual capacities open new dimensions of thinking as subtleties of humor become more apparent and abstract concepts such as environmental interdependence or ethical leadership begin to make sense.

Your Ideas

Psychologist Erik Erikson (1968) explained adolescence as a stage in human development, between middle childhood (6–10 years) and early adulthood (18–34 years), in which young people deal with the psychosocial crisis of defining who they are and where they are going in life. Adolescents are undergoing physical maturation, emotional and moral development, sexual awakenings, and social inclinations for group acceptance and inclusion. They face self-doubt, self-consciousness, and feelings of inferiority; they experiment and try on various roles, some negative; yet through positive guidance and support, they can develop a clearer, more congruent personal, sexual, and social identity.

Adolescence as a developmental time is also characterized by contradiction. Shifts in metabolism can make adolescents squirm in their desks, experience unpredictable bursts of energy, or become listless. In a time when their growing bodies require more sleep, their personal interests expand exponentially through involvement with social events, dating, sports, and other extracurricular activities. Highly desired social relationships can bring disappointment and disillusionment as peer groups shape and include, and reconfigure and exclude. The flip side of heightened intellectual development is awareness that takes various forms: worry about personal appearance, self-consciousness in social situations, confusion associated with puberty, and perplexity over self-identity. It is no wonder that the time of adolescence has been popularized by the term "the roller-coaster years" (Giannetti & Sararese, 1977).

ADOLESCENT LEARNING AND PERSONAL DEVELOPMENT

On a personal level, adolescents need to feel cared about and connected, to be creative and joyful, to have a sense of purpose, and to believe they can exceed the expectations of others (Kessler, 2000). The personal dimension of adolescent learning encompasses these complex and individualized needs, beliefs, and emotions. Adolescents' perceptions about personal ability and effectiveness impact their level of motivation and persistence with new learning tasks. Certain favorable mental "attitudes," such as open-mindedness, tolerance, empathy, and intellectual curiosity, help adolescent thinking to expand and develop at a higher cognitive level. Their learning is enhanced when individual differences are acknowledged, respected, and accommodated; when students are motivated through challenge, relevance, choice, and a sense of accomplishment; and when they feel comfortable to express, create, explore, experiment, take risks, and make mistakes.

Adolescents are more likely to take the risk involved in letting others know what they are thinking, however, when they feel accepted, valued, respected, and supported individually. They need to feel that they belong in the classroom community and to develop a sense of empowerment over their own learning

Your Ideas

management. They are more motivated to learn when they can interact socially and when they are given responsibility (McCombs & Whisler, 1997; Ryan, 1995; Strong, Silver, & Robinson, 1995).

ADOLESCENT LEARNING AND SOCIAL DEVELOPMENT

Adolescents' social and emotional well-being is closely linked to what they believe about other people's perceptions. Adolescents are inclined to be more conscious of the opinions of those around them, especially the opinions of their peers. Elkind (1981) referred to the tendency to be preoccupied with what others think as the "imaginary audience" phenomenon. Many adolescents believe that, in social situations, all attention is focused on them. As a consequence, they may be overly sensitive. They may react emotionally to kidding, for example, and often hold on to personal feelings of anger or embarrassment. Although students become more socially oriented during the period of adolescence, their perspectives remain predominantly "me centered" and limited.

Attention to adolescents' social propensity is important for other reasons. First, this age group needs to be encouraged to develop intellectually and ethically. Adolescence is a formative, tentative, and pivotal time when young people are contemplating significant personal and societal issues. Their ideas may be somewhat confused or misconceived, ill structured or unrefined, yet they need to feel that their contribution in a discussion matters to the teacher (Sizer & Sizer, 1999). They should thus be encouraged to share personal perspectives through persuasive writing, interpretive discussion, and creative approaches; to examine their assumptions through opportunities to express, question, and test original ideas; to consider alternatives through debating, role playing, problem solving, or other "encounters" with differing viewpoints, approaches, or solutions; and to think critically about personal decisions and actions by specifying the consequences in a simulated or real context.

ADOLESCENT LEARNING AND INTELLECTUAL DEVELOPMENT

The intellectual dimension centers on adolescents' cognitive readiness for complexity, reflection, and self-regulated learning. This capacity is affected by varying content knowledge, background experiences, and thinking capacities. Adolescents are prepared to consider more sophisticated content as they build personal knowledge and further understanding. They are intellectually eager to tackle relevant problems, to discuss pertinent topics, to share viewpoints, and to talk about ethical choices that have implications for their actions. They are ready to use expanding capacities for reasoning and conceptual thinking and to reflect upon their own thoughts and feelings. They are also capable of becoming more responsible and competent in learning management.

Perhaps the cognitive development of adolescents can best be understood through contemporary insight into how they experience learning. Their minds

Your Ideas

are continually active and flexible. Since an early age, they have gathered knowledge, organized information, and solved problems in an effort to make sense of what was occurring in their lives (Bransford, Brown, & Cocking, 1999, 2000). Though not as stage discrete and age bound as Piaget (1928) originally proposed, adolescent cognitive development can be viewed as a progression of knowledge acquisition that has been, and continues to be, shaped through interaction with others and with the environment.

Adolescents have the capacity to reason and think abstractly about knowledge that is familiar or meaningful to them, yet when ideas are new or disconnected to what they know, their thinking appears somewhat concrete. Since they have had the opportunity to acquire more knowledge in general than younger students, they deal more successfully with hypothetical situations. They explain their reasoning better and can recognize more readily instances of illogical thinking (Ormond, 2000). Adolescents also tend to show an increasing capability to focus their attention over a longer period of time. They more quickly integrate new information with what they have previously learned, and they are more skilled at drawing relationships among concepts and ideas (Flavell, 1985). Schurr (1989, p. 23) has identified several intellectual content-related capacities of the adolescent. These cognitive capabilities and their implication for adolescent learning are outlined in Table 1.1.

Table 1.1 Cognitive Capabilities and Implication

Intellectual Capacities	*Instructional Implication*
Appreciation for mathematical logic	Complex problems that invite reasoning and alternate approaches Opportunity to explain logic
Analysis of political ideology	Comparative analysis and critique of varying government systems or cultures
Understanding of the nuances of poetic metaphor and musical notation	Interpretive analyses of literary works in which meaning is not readily explicit
Interpretation of symbols, concepts, themes, sayings, and generalizations	An emphasis on broad, abstract ideas and their implication vs. less significant facts
Propositional thinking and deductive reasoning	Opportunities to generate hypotheses, test assumptions, reason through findings, and generate solutions to problems or problem situations

THE INTERRELATEDNESS OF MORAL DEVELOPMENT

The ability of adolescents to make ethical determinations is linked to developing intellectual and personal skills for moral reasoning (Stevenson, 2002).

Your Ideas

The early work of stage theorist Lawrence Kolberg (1981, 1983), augmented by that of Gilligan (1982) and Lickona (1983), explains adolescent moral development in terms of a progression from interpersonal conformity (social approval and self-esteem) to a sense of personal responsibility within the broader social system (Lickona, 1983). The "enterprise of moral growth," according to Stevenson (2002, p. 103), is the healthy exchange of ideas, questions, and differing perspectives or points of view about ethical issues, particularly those that exist in the students' contemporary lives: cheating; honesty; fairness; bullying; drug, tobacco, and alcohol use; sex; juvenile crime; caring for those less fortunate; treatment of the environment; and respect for individual differences, to name a few. Information about a few topics of particular concern for adolescents can be accessed through the following Web sites:

American Psychological Association: Children, Youth and Families
(http://www.apa.org/pi/cyf/homepage.html)

Encyclopedia of Psychology: Adolescent Psychology Resources
(http://www.psychology.org/links/Environment_Behavior_Relationships/Adolescent/)

University of Nebraska–Lincoln: Extension Publications on Adolescence and Youth
(http://www.ianrpubs.unl.edu/epublic/pages/index.jsp?what=subjectAreasD&subjectAreasId=12)

Women's Health Channel: Teen Pregnancy
(http://www.womenshealthchannel.com/teenpregnancy/index.shtml)

Visions Adolescent Treatment Center: Teen Substance Abuse
(http://www.visionsteen.com/articles.html)

Gender Issues Research Center
(http://www.gendercenter.org/)

Advocates for Youth
(http://www.advocatesforyouth.org/index.htm)

A benefit of healthy moral development in adolescents is that they will be able to conceptualize moral and ethical dilemmas and take action to rectify social injustices and improve society. The adolescent classroom provides a prime opportunity for students to grapple with moral issues, to learn cooperation roles and strategies, and to mediate interpersonal differences (Stevenson, 2002). Cooperative learning structures, debates, literature circles, problem-based learning, service projects, apprenticeships, and internships are instructional avenues through which adolescents can delve into ethical issues, work together to solve common problems, and make a contribution to the school and local community.

The literature on learning and learner-centered practice confirms that many personal, intellectual, and social variables interact within the classroom setting and affect adolescent learning (Beamon, 2001; Bransford, Brown, &

Table 1.2 Adolescent Developmental Tendencies and Implications for Learning

Adolescent Developmental Tendencies	*Implications for Learning*
Personal	**Learning Needs**
Anxious for developmental normality	Climate of acceptance, tolerance
Easily angered, slow to recover	Emotional safety, guidance
Push for independence, autonomy	Choice, responsibility, accountability
Easily discouraged if do not achieve	Appropriate challenge, relative success
Intellectual	**Learning Needs**
Have diverse knowledge, interests, abilities	Opportunities to develop range of skill and to pursue variety of content areas
Can see relationships among similar concepts, ideas, and experiences	Complex subject matter, relevant issues
Capable of inferential thinking, reasoning	Higher-level, analytical questioning
Capable of critical evaluation, extended focus	Time and opportunity for critical thinking
Reflective, metacognitive, self-motivated	Self-evaluation, choice
Social	**Learning Needs**
Can be indifferent to adult figures	Opportunity to interact with knowledgeable adults in collaborative projects
Concerned about self-presentation to peers	Emphasis on cooperation, inclusiveness, group contribution
Strive to conform for peer acceptance	Structured, positive student interaction

Cocking, 1999, 2000; Lambert & McCombs, 1998). The broad principles that support an adolescent-centered perspective represent a synthesis of research and theory on teaching and learning (see Table 1.2 above).

ADOLESCENT LEARNING AND THE DEVELOPING BRAIN

Bransford, Brown, & Cocking, (2000), in *How People Learn: Brain, Mind, Experience, and School,* review key findings in the neuroscience and cognitive sciences related to human learning. The authors draw three main conclusions:

1. Learning changes the physical structure of the brain.
2. These structural changes alter the functional organization of the brain; in other words, learning organizes and reorganizes the brain.
3. Different parts of the brain may be ready to learn at different times. (p. 115)

These research-based findings are increasingly pertinent when applied to adolescent development, behavior, and learning (Casey, Giedd, & Thomas, 2000;

Your Ideas

Spinks, 2002). What neuroscientists have discovered through powerful brain-scanning devices is that the post-puberty brain is still developing and evolving. Strauch (2003), author of *The Primal Teen: What the New Discoveries About the Teenage Brain Tell Us About Our Kids*, explains the discovery in this way:

> The teenage brain, it's now becoming clear, is still very much a work in progress, a giant construction project. Millions of connections are being hooked up; millions more are swept away. Neurochemicals wash over the teenage brain, giving it a new paint job, a new look, a new chance at life. The teenage brain is raw, vulnerable. It's a brain that's still becoming what it will be. (p. 8)

SCANNED EXUBERANCE

The neurological research documents rapid brain change in another stage of life other than the first three years. During this second growth spurt, which occurs around puberty, the adolescent brain overproduces both neuronal cells and the synapses that connect them. Neuroscientists refer to this overproduction, which occurs particularly in the frontal lobes, as *exuberance* (Strauch, 2003). Gray matter in the cerebral cortex, the outer area of the brain associated with reasoning, impulse control, and language specialization, thickens "as tiny branches [dendrites] of brain cells bloom madly . . ." (p. 15). It appears that this region of the adolescent brain is the last to mature and does not fully develop until early adulthood.

Sophisticated brain imaging has yielded an additional discovery with relevance to adolescent learning. Between the ages of thirteen and fifteen and following the phase of overproduction, or exuberance, is a "pruning back" phase when a small percentage of synaptic connections are actually lost. Neuroscientist Jay Giedd, in an interview for Frontline's *Inside the Teenage Brain* (Spinks, 2002), noted that "there is a fierce, competitive elimination, in which brain cells and connections fight it out for survival" (p. 2). Referred to as brain sculpting, this finding suggests that adolescent brains go through a period of circuit refinement when synapses that are more frequently activated are strengthened at the expense of those less used (Wilson & Horch, 2002). Brain maturation thus involves a "fine tuning" of neural connections as the brain consolidates, focuses, and prepares for the adult years. Interestingly, during this process some mental capabilities are lost, including the ability to learn a foreign language without an accent (Strauch, 2003).

Important to educators and parents is the implication that the experiences in which adolescents are involved can play a role in determining which neural structures survive (Spinks, 2002). What adolescents do in their social, personal, and academic experiences as they explore and shape identities factors into the brain's maturation process. Those who engage actively in music, sports, or academics, for example, potentially strengthen and sustain synaptic connections in the associated brain areas. An associated and cruel irony, however, is that the maturing teen brain is highly susceptible to drug, alcohol, and nutrition abuse during a time when experimentation, need for social acceptance, and personal perceptions of infallibility are developmentally characteristic. These functional changes in the adolescent brain carry both potential and risk.

Your Ideas

INSIDE THE ADOLESCENT BRAIN

Just under three pounds, the adolescent brain is a complex organ, best understood by its varying parts and their distinctive and interacting functions. The cerebrum, its largest region, covers 85% or five-sixths of the entire brain and is the seat of thinking, learning, and language specialization (Sylwester, 2004; Wolfe, 2001). Covering the cerebrum is an orange-peel-thick layer of tissue, the cerebral cortex, that wrinkles and folds over its surface. The cerebral cortex, often called the gray matter of the brain, is divided into the left and right hemispheres. Information is relayed between the hemispheres by a fiber system called the corpus callosum. The corpus callosum, believed to influence language learning, creativity, problem solving, and associative thinking, is the site of rapid growth spurts before and during puberty (Thompson, Giedd, & Woods, 2000). Figure 1.3 shows the brain's anatomy.

Figure 1.3 The Brain's Anatomy

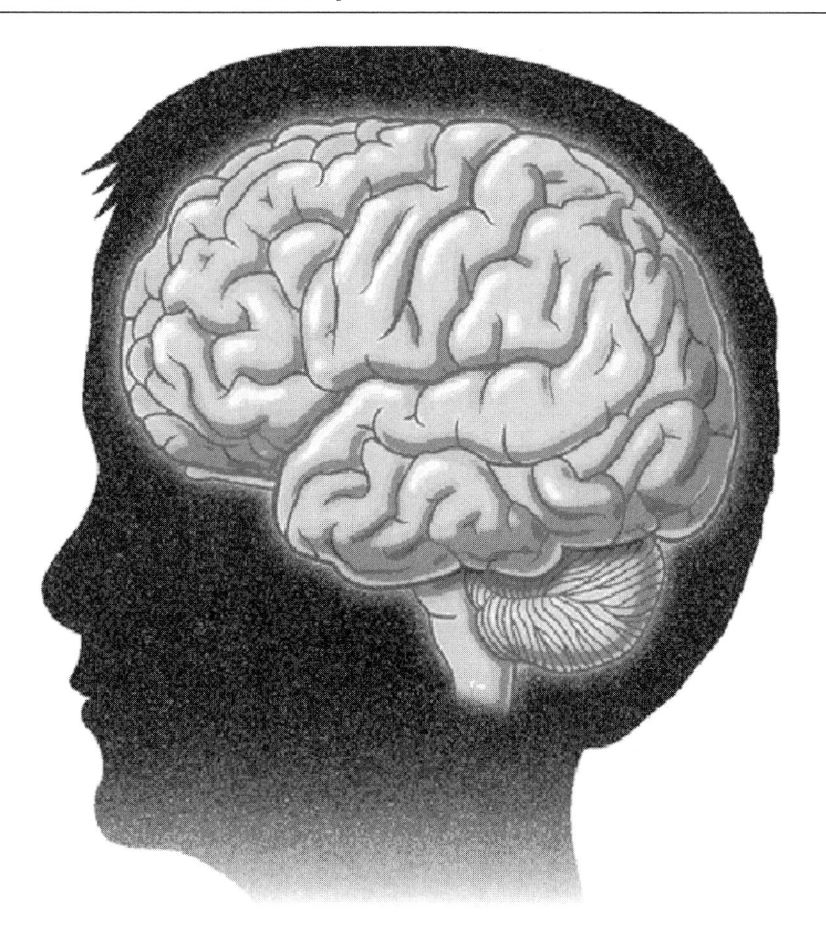

SOURCE: Scientific Learning. (1999). Head 4: Lateral view of the brain against a human profile. *Brain Connection*. Retrieved October 18, 2006, from http://www.brainconnection.com

Your Ideas

The cerebral cortex is further divided into four areas, called lobes, each with a different function (Jensen, 2000; Sylwester, 2006; Wolfe, 2001). The occipital lobe at the central back of the brain, for example, processes incoming visual stimuli; the temporal lobe, located just above the ears, processes auditory data. Located at the top of the brain, the plate-like parietal lobe helps with spatial awareness and orientation. The largest and most highly developed section of the cerebral cortex, the frontal lobe, renders the capacity for metacognition, reflection, problem solving, planning, attention focusing, and emotional self-regulation. The frontal lobe, or prefrontal cortex, is another site of rapid growth and functional change during adolescence (Casey, Giedd, & Thomas, 2000; Strauch, 2003).

Brain growth in the prefrontal cortex is associated with adolescents' development of executive functioning, or the ability to plan and organize thinking, use reason, access working memory, engage in risk assessment, moderate emotions, and reflect on personal strengths and weaknesses (Caine, Caine, McClintic, & Klimek, 2005). While adolescents eventually become capable of executive functioning, it does not happen instantaneously. What remains "under construction," to the dismay of teachers and parents, is the adolescent brain's ability to resist impulses, to control emotions, to think out decisions, and to plan ahead (Strauch, 2003).

Two other regions of interest in the adolescent brain are the cerebellum and the midbrain. A small area located above the brain stem, the cerebellum is responsible for balance, posture, muscle coordination, and physical movement (Jensen, 2000; Sylwester, 2006). Recent brain research, however, associates the cerebellum with more cognitive functions, including the coordination of thinking processes (Wilson & Horch, 2002). Neuroscientists have further speculated that growth in the cerebellum during adolescence is not genetically controlled and thus susceptible to environmental influence. The traditional classroom where adolescents are expected to passively memorize discrete, minimally relevant information is not an environment that facilitates cognitive development. The implication for educators is to create learning experiences whereby adolescents can engage, participate, interact, and reflect in order to become *managers* of their own thinking.

The midbrain, or limbic system, is linked to emotional processing, hormones, sexuality, body regulation, and the production of body chemicals (Jensen, 2000; Sylwester, 2006; Wolfe, 2001). This section includes the hippocampus, thalamus, hypothalamus, and amygdala. Neurological growth and changes in the midbrain, particularly the development of the amygdala and hippocampus as related to adolescents' emotional management, are discussed later in the chapter.

Another interesting anatomical phenomenon is that the brain, adolescent or adult, is approximately three-fourths water (Jensen, 2000). The brain's energy source is blood; however, for optimal functioning, it needs eight to ten glasses of water a day for electrolytic balance. Brain dehydration leads to lethargy and impaired learning, an occurrence that has led many schools to supply adolescents with water during the day and to tout water as a key component of good nutrition.

SIZZLING SYNAPSES

Your Ideas

When one teacher told her eighth graders that she wanted to hear their "synapses sizzling," she was serious! On a cellular level, the adolescent brain is composed of 30 billion intricate nerve cells, or neurons, that connect with trillions of nerve endings, or dendrites, in an elaborate information processing system (Beamon, 1997). Long nerve fibers, or axons, extend from the cell body and serve as transmitters of chemical signals that are picked up by neighboring neurons. The tiny connective pathway between the axon and the dendrites of a nearby neuron is called a synapse. The more often a synapse occurs, the more easily it can operate. An increase in the speed of synaptic activity enables adolescents to process information and make connections between previous and current learning more readily. Hence, the eighth grade teacher's charge to her thirteen-year-olds! Figure 1.4 is a visual of synaptic activity.

Figure 1.4 Synaptic Activity in the Brain

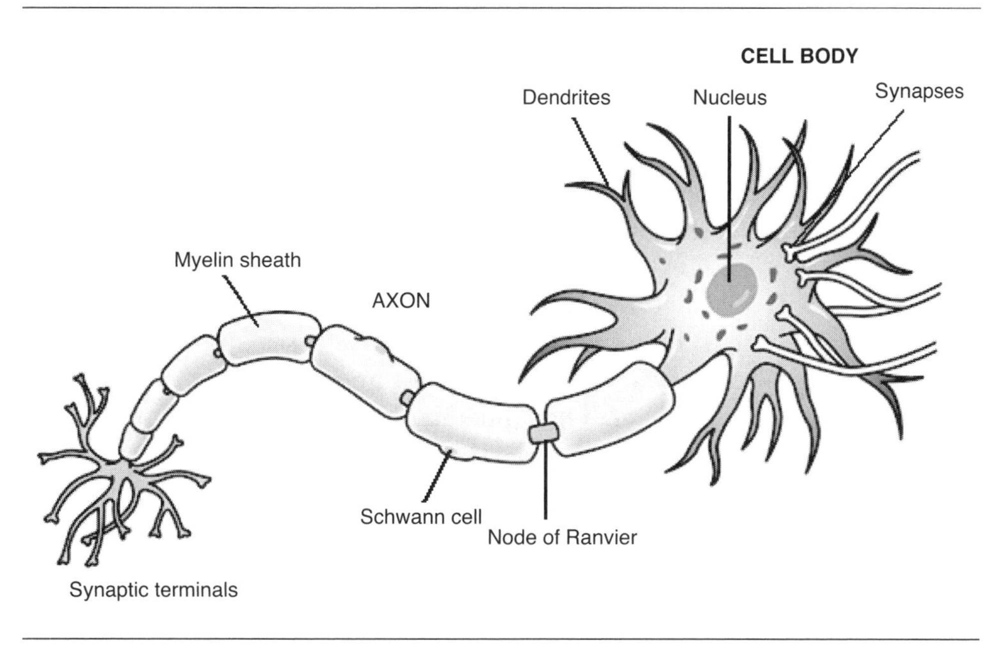

SOURCE: Scientific Learning Corporation. (1999). A myelinated neuron. *Brain Connection.* Retrieved October 18, 2006, from http://www.brainconnection.com

Adolescents' brains are dynamic organs where synapses have been developing since birth as a result of new experiences, impressions, and knowledge accumulation. The number of synaptic connections is believed to be a measure of the complexity of neuron circuitry, or the brain's ability to communicate among its various parts (Wilson & Horch, 2002). As brain schemata form, change, and alter, a white fatty tissue, called myelin, forms around the axons to stabilize and strengthen them. This myelin sheath aids in the transmission of information between neurons and between brain regions, thus facilitating more integrated brain functioning. During adolescence, changes and growth in

Your Ideas

synaptic connections and myelin formation are more dramatic than any time since infancy (Strauch, 2003).

THE BRAIN AND THE INTELLECT

The neurological growth and change observed in the adolescent brain closely parallel documented cognitive development. Once thought of as a period when students' brains were intellectually "arrested" with attention diverted to social and personal concerns, adolescence is clearly a time of rapid and significant intellectual change (Beamon, 1997). Adolescents display a wide range of cognitive ability as they transition from concrete to abstract thinking. They develop the capacity for propositional and hypothetical thinking, deductive reasoning and logic, generalizing, insight and nuance, symbolic interpretation and analysis, and futuristic planning (Lorain, 2002). They also acquire the capacity for metacognition, which enables them to monitor and regulate their own thinking processes.

Cognitive development unleashes in adolescents an intense curiosity and need to know about what interests or fascinates them, and, in many instances, this fascination lies with science fiction, fantasy, mystery, or the macabre (Beamon, 1997; Van Hoose, Strahan, & L'Esperance, 2001). Adolescent intellectual development assumes a continuum of increasing competence in thinking and in emotional management. Interestingly, this development parallels brain functioning development, particularly to related changes in the prefrontal cortex.

Intellectual development additionally brings with it a series of paradoxes that might be related to brain maturation. Adolescents seek peer acceptance, yet are self-conscious of their own awkwardness and perceived shortcomings. They are forming values, yet are often judgmental and hold fast to a strict code of right and wrong. Emerging metacognitive ability brings the unpleasant emotions of worry and self-doubt. Since adolescents lack the knowledge that adults gain through time and experience, they may struggle to put emotions and concerns into perspective.

MIRROR NEURONS AND COGNITIVE AUTONOMY

Well-known authority on brain science Robert Sylwester (2006) explains the brain's maturation during late childhood and early adolescence ("the tween brain") as a progression from "childhood acceptance of dependence" to "an adolescent reach for independence" (p. 1). As the frontal lobe matures during the preteen years, thinking and actions shift from reactive to proactive thinking and behavior. When they were young children, adolescents depended on adults to make executive decisions—what to wear, where to live, what to order to eat from a menu, when to go to bed. With maturation in the frontal cortex, however, young adolescents begin to expect to make their own decisions and solve their own problems. With this cognitive shift, young adolescents crave exploration, peer interaction, and personal autonomy. Though tentative and immature, the competence in the cognitive capacity for self-regulation happens through experience and experimentation.

Your Ideas

Sylwester (2006) explains the impact of families' early mentoring on children's brain development through the recently discovered mirror neuron system. Citing the work of the renowned neuroscientist, V. S. Ramachandran (2006), Sylwester describes the acquisition of language, human movement, and even emotions through the activation of mirror neurons that mimic or reciprocate through the senses. Through the brain's highly interconnected processing systems, mirror neurons simulate both actions and their related properties, such as pain or pleasure. By observing the facial expressions and body language of others, for example, young people begin to develop the cognitive abilities for empathy. These emerging neurobiological discoveries are important in the early years as caretakers nurture children's development. As young adolescents begin to pull away from the immediate influence of family, the mirror neuron system is responsive, and perhaps vulnerable, to human behavior in society—as represented, for example, in the media and in classrooms—because the brain continues to mature.

EMOTIONAL (IM)MATURITY OR "JUST BEING DIFFICULT"

Why did Danielle and her friends decide, on a whim, to have their belly buttons pierced rather than to go to a movie as planned? For years, the erratic, unpredictable behaviors of adolescents have been dismissed as the by-product of an oversupply of hormones. Certainly, hormones rage during this time of development. However, brain research is beginning to shed some light on why teens make impulsive decisions or act out in reckless ways. Strauch (2003) raises this question: "Why do normal, well-behaved teenagers start pouting in their rooms, sneaking out windows, stomping their feet, or making LSD in the school science lab?" (p. 7). It may be that the area of the brain associated with impulse control and self-regulation is still undergoing change. As Strauch humorously writes, "The teenage brain may, in fact, be briefly insane. But, scientists say, it is crazy by design. The teenage brain is in flux, maddening and muddled. And that's how it's supposed to be" (p. 8).

Although neuroscientists are wary of drawing any direct relationship between brain functioning and teen behavior, they do speculate that brain development may explain why adolescents at times have trouble regulating their emotional responses (Thompson et al., 2000). The area of the brain associated with emotional reaction, as opposed to reasoned response, is the amygdala, two almond-shaped structures located in the center of the midbrain near the thalamus and hypothalamus (Wolfe, 2001). Brain scans have revealed that, in responding to emotion-inducing situations, adolescents rely less on the executive or regulating function of the prefrontal cortex and more on the gut responses associated with the midbrain's amygdala. As teens grow older, however, the brain activity shifts to the frontal lobe, and emotional responses are more reasoned and justifiable.

Your Ideas

The emotional turmoil associated with adolescence has less to do with raging hormones than with the "complex interplay of body chemistry, brain development, and cognitive development" (Price, 2005, p. 22). Adolescents' underdeveloped prefrontal cortex is associated with an inability to regulate and refrain from certain behaviors. Not thinking of consequences for potentially harmful decisions and actions, adolescents are more prone to sensation seeking or risky behavior that includes sexual engagement, cigarette smoking, and substance use (Caine, Caine, McClintic, & Klimek, 2005). Even a cognitive awareness of the associated dangers of thrill-seeking behavior does not appear to control adolescents' impulsive actions. With reasonable support and structure by parents and teachers, however, teens can develop the skills for responsible decision making and personal management.

CAUTIONS AND IMPLICATIONS FOR CLASSROOM PRACTICE

Neuroscientists and educators who write about brain-compatible instruction (Beamon, 1997; Brandt, 1998; Caine, Caine, McClintic, & Klimek, 2005; Jensen, 2000; Sousa, 2001; Sylwester, 2003, 2004; Wolfe, 2001) caution against a simplistic interpretation of the emerging brain research as related to classroom practice. The field of neuroscience is far too emergent for causal relationships to be drawn among brain anatomy, cognitive development, and behavior. Adolescents' new intellectual capacities for abstract thinking and abstraction cannot, for example, be equated simply with functional changes in the frontal cortex nor can teenagers' impulsive social behaviors be explained away as mere delay in brain growth.

The brain is too complex a system, and much research is needed before neuroscientists and educators can attempt to understand the interrelationship of brain, individual, others, and the environment. As Wolfe (2001) projects,

> During the past three decades we've learned more about the brain than in all of recorded history, but there is so much to learn. As exciting as the new developments in neuroscience are, the dialogue that has begun between neuroscientists, cognitive scientists, and educators is even more exciting. (p. 191)

With that stated, there is general agreement that brain research can inform classroom methodology as teachers create experiences compatible to student learning. While Wolfe (2001) acknowledges that neuroscience cannot prove that a particular instructional strategy works, she proffers that understanding how the brain learns is "an essential element in the foundation on which we should base our educational decisions" (p. 191).

Wilson and Horch (2002) suggest that, given "the activity in the prefrontal cortex where memory, attention and inhibition [elimination of distracters] are altered as a result of synaptic pruning, certain strategies and methods seem feasible to apply to classroom instruction" (p. 2). These educators and others have bridged a connection between research and application with an emphasis on

Your Ideas

techniques for better memory storage, focusing and holding attention, sensorimotor engagement, relevance and authenticity, challenge, collaborative inquiry, and metacognitive reflection (Davis, 2001; Kolb, 2000; Wilson, 2001; Wilson & Horch, 2002).

Several broad premises generate from the brain research and professional literature, premises that are developmentally responsive for adolescents and have implications for curriculum design, methodology, and the management of the learning environment. These are ordered in relation to the brain's response or receptive capabilities and the role of emotions (input) to the brain's ability to process, connect, and learn (output).

1. The adolescent brain is active, dynamic, and malleable

The brain actively processes new information by seeking connections with what it knows or has experienced. The brain is a pattern seeker that continually attempts to cluster and organize incoming information into previously formed synaptic structures (Caine, Caine, McClintic, & Klimek, 2005; Sylwester, 2003). This new information is sorted by meaningfulness and perceived relevance to earlier learning or personal experiences, and, if these are limited or lacking, the brain is likewise limited in its ability to file the information into its memory system. A child makes no meaning out of a letter in the alphabet, for example, without an existing perception of what a letter is. With ongoing development of neural structures, an individual views letters as words with meaning, and, as happens during adolescence, a more complex ability for interpretive analysis emerges (Wolfe, 2001).

The active and dynamic nature of the brain enables adolescents to construct and reconstruct knowledge as they interact within their learning environment. They respond to cognitively engaging lessons that help them relate to, analyze, and apply new information to the world around them (Beamon, 1997; Caine & Caine, 1997). Active and meaningful learning experiences challenge the brain's growing cognitive capacity. When the adolescent brain is actively engaged with new information, such as through questioning, discussion, problem solving, small group activities, processing, and application, cognitive connections are reinforced, and new learning has more potential of moving into long-term memory (Wolfe, 2001).

Also pertinent to the time of adolescence is the research in neuroscience related to the brain's malleability. Once thought to be fairly "set" at a young age, the brain is now understood to be incredibly "plastic" in its response to experiences and the environment (Diamond, 1967). Within an enriched environment, the brain can literally grow new and increasingly complex synaptic connections. Jensen (2000) identifies the challenge enhanced by variety and novelty and feedback as conditions of an enriched and stimulating learning environment. That the adolescent brain is receptive to environmental context and interaction places great responsibility on the teacher in the design and delivery of instruction. As one neuroscientist indicates, educators need to pay attention to the conditions that enhance plasticity in order to optimize the brain's ability to learn (Giedd, as cited in Spinks, 2002). Inquiry-based instruction, such as problem-based learning or other complex, problem-solving tasks,

Your Ideas

engages adolescent thinking and increases neural pathways. Feedback through peer editing and group interaction, for example, is effective, although it needs to be timely and specific for the brain to incorporate it into its physiology.

2. The adolescent brain responds to emotional arousal

Wolfe (2001) notes that emotion is a primary catalyst in the learning process. Emotion can be likened to a biological thermostat that alerts the brain and body to something in the environment that warrants attention. In response, the amygdala, located deep within each hemisphere, starts a chain of physiological responses that determine the emotional relevance of an experience. Is it harmful or something I'll like? Should I engage or should I withdraw? Approximately a quarter of a second later, the incoming information goes from the thalamus to the prefrontal cortex, which provides a more rational response. This attention focus leads to memory recall—Have I confronted this before?—and to various stored problem-solving and response actions.

Unlike feelings, which are conscious expressions, emotions are beneath the conscious and deeply rooted in memory, and emotional response can impede or enhance classroom learning. "The brain is programmed to attend first to information that has strong emotional content" (Wolfe, 2001, p. 88). Whether the brain determines that information signals a potential danger or not, emotions capture attention and "get a privileged treatment in our brain's memory system" (p. 108). In situations where the brain perceives threat, such as instances of humiliation, embarrassment, or physical harm (e.g., bullying), emotion can dominate cognition and the rational, thinking part of the brain is less efficient. The classroom environment must be physically and psychologically safe for learning to occur.

The new brain research proposes that adolescents tend to respond more in emotion inducing situations, and their responses are gut reactions associated with the amygdala rather than with the executive or regulating function of the prefrontal cortex (Wolfe, 2001). As adolescents age, however, the brain's frontal lobe becomes more active and emotional responses are more rational. With support and structure, therefore, adolescents can develop the skills for responsible decision making and personal management.

3. The adolescent brain is simultaneously receptive and selective

The adolescent brain is naturally designed to be receptive. Wolfe (2001) writes that everything in the brain's memory begins as a sensory input from the environment.

> During any fractional moment in time, an enormous amount of sensory stimuli is bombarding our bodies, giving us much more information than we can possibly attend to. If you were consciously aware of all the images, sounds, tactile sensations, tastes, and smells that were simultaneously impinging on your body, you would experience sensory overload. (p. 79)

Like a sieve, the brain filters out vast amounts of information it considers irrelevant. The key "sorter" is the brain's internal perception as to whether or not incoming information can connect with existing, related neural structures. The brain's filtering activity is directly linked to what it selects to pay attention to. Teachers can be purposeful in the design of instruction that relates to adolescents' prior learning and experiences. They can also create a safe and stable learning environment with resources and sensory stimulation. Several educators who write about brain-based instruction suggest factors that impact the brain's attention (Brandt, 1998; Caine & Caine, 1997; Caine, Caine, McClintic, & Klimek, 2005; Jensen, 2000; Sprenger, 1999; Sylwester, 2003, 2004; Wolfe, 2001). These include the following:

Your Ideas

- Music, art, dance, and sensory enhancements that enable hands-on learning
- Visuals and graphic organizers that help organize and "chunk" information
- Physical movement for its interactive and kinesthetic value
- Periodic processing time, in small discussion groups and individually, that gives opportunity for consolidation and internalization of new learning
- Humor to heighten emotional response and promote relaxation
- Other sensory-engaging experiences such as simulations and role plays, real-life problems, field trips, mock trials or debates related to historical and current issues, experiments, model building, and mind mapping

4. The adolescent brain is motivated by appropriate intellectual challenge

The brain is programmed to make meaning of experience as it rapidly seeks connection with what is stored within its neurological structures. A learning environment characterized by complex, intellectual interactions stimulates the brain and is critical to its development. In a period where rapid growth has been noted in the prefrontal cortex and cognitive capacity is unfolding, the brain is "ripe" for inquiry, critical thinking, and problem solving (Beamon, 1997). Adolescents thrive on challenge that is meaningful, appropriate, and relevant. "They love to play with words, to write limericks, to delve into science fiction, to debate political and environmental issues (the more controversial the better), to give opinions, to solve real life problems—the possibilities are endless" (p. 23).

Intellectual challenge does not come with the passive receiving of information but rather with instruction that includes variety, engagement, and movement. "Challenge gives adolescents the freedom to experiment with their imaginations, to release their passion for make-believe, to explore their fascination for fantasy, and to use developing psychomotor skills" (Beamon, 1997, p. 24). Appropriate challenge brings new learning in contact with prior learning, and a skillful teacher is purposeful in helping adolescents to categorize and integrate new information and experiences with what they already know.

Challenge also means providing the adolescent brain with something substantive to think about. Grappling over essential questions related to human rights issues or solving problems authentic to their experiences, reading and

Your Ideas

thinking about subject matter of consequence, engaging in simulations that bring otherwise meaningless data into real-life situations, and exploring themes that integrate content across disciplines—each of these activities challenges the adolescent brain to process information with more complexity and meaning.

5. The adolescent brain is social by nature

Renate Caine, one expert in brain-compatible learning, stresses the social dimension of the brain (Caine, as cited in Franklin, 2005): "Remember, the mind is social. . . . You're embedding this knowledge in their experiences and everyday worlds" (p. 3). Siegal (1999), author of *The Developing Mind,* suggests that the social interactions among people and within families, classrooms, cultures, or the larger world via the Internet enhance the flow of energy and information into the brain, where it is processed actively by the mind. Not all agree that neuroscientific findings validate the idea that the mind is social; the new research related to mirror neurons reinforces current cognitive theory that emphasizes the social nature of learning (Sylwester, 2006). Current learning theory and the constructivist instructional approach, discussed in Chapter 2, promote the value of social interaction and shared knowledge within a local or global community of learners (Bransford, Brown, & Cocking, 1999, 2000; Perkins, 1999).

Instructional strategies abound that enable adolescents to work in teams to explore problems and discover answers in the real world beyond the traditional setting of the classroom. Problem- or project-based learning, service learning, simulations, cooperative learning structures, literature circles, and numerous other grouping techniques provide opportunities for adolescents to communicate ideas and learn in a collaborative context. Through interpersonal connections adolescents' "brain energy" can be shared, and the cognitive potential of their thinking and learning can be enhanced.

6. The adolescent brain needs assistance, time, reinforcement, and extension

The academic success of adolescents is linked with the brain's ability to intake and retrieve information. As discussed earlier, the adolescent brain attends to information with which it can find a familiar or relevant connection. It is the teacher's task to help these developing brains make meaningful associations with new information so that it can be retained, recalled, and reconstructed. Wolfe (2001) suggests that teachers "hook the unfamiliar with something familiar" by comparing a new concept with one known or by using analogies, similes, and metaphors (p. 104). Knowledge of the circulatory system in the human body, for example, is useful when adolescents learn to dissect frogs. The challenge is to activate what is stored.

Meaning is further increased by active learning strategies that help adolescents process new information and increase the probability that it will be retained. Wolfe (2001) refers to these strategies as the "elaborate rehearsal" needed to process semantic, or word-based, knowledge (p. 170). These varied and motivational strategies engage adolescents through movement, emotion, social interaction, and intellectual challenge. Many active rehearsal strategies have been identified in the brain-based literature (Caine & Caine, 1994; Jensen, 1998; Sousa, 2001; Sylwester, 1999; Wolfe, 2001):

- Writing activities across the curriculum, including journaling, poetry, stories, speeches, letters, newspaper eulogies, dialogues, and quickwrite or quickdraw diagrams or interactive notebooks
- Mnemonic devices, including music, rap, jingles, acronyms, rhymes, phrases, key word imagery, location association, and narrative chaining
- Peer teaching and other cooperative learning structures that enable summarization, discussion, analysis, and evaluation
- Active review, including student presentations and game format
- Reading punctuated with intervals of note taking, discussion, and reflection
- Thinking maps, including webs, graphic organizers, story plots, diagrams, data organization charts, matrixes, and T-charts
- Physical movement, including role play, simulations, and reenactment

Adolescents also need assistance in applying new learning more fully to their own lives. Teachers must be intentional in the use of metacognitive extension questions that explicitly connect classroom learning to the larger world of students' experiences. *Why is it important to consider historical and cultural context? What have you learned about the value of working in groups to solve a problem? What other ways can you engage in community service?* The complex phenomenon of transfer is discussed in Chapter 5.

7. The adolescent brain is physically responsive

The adolescent brain is additionally a physically responsive entity, and movement is closely associated with learning (Jensen, 2000). Multiple studies have linked physical movement and kinesthetic activity such as sculpture and design to better visual thinking, problem solving, language development, and creativity (Greenfield, 1995; Silverman, 1993; Simmons, 1995). The portion of the brain associated with motor function, the cerebellum, according to Jensen (1998), may be the brain's "sleeping giant" because it is so neurologically connected to the frontal cortex (p. 83). The cerebellum takes up approximately one-tenth of the brain's volume yet contains over half of its neurons. Physical exercise fuels the brain with a high nutrient food called neurotropins that enhances growth and connectivity between neurons, thus making a case for sports and recess in schools. In the classroom, physical exercise is also important in adolescents' neural development and can take the form of arts integration (including drama, music, and dance), energizing games, role play, and skits. Other movement activity might include "living" graphic organizers such as the human graph, body sculpture, human bingo, summary ball toss, in-school field trips, or simple stretching exercises. Physical movement is both pleasurable and cognitively stimulating.

A variety of brain-compatible instructional practices have been recommended in the literature and implemented in middle and high school classrooms

Your Ideas

(Caine, Caine, McClintic, & Klimek, 2005; Jensen, 2000; Nelson, 2001; Sousa, 2001; Sylwester, 2003; Wolfe, 2001). The disclaimer stands, however, regarding a simplistic interpretation or the assumption of direct causal relationships among classroom practice, brain anatomy, cognitive development, and behavior.

- **Integrated thematic units of study** encourage adolescents to make thematic connections across disciplines related to social issues and personal concerns.
- **Problem- or project-based units of study** engage adolescents as stakeholders in investigation and advance the critical analysis of authentic problems.
- **Academic service learning units of study** promote collaborative inquiry, civic action, and community outreach.
- **Real-life apprenticeships** involve adolescents in internships with adults in jobs related to the curriculum or based on their personal interests.
- **Simulations** cast adolescents in roles and situations that help them consider alternate perspectives and pertinent ethical issues.
- **Music and arts integration** heighten emotion through sensorimotor stimulation and enhances memory.
- **Peer collaboration and cooperative learning structures** give adolescents the opportunity to share and construct knowledge, problem solve, and hone social and interpersonal skills.
- **Visual maps and graphic organizers** provide a visual and tangible mechanism for adolescents to organize and analyze their thinking.
- **Reflective writing** offers a vehicle for adolescents to process, consolidate, and think metacognitively about personal learning.
- **Puzzles and word problems** serve as "brain teasers" as adolescents improve thinking skills and strengthen synaptic connectivity.
- **Physical movement and exercise** keep the brain alert and attending. Physical group challenges promote collaboration and problem solving.
- **The Internet** opens the world to adolescents as they research relevant and timely issues; collaborate with mentors, experts, and peers; and actively manipulate data and skills.

Table 1.3 offers a summary of these seven brain-based premises and associated developmentally responsive instructional practices. The Adolescent-Centered Teaching (ACT) Model that follows is an example of the way teachers might activate the adolescent brain through interactive, relevant, emotionally engaging, and cognitively compelling instruction. In this first model of adolescent-centered teaching, adolescents are asked to collect information from a variety of disparate national and international sources, through interviews and online sources, on issues related to the justification of the decision by the United States to invade Iraq. They are challenged to evaluate authentic information gathered against the criteria of "just war theory" and to make a determination. The teacher acts as a facilitator who monitors and checks progress as students make sense from the information gathered and share findings through a technology-enhanced presentation. Then, the students explore real-world and current issues related to homeland security, civil rights, and propaganda.

Table 1.3 Adolescent Brain-Based Premises and Suggested Developmentally Responsive Practices

Brain-Based Premise	*Responsive Practice*
Active, Dynamic, and Malleable: The brain constructs and reconstructs knowledge by making meaningful connections through interaction within the learning environment. It is responsive to an enriched and stimulating environment enhanced by variety, novelty, and feedback.	**Cognitively compelling lessons** that help adolescents relate to, analyze, discuss, question, problem solve, process, and apply new information to the world around them **Inquiry-based instruction** (complex problem-solving tasks) and timely feedback (peer editing, writers' workshop, group interaction, conferencing, portfolios
Emotional Arousal: The brain responds naturally and functionally to strong emotional stimuli that it perceives as relevant and safe.	**Classroom environments** that are safe from physical harm (bullying), embarrassment, ridicule, and rote or meaningless seat work Appropriate structure and support to help develop skills for responsible decision making and self-management
Receptive and Selective: The brain pays attention to incoming sensory information that relates to prior learning and experience.	**Sensory-enhanced, hands-on lessons** that integrate music, art, dance, physical movement, and social interaction and humor **Sensory-engaging experiences,** such as simulations, role plays, problem-based learning, mock trials, experiments, field-based projects, and service learning
Appropriate Intellectual Challenge: The brain's rapid development of cognitive capacity makes it "ripe" for inquiry, critical thinking, and problem solving.	**Relevant, varied, and engaging instruction** that provides opportunity to grapple over essential questions, debate real-world issues, and explore cross-disciplinary themes
Social by Nature: The brain's social dimension responds to interaction among people and within families, classrooms, cultures, and the larger global community.	**Collaborative, interpersonal experiences** that enable interaction (cooperative learning, literature circles) and exploration beyond the classroom or via technology (WebQuests, games, simulations, real-life apprenticeships)
Assistance and Extension: The brain may need strategic help to make meaningful associations with new information and to apply new learning more fully to personal lives and experiences.	**Active rehearsal and extension strategies**, such as cross-curricular writing activities (journaling, quickwrite/quickdraw, poetry, dialogues, letters, eulogies, speeches, interactive notebooks); mnemonic devices (music, rap, rhymes, jingles, narrative chaining); peer or reciprocal teaching; active review (game format, student presentations); thinking maps (webs, graphic organizers, story plots, T-charts, matrices); punctuated reading (with note taking, discussion, reflection); physical movement (role play, simulation, reenactment); and metacognitive extension questions that encourage transfer
Physically Responsive: The brain is neurologically responsive to physical movement and kinesthetic activity	**Physically energizing activities** such as arts integration, role plays, skits, and "living" graphic organizers (human graph, body sculpture, human bingo, summary ball toss, field trips, and simple stretching exercises)

Challenging the Adolescent Brain Through Inquiry: A Justifiable War?

The adolescent brain is an active and dynamic meaning maker that is stimulated through intellectual challenge. Authentic inquiry into current and controversial moral issues gives adolescents the opportunity to grapple with ethical questions relevant to their personal lives. Through guided group investigation and interactive technology, adolescent students collaborate with peers, construct and analyze knowledge, draw conclusions, and assimilate expanded learning into their own worldviews.

Content Understanding

Social Studies: The study of the dynamic relationships among individual rights and responsibilities, the needs of social groups, the concepts of a just society, and the critical issues related to human rights, trade, and global ecology; and the recognition of the rights and responsibilities of citizens to impact public policy for the common good

Critical Thinking: An understanding of the principles of logic, reasoning, analysis, decision making, and persuasion

Technology: Using technology as a tool to do the following:

- Enhance learning, increase productivity, and assist in collaboration during the construction of knowledge
- Collaborate with peers, experts, and other audiences
- Communicate information and ideas effectively to multiple audiences
- Locate, evaluate, and collect information from a variety of sources and process data and report results
- Evaluate and select new information resources and technological innovations
- Aid in problem solving and decision making

Key Concepts

Just war theory, justifiable war, conflict, perspective (national and international), power, propaganda, homeland security, human rights, sources of international law (e.g., International Court of Justice, United Nations Security Council, the Geneva Convention)

Learning Outcomes

- Students will discern the standards related to justifiable war through Internet sources and group discussion.
- Through interviews, public polling, and an examination of pertinent Internet documents, students will investigate the varying public perspectives related to the justification of the decision by the United States to invade Iraq.
- Students will draw conclusions about the justification of the U.S. decision to invade Iraq and share the varying perspectives through a technology-enhanced multimedia presentation.

When is war justifiable?

Strategies for Inquiry

The Inquiry Question: Was the United States justified in its invasion of Iraq? This question continues to be a source of heated political debate. On one hand, proponents justify the Iraq invasion by placing it in the context of both the larger global fight against terrorism and the protection and spread of democracy. Protestors, on the other hand, advocate that the Iraq invasion was misguided and perhaps politically motivated. They suggest that the decision to invade was either based on the inaccurate idea that Saddam Hussein's regime had weapons of mass destruction and was connected to the September 11, 2001, suicide bombings of the World Trade Center, or that politicians misled the American public about the Iraqi threat to U.S. security for reasons of their own.

The Invitation: The United States Institute of Peace invites discussion about whether the motives behind the Iraq invasion met the criteria for justifiable war. Is the cause just? Did the United States have legitimate authority to act unilaterally without the support of the United Nations? Your team's challenge is to present both sides of the issue and to make a determination, if possible, based on just war theory. Your team will decide how to show, using technology, findings with classmates: a mini-documentary using iMovie or a multimedia presentation format, a WebQuest, an interactive game, a simulation, a blog, a podcast, a Web page portal, or another form.

Guided Interaction

- Facilitate as small groups of students formulate a working definition of just war theory. What are the criteria that support justifiable war? They can search the Internet for the term "just war standards." Pertinent documents can be found at these URLs, which give national and international perspectives on the invasion of Iraq and the subsequent war.
  - Google News: http://www.google.com/search?sourceid=navclient&ie=UTF-8&rls=GWYA,GWYA:2005-35,GWYA:en&q=Just+War+Standards
  - United States Institute of Peace: http://www.usip.org/pubs/specialreports/sr98.html

- Have students gather information about differing perspectives on the justification for the Iraq invasion by reading and comparing a variety of current and historical perspectives and sources of news coverage. They need to consider U.S. and British sources, United Nations News, and reports from Arab countries, Israel, and other countries. A few Web sites are given for reference.
- Help students to use the following chart as a graphic organizer to compile data concerning the varying perspectives and to determine a source's position related to the justification of the war.
- Question students about the validity of these sources. Who is doing the reporting? What relationship does the source have to the United States and to the conflict in Iraq? What is propaganda, and how does it play into news or governmental reporting?
- Have students conduct a poll in the school related to the question of the war as a just cause and graph findings for analysis.
- Have students poll at least four adults about their views and rationale related to the justification for the Iraq invasion.

Useful Web Sites for Students and Teachers for National and International Perspectives on the Iraq Invasion

U.S. Department of Public Defense: Defend America
(http://www.defendamerica.mil/)

Google News: The Iraq War
(http://news.google.com/news?q=the+iraq+war&hl=en&lr=&rls=GWYA,GWYA:2005-35,GWYA:en&sa=X&oi=news&ct=title)

Google News: War on Terror
(http://news.google.com.au/news?hl=en&edition=au&q=war+on+terror)

"Operation Iraqi Freedom": President George W. Bush's 2003 Address to the Nation
(http://www.whitehouse.gov/news/releases/2003/03/print/20030319-17.html)

The United Nations New Centre: News Focus Iraq
(http://www.un.org/apps/news/infocusRel.asp?infocusID=50&Body=Iraq&Body1=inspect)

Current News From the White house
(http://www.whitehouse.gov/)

Dartmouth College Library U.S. Government Documents
(http://www.dartmouth.edu/~govdocs/iraq.htm)

President Bush's State of the Union 2006
(http://www.whitehouse.gov/stateoftheunion/2006/)

Iraq Veterans Against the War
(http://www.ivaw.org/)

Newslink
(http://newslink.org/)

News From Egypt
(http://weekly.ahram.org.eg/index.htm)

Arab Media Source
(http://english.aljazeera.net/HomePage)

World News Network
(http://www.wn.com/)

The Guardian of the United Kingdom
(http://www.guardian.co.uk/Iraq/Story/0,2763,1188142,00.html)

The Carter Center: Just War–or a Just War?
(http://www.cartercenter.org/news/documents/doc1249.html)

The Iraq Daily
(http://www.iraqdaily.com/)

BBC News
(http://news.bbc.co.uk/)

News From Turkey
(http://www.turkeypost.com/)

News From Saudi Arabia
(http://www.arabnews.com/)

Source:			
When, according to this source, is the invasion of another country justified? Does this source support that the invasion of Iraq was justifiable? What is the evidence?			
How, according to this source, should nations or international bodies make the decision to invade a country? Does this source support that there was legitimate authority for the U.S. to invade Iraq? What is your evidence?			
Does this source support that the American government acted in good faith and responsibly when it took the decision to invade Iraq? What is your evidence?			

Metacognitive Development and Assessment

- Responsibility needs to be placed on the teams of adolescents to explore resources, acquire and analyze information, and synthesize findings to help shape personal perspectives. At various checkpoints, teams need to assess and report progress and productivity.
- Maintain a class pro-con thinking map on chart paper as a graphic organizer on which students can post rationales for both sides.

- The culminating assessment for each group will be the completion and presentation of the technology-enhanced project.
  - Knowledge of key concepts
  - Acknowledgment of varying perspectives on the issue
  - Logical synthesis of data collected
  - Valid support for group's determination
  - Appropriate use of technology
- Individual and peer evaluations can be used to assess group contributions and collaboration skills (see below).
- Reflection and debriefing time needs to be provided for students to think about the value of examining alternate perspectives and rationales related to real-world situations.

Metacognitive Extension

- Students can explore related questions.
  - What is propaganda, and how does it factor into news or government reporting of current events?
  - Does a government have the right to tamper with e-mails or phone calls or in other areas of citizens' rights? Should homeland security preempt human rights in the United States?
  - What was beneficial about gaining personal perspectives on the events you studied?
  - How will what you have learned about getting information from community members help you in the future?
- Students can also examine other instances in history to which the question of "just war" can be applied, such as the Arab-Israeli conflict, the events of the Holocaust, or the dropping of atomic bombs on Japanese cities during World War II, among others.

STUDENT GROUP EVALUATION

Directions: In the space below, honestly evaluate your work and the work of the other member(s) of your group. Please circle the appropriate score for each question.

1 = Never 2 = Sometimes 3 = Frequently 4 = Always

Your name: ______________________________

(Self-evaluation)

Did a fair share of work

1 ———————— 2 ———————— 3 ———————— 4

Contributed ideas

1 ———————— 2 ———————— 3 ———————— 4

Was cooperative

1 ———————— 2 ———————— 3 ———————— 4

Used group time well

1 ———————— 2 ———————— 3 ———————— 4

Took the projects seriously

1 ———————— 2 ———————— 3 ———————— 4

Was fun to work with

1 ———————— 2 ———————— 3 ———————— 4

Overall performance (explain below)

1 ———————— 2 ———————— 3 ———————— 4

Combined score: ___/28

SOURCE: Assessment courtesy of L. Conroy, K. Findley, K. LaVange, J. Moulton, R. Overcash (2005 May). Elon University, NC.

THE POTENTIAL POWER OF ADOLESCENT METACOGNITION

The emerging cognitive aptitude for metacognition affords adolescents the intellectual power to assess reactions in situations, to control impulsiveness and temper negative emotions, to think about the consequence of personal decisions, and to act with healthy judgment in social situations (Beamon, 2001). This intellectual capacity enables them to evaluate the quality of their thinking, to develop a flexible repertoire of thinking and learning strategies, and to decide which strategies to use in certain learning situations. This capacity additionally enables adolescents to reflect upon and more fully understand personal feelings and emotions (Bransford et al., 2000).

Metacognition is a powerful cognitive phenomenon that enables students to set goals, plan, solve problems, monitor progress, and evaluate their own thinking effectiveness, and it is thus associated with thinking management (Paris & Winograd, 1990; Tishman, Perkins, & Jay, 1995). It gives adolescents awareness and control over personal thinking behavior, and enables self-reflection and self-regulation (Costa, 1991; Fogarty, 1995). Accordingly, it provides the

Your Ideas

means for adolescents to oversee thinking as it happens, to determine what they know, to appraise what they need to know, and to orchestrate what they should do in a learning situation. Sizer (1992) described the metacognitive adolescent as "a mindful student . . . who knows where he [or she] is going, is disposed to get there, and is gathering the resources, the knowledge, and the skills to make the journey" (p. 27). This person generally feels personally competent, autonomous, and socially adept.

Metacognition has the capacity to "cultivate cognitive resourcefulness . . . promote responsible and independent thinking . . . [and] foster strategic thinking and planfulness" (Tishman et al., 1995, p. 68). It gives adolescents the mental tools for self-directed learning. Beyer (1987) suggests that teachers ask purposeful cueing questions to prompt metacognitive thinking in adolescents. Examples follow.

- *What are you trying to do?* A teacher might ask this to elicit the purpose for a chosen approach when a student is involved in an academic task.
- *Why are you doing it?* A question such as this shifts the student's thinking to rationale.
- *Is there another way you might do it?* This query encourages a consideration of alternate strategies and supports flexible thinking.
- *How well did it work? Is there a better way?* At the completion of a task, a teacher can promote metacognitive reflection and evaluation with these questions.
- *How can you help someone else do it?* This query reinforces learning and challenges the student to discuss possible strategies with another.

Promoting Metacognitive Development Through Adolescent-Centered Teaching

Swartz and Perkins (1989) distinguish four levels of metacognition—tacit, aware, strategic, and reflective. Many adolescents operate on the tacit, or automatic use, level. They go through the "right" thinking processes without giving much thought as to why. On the aware level, adolescents are conscious of their thinking, and, on the strategic level, they begin to organize their thinking based on an acknowledged strategy. Ultimately, on the reflective level, adolescents continually assess their strategies and evaluate when and how these can be improved. Functioning at the reflective level indicates greater awareness and personal control over thinking at the beginning, middle, and the completion of the learning activity.

Teachers can encourage the development of metacognition in adolescent learners. Current ideas about strategic thinking and mental management indicate several instructional elements that facilitate the process. The initial step is to make adolescents aware of their personal metacognitive power and help them to realize that they can develop strategies that are useful and appropriate for learning situations. Teachers use check questioning to keep the students on the expected "mental track." They ask for the rationale behind their decisions, remind them of necessary steps to consider, arrange for self-evaluation, and give students general feedback and support. Teachers encourage reflective metacognition through the following actions:

Your Ideas

- Discuss the usefulness of students' strategies in organizing for a presentation.
- Have them write about their thought processes in a response journal.
- Ask them to explain their planning strategies to other students.
- Help them to identify strategies they might use in real-life situations.

Scholars and researchers, including Barell (1995), Bransford et al. (2000), Beamon (2001), Costa (1991), Daniels and Bizar (1998), Fogarty (1995), Palincsar and Brown (1984), Paris and Winograd (1990), and Tishman et al. (1995), suggests several instructional techniques that foster metacognitive skills. These include role playing and simulation, journal keeping, problem solving, reciprocal teaching, cognitive coaching, modeling, direct explanation, elaboration, self-questioning, self-assessment, reflection, and planning strategies that emphasize thinking before, during, and after a thinking challenge.

The following Adolescent-Centered Teaching (ACT) Model is an example of science instruction that helps to promote adolescent metacognitive development. Students learn and apply scientific strategies to determine the probability of the transmission of a sex-linked recessive gene mutation connected with the disease cystic fibrosis. The teacher guides as the students diagram the family pedigree, create Punnett squares for problem solving, and simulate strategies for genetic sequencing and profiling on the Internet. They extend learning as they explore ethical issues related to the field of DNA through guided research into selected areas of controversy. The teacher encourages metacognitive reflection through journaling, preparation of a presentation or debate, and reflective questions about personal thought processes and self-management. Through the experience, adolescents enter the real world of scientists and grapple with the ethical dilemmas associated with scientific advancement.

Promoting Metacognitive Development: Who Carries the Gene?

Adolescents are intrigued by realistic and puzzling phenomena that stimulate their curiosity and challenge their thinking. Complex content and ideas can be presented in an authentic format that engages problem-solving skills, allows for choice and creative expression, and promotes metacognitive reflection. The teacher's role is to help students to develop strategies for learning, to ask for rationale, to give feedback, to encourage self-monitoring, and to help them extend the learning into real-life situations.

Content Understanding

Science: Knowledge of chemical reactions and atomic structure (physical science); understanding of the molecular basis of genetics, heredity, and gene mutation (life science); and skills for scientific inquiry and technology

Key Concepts

Cell, chromosome, sex chromosomes, recessive and dominant genetic traits, DNA (deoxyribonucleic acid), genes, heredity, sex-linked traits, phenotype, Punnett square, mitochondria, genome, cystic fibrosis (CF), mutation, homozygous, allele

Learning Outcomes

- Students will explain the concept of sex-linked genetic inheritance by applying it to the genetic disease cystic fibrosis.
- Students will analyze a genetic pedigree using a Punnett square to determine an individual's probability of inheriting this disease mutation.
- Students will consider ethical issues related to technology-supported genetic profiling through research and debate.

ESSENTIAL QUESTIONS

How do sex-linked genetic traits impact the inheritance of related diseases?

How can DNA sequencing be used to determine genetic mutation?

What are some of the ethical dilemmas associated with genetic profiling?

Strategies for Inquiry

Adolescents are motivated and challenged by authentic and intriguing events, problems, and questions. Teachers should consider ways to stimulate their curiosity to explore, investigate, and solve.

The Inquiry Challenge: Mr. and Mrs. Keats are the proud parents of a new baby boy. Their only concern is that Mrs. Keats's only brother died at a young age of cystic fibrosis, a genetically inherited disease. At that time, it was determined that Mrs. Keats's mother was the carrier of the recessive gene for cystic fibrosis. Mrs. Keats's sister has two children, a son and a daughter, and both are healthy. Could Mrs. Keats be a carrier of the cystic fibrosis transmembrane conductance regulator (CFTR) gene, as was her mother? If she is a carrier, what is the percent chance that the Keats's new child will inherit the dreaded disease?

Additional Inquiry Questions:

- Why did neither Mrs. Keats nor her sister contract the disease?
- Could Mrs. Keats's sister be a carrier, even though neither of her children have the disease?
- If the new Keats baby had been a girl, what percent chance would she have had of inheriting the disease?
- If the Keatses have any more children, what is the percent chance they will inherit the disease?
- If no Keats children show traits of the disease, could the Keats's grandchildren inherit the disease?
- If the new Keats child does inherit the disease, what symptoms will he show? Could he live longer than Mrs. Keats's brother? Why?

Guided Interaction

Adolescents need to be guided as they set up strategies for inquiry and as they proceed through learning tasks. While the teacher's role is continually active, it becomes less directive as the experience progresses. Teachers can assist with this challenge:

- Help students to diagram the Keats family's genetic pedigree using the appropriate legend and symbols to denote gender and chromosome structures.
- Teach students to use a Punnett square to show the genetic cross between Mr. and Mrs. Keats.

	X^{CF}	Y
X^{CF}	$X^{CF} X^{CF}$	$X^{CF}Y$
X^{cf}	$X^{cf} X^{cf}$	$X^{cf}Y$

X = X chromosome; Y = Y chromosome
CF = normal allele; cf = cystic fibrosis allele

- Help students respond to the other questions, and have them work in pairs to create different Punnett squares to show that a female can become a carrier from either her father or her mother.

Extended Guided Interaction

- Have student teams access Web sites to learn more about the conditions of cystic fibrosis, such as symptoms or expected life span (http://www.ygyh.org/).
- Download the instructions and a template to fold a paper double helix (http://www.dnai.org/).
- Allow teams to explore interactive Web sites to view the structure of DNA and chromosomes and to learn about genetic sequencing and profiling, as these relate to disease control, cloning, and crime solution. (See below.)
- Involve students in a WebQuest in which they assume the roles of DNA scientist, epidemiologist, pediatrician, and genetic counselor to solve the problem of a mysterious disease affecting babies in a remote community in New Mexico (http://www.koshland sciencemuseum.org/teachers/webquest.jsp).
- View interactive videos and DVDs about DNA and its activity.

Assessment

Have students create poster-sized pedigree charts with legends. See below for directions regarding a project that traces four genetic traits in 12 individuals through four generations of family and for a rubric to assess the project.

Directions for "Trace That Gene"

1. Look at sheets we have used in class for ideas. Choose any four traits that are hereditary and could be traced in your family. They do not have to be your phenotype.
2. Interview family members to determine who has these traits. You must show 12 individuals and three generations.
3. Draw a pedigree chart as a rough draft for the poster. Remember that squares represent male members and circles represent females. Create a color key and fill in squares and circles to show traits.
4. Enlarge your chart to poster size (25" by 22"). Make it neat and colorful for display.

TRACE THAT GENE!

Review different posters, and answer the following for each one.	**Grading Scale**	
____________ name on poster	On time..................	20 pts_____
List the 4 traits traced____________ ____________	Correct spelling..........	20 pts_____
	Neatness, legibility, spacing, ink.....	20 pts_____
Which trait shows the clearest pattern of heredity? ____________	Valid traits and names....	20 pts_____
	Different color/symbol for prototype.......	20 pts_____

Which trait shows the least pattern of heredity? ______________________________ How many people were used to trace the trait? ______________________________ **Rate the following about the poster, 1(low) to 10 (high).** Neatness_____ Spelling ____ Straight lines ____ Clear color marking _____ Symbols/Key ______ **List the symbols you see used on the poster.**	Varied Traits and Names...... 5 pts each_____ 12 individuals/3 generations...... 20 pts_____ Key, clear markings, genetic lines... 20 pts_____ Each generation on same plane... 20 pts_____ Name, title .... 20 pts_____ __________ 100 points

SOURCE: Courtesy of Dennison, P. (2006). Chapel Hill, NC: Peer Assistance and Review (PAR) Teacher, Rashkis Elementary.

Metacognitive Development: The DNA Controversy

Students can explore the ethical issues related to the expanding field of DNA sequencing and profiling through research into areas of controversy. They can discuss the issues; engage in debate, presentations, or simulations; or write position essays to synthesize their findings and conclusions. Here are a few controversial areas:

- Use of genetically modified organs from pigs as transplants for humans
- Use of genetically modified mice for disease research for humans
- Use of universal DNA profiling for certain purposes such as criminal investigations
- Use of embryonic stem cells for scientific research

Other ideas are available in the online article "Dealing With DNA Controversy," available on the DNA Interactive Web site (www.dnai.org).

Ways to Encourage Metacognitive Reflection

- Have students use team journals to record their questions, observations, and thought processes. Periodically ask that these be shared and discussed.
- Have teams prepare an oral report for a simulated research symposium or a debate.
- Work with students to develop evaluation criteria based on content (understanding of concepts related to theory), critical thinking (ability to analyze data and construct explanations), and communication (ability to present findings in a clear manner).
- During the final performance assessment, ask for clarification and elaboration.
- Give other students an opportunity to give feedback on the reasonableness of the teams' explanations.

- As a final reflection, discuss the real-world expectation to make sense of situations based on given evidence. Encourage students to reflect on their level of motivation during the process, how effectively they managed the inquiry, the value of writing out and verbalizing their thinking, the usefulness of sharing ideas, and what they understand better about their own thinking and learning.

Pertinent Student and Teacher Resources

Gene Almanac (http://www.dnalc.org/home.html)

An interactive site created by the Cold Spring Harbor Laboratory. It provides 3D animations of DNA and multimedia guides to genetic disorders and contains links to statistical tools and databases that allow students to manipulate gene sequencing and tabulate findings.

DNA Interactive (http://www.dnai.org/)

An interactive, animated site with teacher resources for lesson building about genetics and DNA. Resource for interactive videos.

DNA From the Beginning (http://www.dnaftb.org/dnaftb/)

An animated primer on the basics of DNA, genes, and heredity. Flash Player and QuickTime are needed.

Your Genes, Your Health (http://www.ygyh.org/)

A multimedia site with information on genetic-related disorders using three criteria: high incidence rate, known genetic cause, and severity of the phenotype (symptoms). Video interviews with researchers and patients provide insiders' views on genetic disorders. Links help users find support groups and additional information.

Cystic Fibrosis Foundation (http://www.cff.org/home/)

Organized to help patients and families with information and referrals about cystic fibrosis. Headquarters: 6931 Arlington Road, Bethesda, MD 20814. Toll-free phone: (800) FIGHT-CF. Or call (301) 951-4422. Email: info@cff.org

Marian Koshland Science Museum of the National Academy of Sciences (http://www.koshlandsciencemuseum.org/)

An interactive site for teaching and learning about genetics.

New Zealand Herald Article: "Screening the Next Generation" (http://www.nzherald.co.nz/section/story.cfm?c_id=2&ObjectID=10387310)

A story on genetic screening for cystic fibrosis.

ACTing

on the Adolescent-Centered Learning Principles Discussed in Chapter 1

Principle	*How I can put it into practice*
❑ Recognize that internal and external factors affect adolescent thinking and learning.	
❑ Acknowledge the personal, intellectual, and social needs of the adolescent learner.	
❑ Recognize that adolescents are developmentally ready for empathy, understanding, reflection, and intellectual engagement.	
❑ Understand the brain-compatible principles and responsive strategies that support adolescent learning.	
❑ Capitalize on the cognitive and metacognitive capacity of adolescents.	
❑ Create challenge that is appropriate to their level of knowledge, skill, and development, and provide opportunity for in-depth understanding and meaningful interaction.	
❑ Structure lessons that allow for student choice and appropriately guided autonomy.	

CHAPTE

2

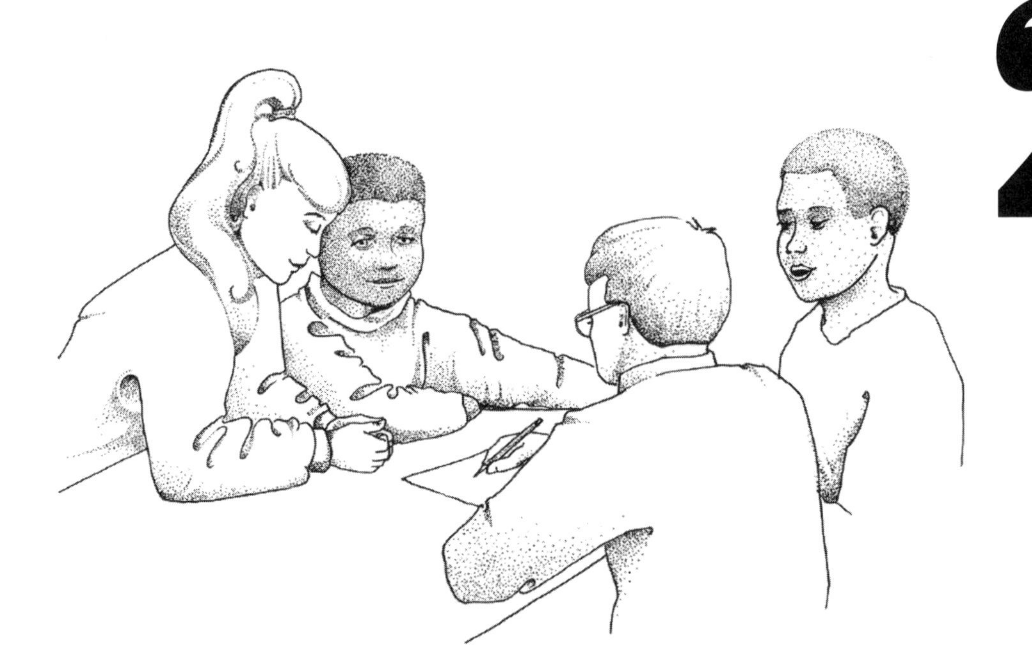

Getting and Keeping Their Attention

THE MILLENNIAL GENERATION

The developmental changes associated with adolescence are not new. The awkward, tentative, yet glorious ritual of youth has long been defined by physical, personal, sexual, and intellectual awakening (Beamon, 2001). What has changed, however, is the context. The adolescent of the twenty-first century is immersed in a world of unlimited access and rapid communication facilitated by technological advancement. Screens instantaneously flash text messages and images; cell phones, as prevalent as backpacks, have taken the place of cameras; personal Web pages can be accessed internationally; MP3 players saturate the gadget market; and blogs (Web logs) serve the purpose of personal diaries "gone public." One need consider the following from the *U.S. News and World Report* (Whitman, 2005) regarding the teens of the millennial generation:

- 51% have their own laptops
- Biggest consumers (collectively spent $175 billion in 2004)
- Love *The OC, Gilmore Girls, Everwood,* and 50 Cent

- Roughly one in six overweight: new teen diabetes
- 8.1 million antidepressant prescriptions given in 2002; one in five get treatment
- Biggest perceived problems: getting good grades, appearance, getting into college
- Most believe in God, go to church, and look forward to marriage and family

Your Ideas

The 34.2 million people aged 12–19 are less likely to smoke, do hard drugs, get pregnant, commit violent crimes, drop out of school, and drive drunk (Howe & Strauss, 2000). Howe and Strauss recognize the millennial generation as one "more numerous, more affluent, better educated, and more ethnically diverse" than any in living memory (p. 4). More are staying in school, selecting academic programs, completing graduation requirements, and attending some form of college. They aspire to professional careers, compete for scholarships, and worry over making the right decisions about their future (Codding & Rothman, 1999; Gibbs, 2005; Howe & Strauss, 2000; Schneider & Stevenson, 1999). A special report in *Time* (Gibbs, 2005) noted that "[t]oday's 13-year-olds, growing up in a world more connected, more competitive, more complex than the one their parents had to navigate as kids, so far show every sign of rising to the challenge" (p. 44). They are physiologically more mature, immersed in a culture of adult images, and the target of mass consumer marketing. These adolescents self-report that they get along fairly well with their parents, plan to wait until marriage to have sex, and worry about the future of this country. The potential of the millennial generation to impact America's future is clear.

On a more cautious note, the new century adolescents are coming of age in a world torn by violent conflict, power struggles, and economic disparity. The circumstances of their lives leave them simultaneously savvy, sophisticated, exposed, and vulnerable. Table 2.1 profiles the current adolescent generation in terms of developmental characteristics and related susceptibilities. Unfortunately, too many adolescents perceive little relevance in schooling and drop out. Some remain in school "simply to get their tickets punched and get on with their lives" (Codding & Rothman, 1999, p. 5), and others express specific concerns about how and what they are taught. In spite of a vigorous and pervasive movement toward higher standards, the academic expectations in many classrooms are far below what students are capable of knowing and achieving, and what they will need to know for subsequent schooling and productive adult lives. Figure 2.1 provides a graphic of an impending disconnect as traditional classroom practices linger behind the needs of a changing generation of adolescents for a world that itself has changed dramatically.

THE NEW GEOGRAPHY OF LEARNING

Bridging the growing "disconnect" between adolescents' lives and school experiences requires tapping into their interests, and one area that cannot be overlooked is technology. A cover story in *Business Week* (Hempel, 2005) refers to twenty-first-century teens as the "MySpace Generation: They live online . . . buy online . . . play online" (p. 1). According to a survey by the PEW Internet and American Life Project (Lenhart, Rainie, & Lewis, 2001), of 13 million

Table 2.1 A Profile of Seeming Contradictions: Today's Adolescent...

May Be	*And Yet, May . . .*
Technological "Savvy"	Lack skill to organize, evaluate, and synthesize data
Multicultural, Multilingual	Feel stymied by one culture's ideas and language
Used to Fast Access	Lack motivation to persevere for task completion
Socially Active	Lack the skills for purposeful social interaction
Peer Oriented	Need assistance with interpersonal relationship
Intellectually Capable	Be unpracticed in higher cognitive thinking
Future Oriented	Lack the skills for self-management and regulation
Exposed to Experience	Struggle with moral judgment and ethical decisions
Information-Rich	Be limited in opportunity to explore broader issues
Independent-Minded	Be personally vulnerable to peer and societal lure
College/Work-Bound	Be limited in content and practical knowledge

Figure 2.1 We're Losing Their Attention

A Different Set of Expectations . . .	*A Growing Disconnect . . .*
Increased Selection of More Academic Courses	Limited Rigor in Preparation Trailing International Test Scores
Higher Graduation Rate	A Curriculum of Diminishing Relevance to Experiences
More Exposure and Access	Traditional Instructional Delivery
Greater Opportunity for Higher Education	"Fragile" Knowledge Underdeveloped Thinking Capacity
Concerns About Preparation for College	Lowered Expectations for Academic Performance
Heightened Career Aspirations	Unpracticed in Decision Making and Collaboration Skills
Greater Potential for the Future	Limited Potential for Professional Contribution

teenagers who use instant messaging (IM) services, one-fifth report that IM is the main way they communicate with peers. Instant messaging, available free online through Yahoo, ICQ, or MSN, offers adolescents real-time, instant written and image connections with the immediacy of a phone call (Renard, 2000). Another recent survey by the Perseus Development Corporation indicates that more than one-half of the 4.12 billion blogs online are created by teens (Twist, 2004). Through a series of postings of text, video, hyperlinks, images, and sound, adolescents communicate instantaneously.

Your Ideas

Adolescents' reality is defined by speed, color, sound, and movement, and data comes easily and quickly to their fingertips. Fast-paced interactive video games have long challenged their mental acuity and dexterity and are integral to their world outside of school. Collections of media have shifted from VHS to DVD to video streaming. Prensky (2005–2006) contends that students of this generation have a better idea of what the future is bringing than many of their teachers.

> They're already busy adopting new systems for communicating (instant messaging), sharing (blogs), buying and selling (eBay), exchanging (peer-to-peer technology), creating (Flash), meeting (3D worlds), collecting (downloads), coordinating (wikis), evaluating (reputation systems), searching (Google), analyzing (SETI), reporting (camera phones), programming (modding), socializing (chat rooms), and even learning (Web surfing). (p. 10)

These digital tools are like extensions of students' brains; educating or evaluating without them "makes no more sense than educating or evaluating a plumber without his or her wrench" (p. 12). Prensky challenges that for schools to have relevance in this century, students must be engaged in the twenty-first-century way, electronically.

With new digital tools and supporting software, adolescents can construct Web environments where they interact about common interests, tasks, and ideas. Within these virtual spaces, they collaborate, collect, store, and share information and resources, including graphics, and create products for authentic audiences (Richardson, 2005–2006). These include Web logs, wikis, Really Simple Syndication (RSS), social bookmarking, and podcasting, to name a few. Web logs, or blogs, enable the creation of personal or group sites without having to learn hypertext markup language. Social blogs, such as MySpace.com and Facebook.com, among others, enable adolescents to "hang out" virtually. Wikis are open content creation tools that anyone can contribute to or edit at any time.

Through Really Simple Syndication (RSS), students can subscribe to various "feeds" of information from the Internet (e.g., blogs, Web sites, or traditional media outlets like the *New York Times*) that are continually streamed and aggregated into a file. Social bookmarking sites such as Furl.net and del.icio.us expand the capacity of traditional bookmarks to save a copy of Web sites in a searchable folder. The tool of podcasting enables students to produce and broadcast multimedia creations, including oral histories, interviews, and weekly news from classrooms. See the following box for definitions and resources related to these new technologies.

Your Ideas

Web Environment Technologies

WebQuest: A Web-based scaffolding tool for interactive real-world problem solving that promotes collaborative group work through authentic roles, research skills, and higher-level thinking skills

Selected WebQuest Resources

Tom March's Portal (http://tommarch.com)

The central location for all Tom's "Bright Ideas for Education"

Celebrating the Best in WebQuests (http://bestwebquests.com/)

View highly rated WebQuests and get personal feedback from Tom March

WebQuests for Learning (http://tommarch.com/learning/index.php)

WebQuests and materials created by Tom March

WebQuest News: Bernie Dodge's Portal (http://webquest.org)

Interactive WebQuest community from Bernie Dodge

The WebQuest Page: San Diego State University (http://webquest.sdsu.edu/webquest.html)

Features WebQuest construction, samples, and portal

Filamentality (http://www.kn.pacbell.com/wired/fil/)

An online WebQuest maker

Web-and-Flow (http://www.web-and-flow.com/)

A comprehensive WebQuest maker

Web log: Referred to as a blog, this tool enables the creation of personal or group Web sites for content sharing and online conversations. Graphics and multimedia can be incorporated (Richardson, 2005–2006).

Web Log Resources

WordPress (http://wordpress.org/)

Blogger (www.blogger.com)

Edublogs (www.edublogs.org)

Schoolblogs (www.schoolblogs.com)

Movable Type (www.sixapart.com/moveabletype)

Sample Blog: Mr. Blake's ClassBlog (http://incsub.org/wpmu/nwa/index.php)

Social Blogs: MySpace.com; Facebook.com; Xanga.com; StudyBreakers.com; and Photbucket.com

Your Ideas

Web Portals: Interactive Web sites constructed and grown by a group around a common interest, such as a curriculum topic, or need, such as networked resources for rainforest conservation. Content can include pertinent Web links, such as to databases, blogs, student communication, and archives of student writing.

Portal Resources

ClassAct Portal (http://classactportal.com/)

Sample ClassAct Portal: IHS Child Slave Labor (http://ihscslnews.org)

Forest Conservation Portal (http://forests.org/)

Wiki: Hawaiian for "quick," a wiki is a collaborative content creation tool that enables contributors to share and access resources, such as Wikipedia.org, an online encyclopedia of one-half million entries (Richardson, 2005–2006).

Wiki Resources

Wikipedia: The Free Encyclopedia (www.wikipedia.org)

Seed Wiki (www.seedwiki.com)

Wiki Software List (http://en.wikipedia.org/wiki/List_of_wiki_software)

Podcasting: An audio program broadcast over the Internet that can be downloaded to a portable MP3 player. Can feature class-produced talk shows, audio files of books, vocabulary, articles, and poems.

Podcasting Resources

Podcast Directory (www.podcast.net)

Sample Podcast: Recording *Romeo* (www.netc.org/focus/examples/record.pdp)

Other Resources

Social Bookmarking Tools (http://www.furl.net) and (http://del.icio.us)

Free or low-cost online photo sharing (http://www.flickr.com)

Tom March (2005–2006), who has published widely about the WebQuest as a Web-based scaffolding tool for interactive, real-world problem solving, describes another instructional phenomenon that is gaining popularity in support of active, meaningful learning: a ClassAct Portal. Teachers choose a topic of

Your Ideas

personal interest that will also engage students. Topics could be grounded in the traditional curriculum, related to world or environmental issues, or based on the hobbies or interests of students, such as hip-hop music. March cites an exemplary ClassAct Portal that was created by students in a U.S. history course in a New Jersey high school. The site, entitled *Child Slave Labor News* (http://ihscslnews.org/), provides links to organizations opposing child labor, invites responses, and contains an archive of articles written by the high school students.

March (2005–2006) has created a site with suggestions for ClassAct Portal topics that also includes articles, example sites, and user-friendly tutorials for setting up a personal blog or wiki (http://classactportal.com/). He suggests the following steps for ClassAct Portal building (p. 18):

- Locate a site from a free online blog, such as Blogger or WordPress, or have students set up their own Web space through a Web host that provides "cPanel" and "Partastico."
- Create content for the Portal by gathering hotlists of links from the Internet, and have students critique or annotate these links.
- Build community by having students send e-mails of appreciation to hosts of the most interesting sites.
- Grow the site by adding wiki or photo gallery options.
- Personalize the site with extensions of lesson plans, bulletin boards, student written work, and classroom persona.

Another technological phenomenon that is surfacing in the educational arena is gaming (Jenkins, 2000). Building upon the intrinsically motivating draw of recreational video games, researchers are touting the pedagogical potential of electronic games in instruction. Simulation and strategy games in the area of social studies, for example, allow adolescents to immerse themselves in authentic social contexts as they explore and think critically about issues in history or in current events.

TECHNOLOGY AS A BRAIN/MIND TOOL

Instructional technology is a natural "fit" with the functioning of the adolescent brain, and, used meaningfully, it can be a tool to develop students' thinking and learning. The brain-based premises identified in Chapter 1 are supported within the learning opportunities afforded by Internet resources and interactive software applications. The brain is active, dynamic, malleable, receptive, and selective, for example, as it interacts with knowledge and new information. Technology brings real-world problems into the classroom for adolescents to explore, and it connects them with others in a networked knowledge-building community (Bransford et al., 1999, 2000). Through databases, digital libraries, videodisks, simulations, and the limitless communication and management tools afforded by the World Wide Web, teachers can use technology to help adolescents learn to analyze, synthesize, and make more informed judgments about the vast amount of information so readily available.

When used actively and interactively (versus a passive, presentation mode or "cut and paste" exercise), technology can be an intellectually challenging and social tool for shared inquiry, critical thinking, and collaborative problem solving. Spreadsheets and databases demand the critical thinking skills of abstract and concrete reasoning, deductive and inductive thinking, analysis, logic, and problem solving (Adams & Burns, 1999; Burns, 2005–2006; Jonassen, Carr, & Yueh, 1998). Instantaneous electronic access enables teachers, adolescents, and expert practitioners, including scientists and engineers, to form telecollaborative learning communities whose purpose is to build knowledge jointly through inquiry. Through these experiences, adolescents follow the rigorous procedures of professionals in the field; these learning "partners" collaborate about real-world problems (Bransford et al., 1999, 2000).

Your Ideas

In GLOBE (Global Learning and Observations to Benefit the Environment), for example, an international community of schools forms an electronic network to research large-scale global problems related to earth science. Students research a local problem, share findings with international peers, and interactively identify common environmental phenomena across the world. These students collaborate with real scientists to design experiments, conduct peer reviews, and publish findings. Geographic information systems (GIS), a computer-aided simulation program, is another example. Adolescents use GIS to determine the vulnerability of a geographic region to natural disaster by identifying constraints and creating an alternative land use option. With the free tool Google Earth, students can scan historical photos of a specific city and superimpose the images onto a current satellite view to contrast topography (Burns, 2005–2006).

Project and problem-based learning, WebQuests, ThinkQuests, CyberGuides, and ClassAct Portals are other inquiry-based learning approaches that require students to think, collaborate, problem solve, and build new knowledge (March, 2005–2006; Yoder, 1999). These experiences promote student inquiry, discussion, teamwork, and an understanding of multidisciplinary concepts, and they appeal to the adolescent brain's need for emotional engagement, assistance and extension, and intellectual stimulation. Adolescents use traditional and Web-based resources, and usually work toward a common product or project, for example, a multimedia presentation, a dramatic performance, an interactive Web page, a debate, or a written document. Beyond higher order knowledge and critical inquiry skills, adolescents also learn to differentiate Web sites that are educationally appropriate. General guidelines for designing Web-based inquiry follow (Yoder, 1999, pp. 3–4).

Designing Web-Based Inquiry

- Design a compelling inquiry task that captures adolescents' interest. These situations may ask them to (1) investigate contemporary problems, such as global warming; (2) evaluate historical events; (3) create products; (4) deal with real-life encounters, such as planning a trip, or (5) use their imagination, such as a journey in time or space. A task introduction will help "set the stage."
- Guide adolescents through the process. Teachers should facilitate student questioning, assign roles, and help with data collection and time

Your Ideas

management. Strategies for effective group work or problem solving should be posted.

- Gather relevant materials and links. Resources include people, texts, videos, places, and relevant Web sites identified in journals and through search engines.
- Evaluate final products. A rubric, designed by teachers and students, which has a variety of criteria and benchmark levels in each category is the best tool.
- Conclude. Adolescents need time to review and reflect on the process of learning and the skills gained through the inquiry.

When technology is used as a tool to cultivate higher order thinking skills, "[s]tudents and teachers must become creators of information and ideas, not simply users of technology" (Burns, 2005–2006, p. 52; Gibson, 2005).

TECHNOLOGY AND MULTICULTURAL DEVELOPMENT

Technology has the potential to diminish cultural barriers and promote multicultural awareness among adolescents. They become more aware of an accessible global community when they observe a full solar eclipse transmitted from a prime vantage in the Middle East simply by visiting a Web site. They experience an ancient culture when they view an online exhibition in the Egyptian Museum in Cairo, post questions on instant message centers, contribute ideas to youth forums, and "chat" with other young people throughout the world. Within the classroom and beyond, technology can have an impact on adolescents' attitudes and perceptions toward peers and people of differing cultures and worldviews. Several examples of the role of technology in adolescents' multicultural development follow:

- In a sixth grade language arts class, a student from rural China was able to share the story of how her parents came to the United States; her digital story included cultural music, authentic photographs, and original drawings. She used movie making software, a digital camera, microphones, a flatbed scanner, and a video camera (Ohler, 2005–2006).
- Students in a graphic arts class gained a deeper understanding of cultural heritage and counteracted negative stereotypes through an Internet-based project about *Amistad.* Using software programs such as PowerPoint, PhotoDeluxe, and Microsoft Word, they designed and reproduced images of the passage of this slave-carrying merchant ship (Frederick, 2005–2006).
- High school students in a low income and ethnically diverse area of Washington, with grants from Microsoft and other companies, sent refurbished computers to schools and orphanages in developing countries and taught their peers how to use them (DePillis, 2005–2006).

The following box offers other classroom examples of how teachers are using instructional technology and the power of the Internet to make learning relevant and real for adolescents and to increase multicultural awareness.

Your Ideas

Technology Changes Learning

Digital Story Telling: Sixth grade students create multimedia personal narratives that include music, photographs taken by the young adolescents and scanned images, and personal artwork. They map and storyboard the narratives, compose and narrate the scripts, produce soundtracks using composition software, and add titles and credits. Technology needed: iMovie software (for Macintosh), MovieMaker (for PC), digital camera, microphones, flatbed scanner, video camera (Ohler, 2005–2006).

WebQuests: Eighth grade language arts students create a WebQuest titled "To Choose Freedom" (http://www.lausd.k12.ca.us/Emerson_MS/levin_wq/), which raises this question: "As a slave, would you be able to escape?" Students research risks associated with attaining freedom, compare lives of escaped slaves with those who remained enslaved, and write essays defending their decision. Authentic group roles include risk assessor, historian, or Underground Railroad expert (Renard, 2000).

Gaming: Adolescents in U.S. history classes used the simulation game "Revolution" to assume the roles of citizens in Colonial Williamsburg, Virginia during the political time of the American Revolution. Students learn from primary sources of historical accounts, assumed authentic roles, and shared perspectives through class discussion (Jenkins, 2000).

Web Logs: Adolescents use blogs for reflective journaling, submitting and reviewing assignments, creating online portfolios, dialoguing about group work, exchanging response comments concerning peer work, and sharing resources. Adolescents also contact and collaborate with authors of books read in literature class; with professional mentors in journalism classes; and, during a unit on the Holocaust, with peers in Krakow, Poland (Richardson, 2005–2006).

The Virtual Library: High school librarians create virtual libraries with online databases such as Galenet and EBSCO, reference tools and bibliography links, search tool pages, strategies for evaluating Web resources, tools for writing research papers and making professional presentations, and links to outside professional services sponsored by state and regional libraries (Valenza, 2005–2006).

Podcasts: Groups of high school students, using a computer and microphone, create Web-based "radio shows." Others use this format for book discussions, poetry slams, or historic reenactments (Valenza, 2005–2006).

Internet 2: Through this faster access Internet, formerly used only by universities and researchers, a gifted high school class is able to meet with a

Your Ideas

postdoctoral fellow at the University of Pennsylvania to discuss concepts and questions following a unit on the brain. Advanced French classes join others in the region for an online bilingual seminar with graduate students in French West India.

Technology has restructured curriculum and changed the social, intellectual, and personal culture of adolescent learning across the world. The time, energy, personal expertise, and resources needed to use technology effectively in the instruction of adolescents are immense; however, resources abound. An excellent resource is the In Time Web site (http://www.intime.uni.edu) where teachers can access lesson plans and videotapes that integrate technology into regular content instruction, using a pedagogically sound, student-centered model. This site also includes lessons and media for multicultural development. For educators' professional development and networking, Tapped In (http://tappedin.org/tappedin/) offers a useful online community. The box "Teacher Resources for Integrating Technology" gives a sampling of Internet locations that might be useful as teachers seek to integrate technology into the daily instruction of adolescents. Others are interspersed throughout the book within content-based examples.

Teacher Resources for Integrating Technology

For General Information, Resources, and Learning Interchange

Apple Learning Interchange (http://www.ali.apple.com/)

Center for Media Literacy (http://www.medialit.org/focus/tea_home.html)

EducationNow.com (http://educationnow.com)

In Time (http://www.intime.uni.edu)

In Time Multicultural (http://www.intime.uni.edu/multiculture/)

National Service Learning Clearinghouse (http://www.servicelearning.org)

Tapped In (http://tappedin.org/tappedin/)

Technology Education Lab (http://www.techedlab.com/k12.html)

Your Ideas

For Technology-Supported Learning Communities

Berkeley (http://www.kie.berkeley.edu/KIE.html)

Global Learning and Observations to Benefit the Environment (GLOBE) (http://www.nsf.gov/pubs/2006/nsf06515/nsf06515.htm)

Global Schoolhouse Project (http://www.virtualschool.edu/mon/Academia/GlobalSchoolhouseProject.html)

Journey North: Annenberg Media (http://www.learner.org/jnorth/)

Knowledge Integration Environment (KIE): University of California at

For Teleconferencing

Global SchoolNet (http://www.gsn.org/cu/)

For ThinkQuests and Other Inquiry-Based Learning

Academy (http://www2.imsa.edu/programs/pbln/)

Classroom Connect (http://www.classroomconnect.com/)

The Exploratorium: Institute for Inquiry (http://www.exploratorium.edu/ifi/)

International Society for Technology in Education (http://www.iste.org/)

Oracle ThinkQuest International Challenge (http://www.thinkquest.org/)

Problem-Based Learning Network: Illinois Mathematics and Science

For Interactive Learning Labs

TechLearning (http://www.techlearning.com/)
Texas Computer Education Association (www.tcea.org)

Using Computers Across the Disciplines

Center for Arts Education (http://www.cae-nyc.org)

Development Education Program: World Bank (http://www.worldbank.org/depweb)

MATHCOUNTS (http://mathcounts.org/)

The Math Forum (http://mathforum.org/)

National Council for the Social Studies (http://www.socialstudies.org)

Project-Based Science: University of Michigan (http://www.umich.edu/~pbsgroup/)

World Resources Institute (http://www.wri.org)

Your Ideas

PROMOTING MEDIA LITERACY

With the vast amount of information available at their fingertips, adolescents need critical literacy skills not only to learn with media but also to learn to think critically about media (Ohler, 2005–2006). Alvermann (2000), in *Adolescents and Literacies in a Digital World*, edits a series of case studies that address the growing need for educators to provide adolescents with the skills for critical inquiry in this age of information overload. The Center for Media Literacy (2002–2006) educates that media messages are value laden, constructed creatively, and organized for commercial reasons. The Center suggests five key questions to consider when assessing the quality of media messages.

1. Who created the message?
2. What creative techniques are used to attract my attention?
3. How might different people understand this message differently from me?
4. What values, lifestyles, and points of view are represented in, or omitted from, this message?
5. Why is this message being sent?

Ohler (2005–2006) proposes digital stories as powerful learning opportunities for students to develop media literacy because they must analyze information in order to create the stories. In this way, adolescents learn with media *and* learn to think critically about it. The ACT Model "The Information Challenge" illustrates another way to help adolescents learn to evaluate the vast amount of information so readily available. In this interdisciplinary ACT focused on the theme of commercialism, teams of students critique various advertisements in print and nonprint media and other consumer sources in terms of targeted marketing appeal, accuracy of information, and truthful representation. As a culminating assessment, students design multimedia commercials to market an original product to their peers.

The Information Challenge: Deceived by the Truth?

Adolescents are bombarded with advertisements and luring messages on the Internet, television, and radio, and from audio and print sources, such as billboards and newspapers. According to the *U.S. News and World Report* (Whitman, 2005), the commercial market purposefully targets, through emotional appeal and persuasion, adolescents as consumers who spend hundreds of billions of dollars per year in the areas of music, fashion, sports, and entertainment, and pursuing pseudosophisticated lifestyles. The challenge to youth is to sort through the marketing blitz, recognize the method of attraction, and determine fact from fiction or embellishment. At times, they may have to realize that even the truth can be deceiving. This thematic unit focuses on the impact of commercialism on adolescents' social, emotional, and intellectual development.

Content Understanding

Theme: Commercialism

Interdisciplinary: To help adolescents learn to evaluate the print and nonprint communication for bias, sensationalism, and advertising appeal and to apply the skills of statistical data analysis and decision making as potential consumers.

Technology Standards: Consider student use of technology to do the following:

- Locate, evaluate, and collect information from a variety of sources
- Process data, report results, and evaluate and select new information resources and technological innovations based on their appropriateness for specific tasks
- Solve problems and make informed decisions

Key Concepts

Advertising, personal bias, sensationalism, marketing, embellishment, consumer, commercialism, anecdotal testimonial, nonrandom and nonrepresentative sampling

Learning Outcomes

- By viewing popular "infomercials" and by examining facts about consumerism, students will discern the differences between sensationalized marketing blitz and credible advertising.
- By examining consumer information data, students will investigate instances in which various populations have been used as target groups for advertising.

- By evaluating advertisements containing cultural material, students will consider how advertising can perpetuate stereotypes.
- By critiquing tabloids and Web sites, students will use scientific inquiry to determine the sensationalism of written and electronic media.
- By examining specific products and written and online documents, students will use mathematical skills to determine discrepancies in food labels and consumer reports.

ESSENTIAL QUESTION

How does commercialism affect the lives of teens?

Strategies for Inquiry

Precipitating Question: If you wanted to market a product to your peers, what techniques would you use to make it appeal to them?

Teachers ask students to consider the following challenge:

Ongoing allegations by consumers against large tobacco companies have resulted in multimillion dollar fines and judgments.

- Do you think these are justified?
- Should consumers be more responsible for their actions?
- Would your ideas change in any way if you were told that a high percentage of smokers begin smoking before the age of 12?
- What if you found out that many cigarette machines were intentionally placed near middle schools?
- How do you feel about the use of cartoon figures in tobacco ads?

Teachers show a popular television commercial and have students critique the appeal to the adolescent market.

Guided Inquiry

- In language arts, students view videotapes of popular "infomercials" (exercise programs, skin products, sports equipment) and other advertisements on the Internet, television, or in print. Guiding questions include the following: What is the emotional appeal? What tactics are used? Who is the targeted audience? Why? Where are any discrepancies or use of generalizations? How are testimonials used? What statistics are used? Are they valid? In small groups, students discuss the validity of the information and discern the rationale for consumer appeal.
- In social studies, students can evaluate local and international media portrayals of Middle Eastern cultures through an evaluation of political cartoons or advertisements that perpetuate the stereotyping of African, Arab, and Israeli cultures.

- In science, during a study of genetics, students use the scientific method to explore the sensationalism of tabloids and Web sites.
- In math, students calculate the discrepancies in food labels and advertisements, or use statistical knowledge and online consumer reports to determine the best car deal.

An excellent site with numerous ideas for activities aligned with the National Education Technology Standards (NETS) for Grades 6–8 and the topic of advert sing can be accessed through the NETS Web site (http://cnets.iste.org/students/pdf/6-8Advertising.pdf).

Metacognitive Development and Assessment

Teachers pose extension questions that promote reflection on observations. Examples follow:

- If testimonials, surveys, and statistical reports are truthful, how might they misrepresent the truth? (personal bias, nonrandom and nonrepresentative sampling, anecdotal testimonials)
- How do ads target certain audiences? (billboard location, Internet games, music, Web sites, television and radio timeslots)
- What makes advertising truthful? How can the accuracy be checked?
- Why is emotional appeal more effective? Can there be a balance, for example, truth and strategic appeal?

Student understanding is assessed through various content products:

- A language arts persuasive paper on the effect of commercialism on them and society
- A social studies advertisement to attract new British settlers to South Africa in the 1770s
- A role play to promote a new scientific advancement in DNA profiling
- A statistical analysis report of the truthfulness in the advertising of food companies

As a culminating assessment, teams of students create a multimedia commercial to promote an original product. Within groups, students assume various roles, including commercial designer, product designer, reporter, money manager, or research manufacturer. Teachers serve as advisors for each role, and a "loan" is extended for product and commercial development.

Other Helpful Online Resources for this ACT

Consumer Reports
http://www.consumerreports.org/

Corporate Watch
http://www.corpwatch.org/

Federal Citizen Information Center
http://www.pueblo.gsa.gov/

Federal Trade Commission
http://www.ftc.gov

Weekly World News Online
http://www.weeklyworldnews.com

SOURCE: Web site research courtesy of E. Crowell, A. Peoples-Robinson, and M. Swanik, May 2000, Elon University, North Carolina.

Evaluation criteria for the final presentation may include the following:

- Targeted audience appeal
- Accuracy of information
- Strategic (yet "truthful") persuasiveness
- Appropriateness of technology (graphics, audio enhancement)

Cross-Disciplinary Applications

- In English, in preparation for a research paper, adolescents might evaluate the credibility of Web sites for information.
- In science, students might interview NASA scientists (online) to check the validity of regional newspapers in reporting coverage of ongoing missions.

TECHNOLOGY AND CLASSROOM DIVERSITY

With the range of diversity in classrooms, the question of technology access and equity arises. Which students have an advantage over others because they have computers at home with fast Internet access? How does the economic gap impact students' opportunities to learn technology skills and acquire information over the Internet? A recent study by the Children's Partnership, entitled *Measuring Digital Opportunity for America's Children: Where We Stand and Where We Go From Here* (Lazarus, Wainer, & Lipper, 2005), offers both positive and negative information related to the digital divide. While the percentage of students and teachers using technology at home and in classrooms is increasing, a gap exists between higher-income households (earning more than $75,000 annually) and lower-income households (earning less than $15,000 annually). The disparity further exists among ethnic populations.

In steps toward more equitable access in the twenty-first century, schools are purchasing laptops for individual use and checkout, and libraries are loaning digital cameras and flash sticks (Valenza, 2005–2006). Librarians and teachers assist students by downloading on CDs alternative software, such as Open Office in lieu of the pricy PowerPoint package. Computer labs are open before and after school.

The fast-expanding technologies enable teachers to create learning environments that better respond to the social, cognitive, and personal needs of adolescents. These environments support sustained exploration and collaborative inquiry about relevant, authentic, and challenging problems. Adolescents assume responsibility, develop confidence, and become competent as they share expertise and construct personal understanding about important knowledge.

Affirming Diversity

American classrooms are becoming increasingly diverse. Students from non-English-speaking backgrounds, for example, represent the fastest growing subset of the preK–12 student population (Short & Echevarria, 2004–2005).

The proportion of students of color will approach 50% of the nation's school-age youth by the year 2020 (Banks & Banks, 2001). These demographic, social, and economic trends have important implications for the classroom environment, curriculum design, and teaching. Banks and Banks promote the integration of multicultural education to promote positive relationships among varying races and ethnic groups.

Your Ideas

Gay (2002) stresses the need to recognize, honor, and incorporate the personal abilities of ethnically diverse students into instruction because their intellectual potential often goes untapped. Culturally responsive teaching uses the cultural characteristics, experiences, and perspectives of ethnically diverse students as conduits for teaching them more effectively. When academic knowledge and skills are situated within the lived experiences and frames of references of students, they are more personally meaningful, have a higher interest appeal, and are learned more easily and thoroughly. Here are some elements of culturally responsive teaching:

- Developing a knowledge base about cultural diversity and including ethnic and cultural diversity in the content of the curriculum
- Demonstrating caring and building learning communities
- Communicating with ethnically diverse students
- Responding to ethnic diversity in the delivery of instruction

Short and Echevarria (2004–2005) reiterate that students who are English language learners have diverse backgrounds, languages, and education profiles that impact their potential for school success.

> Some read and write above grade level in their own language; others have limited schooling. Some enter school highly motivated to learn because of family support or an innate drive to succeed; others have had negative experiences that squelched their motivation. Many come from middle-class families with high levels of literacy; others live in poverty without books in their homes. Those whose native language is based on Latin can recognize English words with the same Latin derivatives; those who have different language backgrounds, such as Mandarin or Arabic, lack that advantage. Some students' native language does not even have a written form. (pp. 9–10)

It is also important to acknowledge that English language learners have two jobs in the classroom: learning a new language and learning new academic content (Carrier, 2005). The time required for second language acquisition is one to three years to develop conversational proficiency and five to seven years to develop academic content area English. The following box summarizes several instructional strategies that promote learning while affirming the identity of adolescents in multicultural and multilingual classrooms (Aronson, 2004; Carrier, 2005; Cummings et al., 2005; Landsman, 2004; Short & Echevarria, 2004–2005). Additional ideas for teaching adolescents who are English language learners can be found at the National Clearinghouse for English Language Acquisition (NCELA), accessed at http://www.ncela.gwu.edu/practice/itc/secondary.html.

Affirming Identity in Multicultural and Multilingual Classrooms

Multicultural Strategies

- Overcome negative stereotypes through use of cooperative learning structures and by creating a climate of respect.
- Experience other cultures through multicultural literature, class discussions, and literacy circles.
- Build awareness of diverse cultures through displays in classrooms, hallways, and media centers.
- Strengthen interaction between families and school through letters, school events, and positive communication.
- Enrich curriculum by weaving in achievements and ideas of diverse writers, thinkers, and historical figures.
- Hold high expectations for *all* students in work completion, answering questions at varying cognitive levels, and adherence to classroom procedures and policy.

Multilingual Strategies

- Modify lessons to address language needs by identifying language demands on the content and providing extra support in developing content specific vocabulary through word walls, word sorts, semantic webs, and sentence structures.
- Use multiple modes of input that increase comprehension, including manipulatives, pictures, videos, demonstrations, movement, games, drama, gestures, multimedia, and hands-on activities.
- Incorporate multiple modes of output that reduce need for a high level of language proficiency, such as pictures, graphic organizers, demonstrations, and drawings.
- Activate and strengthen background knowledge by tapping into what students know, for example, about conflict to understand the U.S. Civil War.
- Promote oral interaction and extended academic talk by talking less and engaging through probing questions and writing key phrases or terms on the board.
- Affirm identity by allowing students to create an expressive written, oral, dramatic, or artistic product, or to write dual language books.

CONNECTING THROUGH SUBSTANTIVE CONTENT

Adolescents face a world where complex ethical issues vie for their attention. Human cloning and genetic engineering define the landscape of biotechnology, international peace is negotiated with chemical warfare, and medical advancement competes with cultural preservation. Students struggle regularly with moral decisions and social actions, and society puzzles over the motivation behind teen violence. In his book, *The Disciplined Mind: What All Students Should Understand*, Howard Gardner (1999) describes the importance of educating today's students for a world that has changed dramatically and is continuing to change rapidly: "I envision a world citizenry that is highly literate, disciplined, capable of thinking critically and creatively, knowledgeable about a range of cultures, able to participate actively in discussions about new discoveries and choices, willing to take risks for what it believes in" (p. 25).

Your Ideas

Unfortunately, classroom learning experiences are often dictated by a curriculum that puts heavy emphasis on textbook knowledge, definitive solutions, and predictable steps. The pressure of end-of-course tests and advanced-placement examinations has forced many teachers to cover information so rapidly that the opportunity to delve into meaningful content issues is limited. Opportunities to think conceptually about the significant ideas that endure beyond the classroom experience are often minimal (Sizer & Sizer, 1999; Wiggins & McTighe, 1998). Regardless of the circumstances, the need to deal with matters of greater significance remains in adolescents' lives.

The Shortfall of Fragile Knowledge

Challenging adolescents to think more deeply about content begins with a look at the content itself. In many instances, adolescents are asked to "learn" content that lacks purpose, relevance, connection, or meaningfulness to what they know, can relate to, or have experienced. Also, rather than stimulating and challenging adolescents' intellectual curiosity about important content issues, some teachers merely tell students what they need to know. They may not allow for meaningful interaction with the content.

For a number of years, educators have been concerned that students' practical understanding of pertinent concepts and underlying principles is limited (Gardner, 1991, 1999; Resnick, 1987, 1999; Sizer, 1996; Sizer & Sizer, 1999). Perkins, in his book *Smart Schools: From Training Memories to Educating Minds* (1992), writes of a shortfall in students' ability to retain, apply, and use knowledge in a way that helps them to benefit and understand their world. He describes this knowledge as "fragile" in terms of its being incomplete, misconceived, ritualistic, or even just retained long enough for a test (p. 26). Adolescents may have simplistic theories about scientific principles or mathematical concepts. They may lack knowledge about geographical location, be confused about historical phenomena, or be too literal in interpretation. They may also cling to stereotypical perceptions of culture, race, or ethnicity.

Not confined to a particular discipline, fragile knowledge is perpetuated when information is simply added on rather than connected to what students already know. Perkins urges teachers to structure learning experiences in which students are challenged to "learn about and think with what they are learning" (1992, p. 8). In his 1933 book, *How We Think*, John Dewey expresses early dismay for an education system that viewed young people as passive recipients in the learning process. His continuing concern for the detrimental effect

Your Ideas

of education that does not focus on students and their learning is evident in the questions he raises in a later book, *Experience and Education* (1938, pp. 26–27):

> How many students . . . were rendered callous to ideas, and how many lost the impetus to learn because of the way in which learning was experienced by them? How many acquired special skills by means of automatic drill so that their power of judgment and capacity to act intelligently in new situations was limited? How many came to associate the learning process with ennui and boredom? How many found what they did learn so foreign to the situations of life outside the school as to give them no power of control over the latter?

The Danger of Low Expectations

Setting expectations too low may be linked to an underestimation of adolescents' capabilities. There might be the fear that struggling students will "give up" under the pressure to work harder or if they are expected to put more thought and energy into an assignment. Teachers may think that some adolescents lack the background experience, knowledge, or ability to handle a complex task. In some instances, the climate of the entire school revolves around the philosophy that adolescents should not be pushed too hard academically and that their educational experiences should be the last safe haven "before the world turns serious on them" (Gibbs, 1999, p. 70).

For whatever reason, expectations are often set lower than what adolescents can handle. Teens are frequently given limited opportunity to wrestle mentally with substantive subject matter. In their recent book, *The Students Are Watching: Schools and the Moral Contract*, Sizer and Sizer (1999) use the term "grappling" to denote the process of striving to know important content on a level that reflects true understanding. Grappling involves the discussion of content-related issues and problems pertinent to the ongoing experiences of adolescents. Grappling also assumes that these students have something meaningful to contribute, such as relevant knowledge or ventured opinions. Because adolescents are considering, questioning, and formulating beliefs that will affect their decisions, they should be encouraged to express themselves, so their thoughts can be developed, refined, and strengthened. To underestimate what adolescents have to offer or to believe that a certain level of thinking is beyond them is expecting too little.

CHALLENGE AND BRAIN-BASED INSTRUCTION

Adolescents are forthright about what helps and motivates them to think and learn. They want to know the reasons behind historical trends, and they enjoy designing their own art projects. They learn biology better when they work in a school greenhouse, learn math better when they help to construct a shed to house the football team's athletic equipment, and learn music theory better when they write their own compositions. They like to discuss books that relate

Your Ideas

to their lives, to consider questions that have more than one answer, and, as one ninth grader volunteered, they actually prefer assignments that "make you think." They also prefer teachers who understand that "one style won't always work." They are bored by meaningless facts in a chapter-by-chapter progression. They are frustrated by busy work, by having insufficient time to complete an assignment, and with unvarying teaching methods.

Conversely, adolescents are motivated and their brains are stimulated by complexity, challenge, and intellectual stimulation (Strong, Silver, & Robinson, 1995). As discussed in Chapter 1, adolescents are naturally curious, and they are intrinsically motivated to find answers to perplexing questions or solutions to unresolved problems. Their intellect is stimulated by tasks that are novel, personally interesting, authentic, and "perceived as worthy by both adolescents and by the larger society" (Sizer & Sizer, 1999, p. 5). They can be expected to grapple with intricate content and to gain genuine understanding.

In making curriculum and instructional decisions in support of brain-based learning, teachers might ask the following questions:

- Has time been allotted to identify the important knowledge, including facts, concepts and principles, or the essential understandings of a discipline?
- Is the content too broad, too unconnected, or too prescriptive, in what has been referred to as "broad-brush knowledge" (Wiggins & McTighe, 1998, p. 9)?
- Has consideration been given to what is known and is familiar to adolescents?
- Has thought been given to the manner in which students can be intrigued and actively involved?
- Have students been encouraged to question or speculate?
- Will they be allowed to simulate, debate, discuss, reflect, or err?

The ACT Model "Technology and Interdisciplinary Learning" provides an interdisciplinary example that is interactive, engaging, and appropriately challenging for adolescent learners. Adolescents explore the theme of interrelationship as it applies to the balance between, on the one side, commercial and industrial progress and, on the other, the conservation and protection of natural resources. They assume the role of real-world stakeholders in a team project about diminishing rainforests, participate in guided online research to gather data, write position papers, and prepare and participate in a podcast debate about the pertinent issues. Throughout this motivational experience, adolescents have opportunities to explore; use technology as a tool for research, problem solving, and decision making; and assume responsibility for their own learning management.

Technology and Interdisciplinary Learning: Transitions in the Rainforest

Adolescents learn better when they are allowed to work together on relevant tasks and problems. An interdisciplinary team project revolving around a pertinent theme immerses them in a learning experience across content areas. Other benefits include challenging tasks, ongoing feedback on personal progress, a variety of learning products, and a culminating performance assessment. Throughout the experience, adolescents are given opportunities to explore ideas, research using technology, and make decisions and choices. Adolescents are highly motivated as they assume increasing responsibility over learning management.

Content Understanding

Theme: Interrelationship

Science: Help students construct knowledge of population dynamics and analyze practices that affect the use and management of natural resources.

Mathematics: Help students acquire skills for understanding graphing, probability, and data analysis.

Social Studies: Help students discern the interrelationship among resources, people, plants, and animals.

Language Arts: Help students use language to express individual perspectives and to develop critical thinking skills for persuasive writing.

Technology Standards: Using technology to locate, evaluate, and collect information from a variety of sources; to process data, report results, and evaluate; to select new information resources and technological innovations based on their appropriateness for specific tasks; and to problem solve and make informed decisions.

Key Concepts

Natural resources, conservation, environmental interrelationship, stakeholders, commercial and industrial progress, and persuasive writing and debate

Learning Outcomes

- By assuming roles and participating in guided online research, students will recognize the varying viewpoints of stakeholders in problems that pit commercial and industrial development against conservationists.

- Students will relate to the causes of diminishing rainforests in various parts of the world by gathering and comparing trends.
- Students will develop skills and techniques for persuasive writing and debate by writing position papers and by preparing and participating in a podcast debate.

ESSENTIAL QUESTION

What is the interrelationship among people and natural resources in the environment?

Strategies for Inquiry

A Problem-Based Role Play

Four students will assume the following parts (with props) and present a role play:

- Rainforest Native complains about the land, home, and food disappearing.
- Business Person/Logger says that the company is taking the trees and land to make a living.
- Scientist/Researcher expresses concern for the loss of raw materials for medicines.
- Environmentalist takes the side of the Rainforest Native in protection of the land and its resources.

A video documentary about rainforest destruction can be shown, followed by questions such as these: What is the major problem? Who are the groups involved in the conflict? What do you currently know about the argument of each?

Guided Interaction

- Teachers divide students into the four representative groups with the task of researching this perspective over a two-week period in preparation for a podcast debate as a culminating technology-enhanced presentation.

Supporting Learning Experiences Across Classes

- In science, students explore the geographical location, climatic conditions, and plant life of rainforests. Comparisons are made with areas in the United States and graphs are produced. Students respond to this question: Should plant life be preserved in rainforests? Students interview real conservationists through Internet sources. Students research selected environmentalists.
- In math, students learn graphing techniques, including the creation of histograms, stem, pie, and bar graphs, and spreadsheet applications to use with rainforest data. Data is accessed to interpret trends, such as the increase in paved roads or decrease in a kind of vegetation.
- In social studies, students participate in guided research according to assigned roles using Internet search engines and Web sites shared by teachers, such as Amazon Interactive. (See sidebar on the next page.) Their perspectives are represented by a creative rainforest brochure. They also learn the techniques for debate.

- In language arts, students learn the techniques of persuasive writing. Model essays about other environmental issues, such as global warming, forest conservation, or strip mining, are analyzed. Students ultimately develop a persuasive essay representing a stance on the rainforest issue.

Metacognitive Development and Assessment

- The culminating project is a podcast debate that is broadcast for other students in the school or community. Students engage in a structured debate that sheds light on this real-world issue and on the varying perspectives of authentic stakeholders. A student representative from each group sits on the debate panel. One or two other students per group sit on a questioning panel, and the remaining students and teachers form the audience. Debate criteria include logic of presentation, credibility of information, persuasiveness of argument, representation of role, verbal delivery of speech, and involvement in counterquestioning.
- Other ideas for technology-enhanced products: a class Web portal that identifies issues related to rainforest conservation, a blog on related issues, or an interactive WebQuest.

Metacognitive Extension

Student learning can be transferred through discussion and extended research to other instances when commercial progress and the conservation of natural resources collide. Here are some sample topics:

- Conflicts between commercial developers and those protecting diminishing wetlands
- Issues between the logging industry and those protecting the natural habitats of wildlife
- Tensions between oil refinery policies and the protection of ocean birds and animals
- Effects of strip mining (soil erosion and contamination of rivers and streams)
- Problems associated with industrial pollution and global warming
- Concerns over the disposal of industrial waste and the toxic effect on fish in rivers and on humans through drinking water

Additional Teacher/Student Internet Resources to Facilitate Inquiry

The Smithsonian Center for Tropical Forest Science (http://www.ctfs.si.edu/)
Educational Web Adventures: Amazon Interactive (http://www.eduweb.com/amazon.html)
Forest Conservation Portal (http://forests.org/)
Wealth of the Rainforest: Help With Rainforest School Reports (http://www.rain-tree.com/schoolreports.htm)
Skyrail: Tropical Rainforests (http://www.skyrail.com.au/rainforests.html)

SOURCE: Web site research courtesy of S. Howard, S. Simpson, C. Spigle, and K. Stack, May 2000, Elon University, North Carolina.

Cross-Disciplinary Applications

- The standard curriculum is a rich source of problems, issues, and themes that connect the content areas. A few that are pertinent to adolescent learning include transitions, identities, interdependence, independence, conflict resolution, justice, social structures, caring, and wellness (Stevenson, 2002).

CREATING A SAFE PLACE TO THINK AND LEARN

Your Ideas

When adolescents are asked what they like best about classes where they learn the most, they frequently begin by identifying the personal traits of the teacher. "He has a sense of humor." "She is friendly." "He is patient." "She cares about us." "He always found a way to connect with every student." Parker Palmer, in his book *The Courage to Teach*, describes teachers who attend to the personal dimension in this way: "Good teachers possess a capacity for connectedness. They are able to weave a complex web of connections among themselves, their subjects, and their students so that students can learn to weave a world for themselves" (1998, p. 11). On a simple level, personal connection with adolescents is made through teacher gestures that convey interest, caring, or thoughtfulness. These small acts might include the following:

- Baking a cake to celebrate a class accomplishment
- Using some Spanish terms to help explain a geometry concept for Spanish-speaking English language learners
- Giving students an opportunity to write about their feelings in journals

On another level, personal connection is made through teacher actions that give adolescents opportunity and choice:

- Allowing a highly gifted student to do independent work with more advanced concepts
- Helping students draw relationships between historical events and current events
- Permitting students to choose the artistic style for a self-portrait assignment

Connecting with adolescents on a personal level is needed to help them develop intellectually and ethically. Adolescence is a formative, tentative, and pivotal time when students are contemplating significant personal and societal issues. Their ideas may be somewhat confused or misconceived, ill structured or unrefined, yet adolescents need to feel that their contribution in a discussion matters to the teacher (Sizer & Sizer, 1999). Adolescents can be encouraged to do the following:

- Share personal perspectives through persuasive writing, interpretive discussion, and creative approaches
- Examine their assumptions through opportunities to express, question, and test original ideas
- Consider alternatives through debating, role playing, problem solving, or other "encounters" with differing viewpoints, approaches, or solutions
- Think critically about personal decisions and actions by specifying the consequences in a simulated or real context

Adolescents are more likely to take the risk involved in letting others know what they are thinking, when they feel accepted, valued, respected, and supported on a personal level.

Your Ideas

The feeling of personal connectedness is closely aligned with perceived emotional safety, which is a brain-compatible condition for thinking and learning. In this period of developmental upheaval, when students' thoughts are more socially than academically oriented, emotions are confusing and quick to surface. The naïve sense of security of childhood has turned into an uncomfortable time of self-consciousness and awkwardness. Students are pulling away, testing limits, exploring sexuality, questioning identity, and negotiating relationships. To confound the situation, as discussed in Chapter 1, adolescents' immature capability for emotional management closely parallels underdeveloped areas of the brain. Emotionally charged neural responses may lead to quick reactions and self-protective actions (Sylwester, 1999). Because of the range of their prior experiences, some supportive and caring and others not so healthy, adolescents bring different kinds of personal and emotional needs. The following box lists a few signs of emotional and social distress that may signal problems.

Signs of Emotional and Social Distress

Social withdrawal

Excessive feelings of isolation, loneliness, or rejection

Excessive feelings of persecution

Uncontrolled anger

Patterns of impulsive and chronic hitting, intimidation, and bullying behaviors

Low school interest, low academic performance

Consistent alcohol or drug use

Affiliation with gangs

Expression of violence in writings or drawings

Serious threats of violence

Accessing, possessing, and using firearms inappropriately

History of discipline problems and violent and aggressive behavior

Intolerance for differences, prejudices

Similarly, adolescents' emotions under negative conditions, such as fear of failure, embarrassment, or physical harm, can overpower cognition and thus impede thinking and learning (Beamon, 1997; Wolfe, 2001). These students need the personal stability of a learning environment where they feel accepted, valued, and physically and emotionally "safe." When classroom climate is characterized by personal connection, positive interaction, and trust, adolescents' social and emotional behaviors can be positively directed, and they can develop healthy behaviors.

GIVING ADOLESCENTS THE CHANCE TO SUCCEED

Adolescents still read aloud passages from Tennessee Williams's poignant script of love and betrayal, discuss the causes of major world conflict, solve algebraic equations, and struggle with periodic tables. They face the confusion of identity, the fear of belonging, and the uncertainty of future direction. While the rituals of their daily existence seem perennial and they are perplexed by the changes that have characterized the period of youth for centuries, adolescents of the new century represent a group more diverse, more experienced, more aware, more expectant, and yet more vulnerable than in past decades. Their world is extensive and compelling, and their future promises to be fast-paced and intellectually demanding. Technology has given them new autonomy over learning, broadened their avenues of communication, and heightened their awareness of a sophisticated world.

Your Ideas

Teachers who teach with adolescent learning in mind plan differently for instruction and create responsive environments for adolescents' cognitive, social, and emotional development and learning. They model adolescent-centered instruction in various ways:

- Giving students more opportunities to solve mathematical word problems
- Allowing students to work in pairs or small groups
- Expecting students to share their views on current social issues and to debate different sides
- Stressing critical thinking daily
- Conducting inquiry-based discussion and Socratic seminars
- Using technology instructionally as a thinking tool
- Spending time talking about what it means to walk in another person's shoes
- Talking about feelings and emotions, and about positive actions and negative reactions

These teachers realize the importance of active learning experiences that challenge adolescents to discuss ideas, to ask questions, and to work together to solve problems. They use seminars, debates, and case studies and simulations to bring real experiences into the classroom. They understand that knowledge building is not limited to the local setting, and they plan inquiry-based projects that enable students to use technology for communication and information gathering. These teachers are more mindful of adolescents' learning preferences and capabilities as they plan, and they consider content and challenge when they make decisions about instruction. They also pay attention to students' emotional and personal needs.

Teachers who focus on adolescent learning in a brain-based approach also consider their relationship with their students in terms of role and responsibility. They realize that they need to facilitate understanding rather than to deliver information; they strive to connect with what students know, to demonstrate and model, and to support and give feedback as students work. They recognize that for adolescents to think and learn better, they must interact meaningfully with knowledge, with each other, and with resourceful others. These teachers also realize that for adolescents to become independent, they need some degree of choice in how they pursue learning and demonstrate understanding. Their students also must think together about substantive content and take responsibility for their achievement and progress. In the future, adolescents must be versed in problem solving and teamwork skills, and they will need to be able to take charge and monitor their own thinking and learning. The quality of their experiences in middle and high school classrooms can provide this preparation.

ACTing

on the Adolescent-Centered Learning Principles Discussed in Chapter 2

Principle	*How I can put it into practice*
❏ Prepare students for the high expectations of the new millennium.	
❏ Broaden avenues of communication among all partners in education.	
❏ Allow for students to share their ideas with others in and beyond classrooms.	
❏ Use technology appropriately as a tool to enhance student thinking and learning.	
❏ Affirm students' individual cultural and language differences.	
❏ Build meaningful relationships with students' families.	
❏ Create classrooms characterized by respect, inclusion, interaction, and appropriate challenge.	
❏ Give students a chance to produce high quality work and see the relevance and purpose in what they are being asked to learn.	

CHAPTER

3

Creating a Community of Learners

A BETTER UNDERSTANDING OF LEARNING

The differences between the two classrooms are remarkable. In the first, rows of students focus on the task of copying a hastily written geometry problem from an overhead screen in the front of the room. A couple of motivational sports posters are stapled to a side bulletin board. The teacher stands behind the projector, reminding students to work quietly and waiting for a hand to indicate that an answer has been found. A female student asks, "Is that a one or a seven?" Another puts down her pencil and slumps in her desk with the frustrated comment, "I don't even know what a hypotenuse is! I've never done this in my life. I come here every day and have never understood this." A guy in the back calls out an answer, and the teacher writes the solution. Around the room conversations begin as another triangle is drawn on the acetate.

Your Ideas

In contrast, in the second classroom, pairs of students with rulers, notes, markers, and calculators in hand pore over chart paper. An earlier walk around the school has given them ideas for geometry word problems that they are now composing with a partner to pass for other classmates to solve. The teacher is spotted, after a couple of minutes, kneeling beside one team whose problem involves finding the area within the triangular support beams of the gym bleachers. Student work peppers the walls. The bulletin board challenges students to post different and creative ways to solve a mystery problem. Over the door frame, an encircled word "EXCUSES," crossed by a diagonal line, clearly specifies the teacher's expectations.

Educators committed to the study of learning and the craftsmanship of teaching share similar ideas about adolescent learning (Resnick, 1999). A goal of learning, for example, is to help students become responsible managers of their own cognition. Knowledge is not a collection of facts but rather the meaningful interpretation of ideas. Learning is contextualized and thus related to the situation in which it is learned. Learning is the socially shared construction of knowledge, and thinking is highly dependent on the mental manipulation of the individual learner. Four interrelated strands (see Figure 3.1) are common across the cognitive science, socio-cognitive, and brain-based learning literature. These are listed below and detailed in the following sections.

Adolescent learning . . .

involves active mental processing by the learner,

is enhanced by purposeful interaction,

necessitates thinking about knowledge in meaningful ways, and

thrives in a context of social-emotional support.

Figure 3.1 A Convergence of Theory About Learning

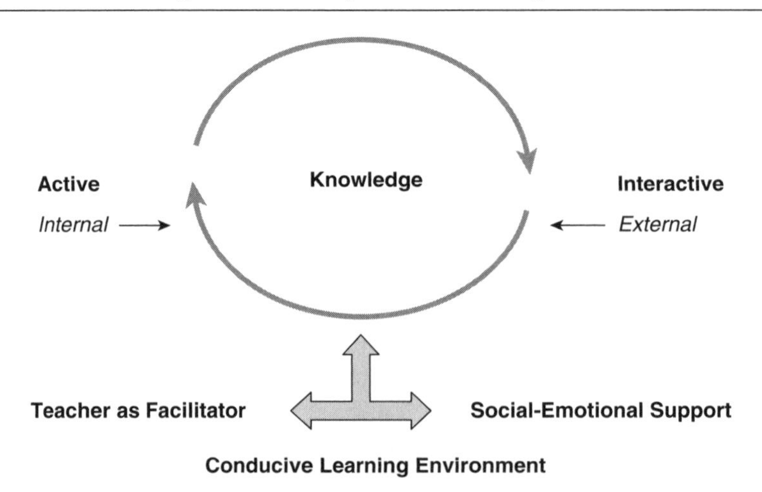

LEARNING IS ACTIVE

Your Ideas

Adolescents do not merely "absorb" information to reproduce it: they actively construct personal meaning based on how they relate to or make sense of what they are trying to learn or understand. Current studies of the brain's activity during learning show that the mind constantly attempts to "chunk" together and organize pieces of new information, connecting these with what is already familiar in the individual's knowledge base or personal experience (Caine & Caine, 1997; Jensen, 2000; Sylwester, 2003). The cognitive structures, or schemata, that form a network of unrelated information can be accessed through memory and future associations. The learning process is highly individual and internal, and it depends heavily on the knowledge, experiences, and other schemata in place at the time. Teachers may try hard to impose knowledge upon adolescents; however, the extent that students internalize and remember it is based on how well they are able to connect the new learning with what they know, believe, and feel. The ACT Model "Learning as Active Meaning Making" provides an example. Adolescents explicate a poem by T. S. Eliot to understand how poets convey personal feelings through imagery. They construct their own poem as a personal expression, which is also used as a performance-based assessment, and consider comparable ways of creative expression in the fine arts as a metacognitive extension.

Learning as Active Meaning Making: Can You Think Like a Poet?

Adolescents at times have a perception that poetry is boring and difficult to understand. Teachers have to work strategically to help them relate poetical imagery and abstract ideas to personal experiences. One instructional strategy is to enable them to think like poets. Here, T. S. Eliot is the poet studied.

Content Understanding

To help adolescents learn to explicate metaphorical imagery in poetry.

Key Concepts

Explication, metaphor, imagery, expatriate, verse, free verse

ESSENTIAL QUESTION

How do poets use metaphorical imagery to convey personal feelings?

Strategies for Inquiry

- As a preliminary exercise, students write a personal interpretation of abstract images. These concepts include peace, silence, loneliness, relationship, betrayal, or others that seem relevant to their lives.
- After a few students share aloud, the teacher asks if the images they created with words sound poetic. The teacher explains that poetry is written about something that is important to someone. Poems have a meaning that is personally relevant to the poet. Each word of a poem is carefully chosen by the poet to convey this meaning.
- Students need prior knowledge of the political and social nature of early-twentieth-century America. The novels of F. Scott Fitzgerald, Ernest Hemingway, and John Steinbeck, for example, provide rich fictional accounts of this historical period.

The Inquiry Mind-Set

Imagine yourself as a poet living during a time when you feel personal frustration about what is happening in your native country and in your own life. Imagine you are so frustrated with what you perceive as a society devoid of values or morality that you decide to renounce your citizenship and move to another country.

Guided Interaction

- The teacher reads aloud the first stanza of Eliot's "The Hollow Men" and asks students to visualize the figurative images conveyed. Guiding questions may include the following:
  - Can a person's head seem like it's full of straw?
  - Can there be shape without form? Or shade without color?
  - When can a gesture be without motion?
  - Can someone be alive but still feel dead? When?
- Students visualize a cartoon box out of which a character cannot escape or someone trapped in jail looking out on life.
- An explanation of the term "oxymoron" as a contradiction of words is constructed. Examples include deafening silence or blind vision.
  - Can a person be blind to life? How?
  - How do Eliot's words make you feel? Have you ever felt "hollow"?
- The remaining stanzas are read aloud by various students. Groups of students are assigned specific verses to explicate, and interpretations are shared and discussed.
- Students read about another early-twentieth-century poet and analyze at least one poem in terms of this poet's personal, political, or religious beliefs or cultural context. These are discussed and contrasted.

Metacognitive Development and Assessment

- Students work individually or in pairs to construct a short poem (free verse is acceptable) that conveys a relevant message, personal feeling, or concern they have as adolescents. A software program, such as Inspiration, is used to help students organize ideas graphically, and drafts are typed and edited on the computer.
- Finished products are published on the class Web page or blog for other adolescents to read, critique, and respond to; poems may also be printed in a school publication, sent to a publisher, or shared with a poet.
- Adolescents reflect on their own (possibly changed) beliefs about poetry and on their ability to make meaning.

Metacognitive Extension Question

What other ways are feelings conveyed through creative media (e.g., art, dance, sculpture)?

Your Ideas

LEARNING IS INTERACTIVE

Current theorists additionally acknowledge that learning is a social process supported through meaningful interaction with resources in the learning environment (Perkins, 1992; Resnick, 1987). Resnick notes that "human cognition is so varied and sensitive to cultural context" that ways must be found for people to "actively shape each other's knowledge and reasoning processes" (1987, p. 2). When thinking is socially shared, she suggests, adolescents' internal mental conversations are made visible, and the knowledge they bring to the learning experience can be examined, built upon, strengthened, and, if necessary, reshaped. This social-intellectual interaction with internal and external resources is known as *shared cognition.*

The external resources that support adolescent learning may be human, such as the teacher, other students, and other adults, or they may be symbolic tools that enable students to retrieve, manipulate, and organize information. These symbolic supports can include various technologies, such as computers or graphing calculators, or they may be graphic organizers, such as K/NK charts, diagrams, observation reports, sequence chains, decision-making structures, dialectic journals, concept webs, story maps, ranking ladders, flow charts, and analogy links (Daniels & Bizar, 1998; Fogarty & Bellanca, 1995b). Perkins (1992) uses the term "person-plus" to explain this purposeful interaction of the learner's inner resources with the range of supports in the learning surroundings (p. 134). The following examples illustrate.

Visual Organizers

- A teacher helps students use a large Venn diagram drawn on the board to compare and contrast the cultures of two Native American groups. This graphic design enables adolescents to view information and organize the knowledge so that differences and similarities are more visually apparent.
- Students use a dialectic journal (divided notebook page) to show problem figuring and mathematical reasoning in trigonometry. This graphic format helps to make their mental processes visible so that they can be examined, expanded, and improved.

Technology

- For the task of evaluating the visual impact of cultural portraiture, students in an art class visit the Web sites of the Louvre, the Tate Gallery, the National Portrait Gallery, and the Metropolitan Museum of Art. In this way, technology gives adolescents an interactive learning experience more authentic and effective than looking in the pages of an art book.
- Students in a health class use computerized exercise machines to gather data on the impact of aerobic conditioning on heart rate. Technology generates pertinent information easily, thus enabling adolescents to move more quickly to the analysis stage of the research process.

Your Ideas

Newspapers

- Students in an economics class analyze the causes of the stock market crash of 1929 by reading newspaper archive articles and talking with business students at an area college. These print and human resources provide rich historical information and current expertise that contribute to the adolescents' understanding of a complex economic phenomenon.

Noneducators

- An interview with a local author helps adolescents understand the literary elements of setting, characterization, and style. This real-world figure provides a credible and authentic resource as they learn firsthand through the words of a literary expert.

Peers

- A teacher arranges a tutoring partnership between students in two levels of math classes.
- Other students share perspectives with teens in Japan on world trade negotiations. The exchange of ideas with peers who may have alternate perspectives challenges and expands adolescents' learning.

DISTRIBUTED INTELLIGENCE

A phenomenon closely linked with the concept of shared cognition is *distributed intelligence* (Pea, 1993). Gardner (1999) theorizes that knowledge is distributed. Instead of residing "exclusively within the head of an individual . . . it emerges jointly from one's own perspective, the perspectives of others, and the information that is derived from available human and technical resources" (p. 98). When adolescents are permitted to interact cognitively with peers and to capitalize on other available resources in and beyond the classroom, their learning is expanded and enriched. As will be discussed later in the chapter, Vygotsky's (1978) concept of zone of proximal development suggests that when adolescents are guided by teachers or other competent adults, when they collaborate with more capable peers, or when they are assisted by pertinent learning devices, they achieve a level of competence beyond what they would have reached on their own (Bransford et al., 1999, 2000).

LEARNING AND KNOWLEDGE

Central to current theoretical agreement about learning is the importance of knowledge and how it is constructed during the learning process. Learning depends on the way adolescents deal internally and externally with knowledge (Resnick, 1999). Both the construction of knowledge and the acquisition of cognitive strategies to process information and solve problems are critical in

Your Ideas

this era of information explosion. Thoughtful learning, however, is more than simply adding, expanding, organizing, and reorganizing cognitive structures, although information-processing theorists of past decades have sometimes viewed it this way (Bransford et al., 1999; Perkins, 1992). Memory is important, yet knowledge needs to be related, extended, refined, and applied to new situations to be internalized (Marzano et al., 1992). The rapid cellular transactions that take place when such connections are made strengthen adolescents' understanding and provide a stronger knowledge base for future learning (Caine & Caine, 1997; Caine, Caine, McClintic, & Klimek, 2005; Jensen, 1998).

For adolescents to think about knowledge in a thoughtful way, four conditions are important (Beamon, 2001; Bransford et al., 1999, 2000; Perkins, 1992).

1. The knowledge needs to be substantive and considered "worthy" of adolescent thought. Though the attainment of facts or isolated information may be necessary in certain instances, adolescents' minds are more likely to relate to the broader ideas with which they can grapple or the intriguing problems that they can approach.
2. Adolescents should be expected to think critically about the knowledge they are acquiring. While adolescents need a solid foundation of basics—formulas, theorems, steps, principles—they need to interact with the knowledge in a meaningful way. They should question, apply, compare, adapt, speculate, analyze, synthesize, hypothesize, and draw conclusions about information.
3. Adolescents need an opportunity to construct an understanding of the knowledge in collaboration with others, including the teacher. Intentional and sustained interaction with supporting resources in the learning environment strengthens learning. Adolescents' knowledge base broadens as expertise is shared through collaboration.
4. The classroom climate needs to be conducive to intellectual, social, and emotional growth. In a learning environment where adolescents feel individually valued, accepted, and challenged, they will take a risk with higher level thinking, rise to teacher expectations, and progress toward improved thinking and understanding.

NONACADEMIC INFLUENCES ON LEARNING

Adolescents bring a host of individual differences to the classroom that affect learning. Students' race, religion, socioeconomic status, ethnicity, first language, and gender are critical factors that impact success and achievement. Each culture represented in the classroom, for example, brings its own set of social values, worldviews, behavioral standards, and beliefs that continue to shape students' lives (Delgado-Gaitan & Trueba, 1997). Teachers who perceive cultural diversity as significant will practice culturally responsive pedagogy that includes sensitivity to and knowledge of students' backgrounds; an awareness of learning styles; and a recognition of racism, classism, and sexism

(Larke, 1992, as cited in Darling, 2005, p. 47). Ladson-Billings (1995) defines culturally responsive pedagogy as

Your Ideas

> A theoretical model that posits effective pedagogical practice through addressing student achievement, helping students to accept and affirm cultural identity while developing cultural perspectives that challenge inequalities that schools perpetuate. (p. 469)

Other writers (Banks, 2001; Delpit, 1995; Gay, 2002; Nieto, 2000) recognize the critical need for culturally relevant pedagogy.

In the past decade, the number of students for whom English is a second language has increased 95% (National Clearinghouse for English Language Acquisition, 2004). Languages can vary from Spanish to Vietnamese to Russian to Arabic to Hmong, among many others. As mentioned earlier, the amount of time that it takes for an English language learner (ELL) to develop conversational proficiency ranges from one to three years; however, to develop academic English, the language of content learning, adolescents need five to seven years (Carrier, 2005). Teachers in core content areas face the simultaneous challenge of helping students to learn content and the English language and of developing literacy.

Several recommended strategies respond to the range of individual differences in culture, language need, and socioeconomic status. Curtin's (2006) research indicates that ELL students preferred an interactive teaching model, based on Bank's (2001) multicultural teaching behaviors, to a didactic, teacher- and subject-centered traditional model. Here are some components of pedagogy more responsive to cultural and linguistic differences:

- Personalization (knowing students' names, knowing and incorporating students' home and cultural backgrounds, communicating with families, using humor)
- Cooperative Learning (grouping students in pairs or small clusters regularly)
- Student-centered teaching (individualizing instruction, planning for different learning styles, expecting all students to interact, presenting instruction in multiple ways)
- Focus on the Process of Teaching (continually improving and adapting instructional delivery)
- Personal and Nonverbal Communication (intuition, empathy, classroom "with-it-ness," flexible management, walking around and gauging student reactions)
- Interaction (students and teachers involved in active and constant discussions and conversations)
- Democratic Discipline Style (less emphasis on silence and behaviors)

Payne (2006) advocates for a better understanding of the implicit middle class rules that often define a classroom culture. She offers ideas for designing classroom learning environments that are more responsive to children of poverty. (See http://homepages.wmich.edu/~ljohnson/Payne.pdf)

Your Ideas

The likelihood of academic success for students is closely tied to the connectedness in schools and classrooms (Blum, 2005). In connected classrooms, learning is relevant, expectations for behavior and performance are consistent, and students practice decision-making skills and exercise autonomy. Teachers use team and cooperative learning to build collaboration among differing populations, and they recognize a variety of student accomplishments. Stevenson (2002, p. 88) delineates specific attributes that define the resilience in adolescents who have overcome social and academic challenge in the classroom and out, including the following.

- Social competence, or the skills for flexibility, empathy, communication, responsiveness, and humor in relationships
- Problem-solving skills, or planning, resourcefulness, creativity, and reflection
- Critical consciousness, or understanding one's disadvantages and having the ability and disposition to overcome them
- Autonomy, or an integrated and healthy sense of personal identity that includes an internal locus of control and self-efficacy
- Sense of purpose, or optimism about the future

Helping all adolescents reach this level of personal growth is a key goal of the educational experience.

THE SOCIAL-EMOTIONAL CONTEXT

Adolescents often give the impression that they are secure, confident, calm, in command, and in need of no one, when, in actuality, they may be dealing with a range of emotions: How do I fit in? How can I fit in? How dumb does that sound? I know I can't do this. I hope no one finds out what I'm really feeling. I wish I could be more. . . . I wish I could be more like. . . . Their internal thoughts are preoccupied with questions about personal and social identity, yet they try hard to project an image of self-assuredness. The way adolescents feel about themselves and how they think others perceive them affect their learning.

While current theorists propose that learning is an active process enhanced through social interaction, they also agree that classrooms are not emotionally neutral places (Wolfe & Brandt, 1998). Adolescents' feelings, emotions, beliefs, and perceptions affect how they interact with each other, the attitude they have in general toward learning, and their motivation to commit to its challenge. "[L]earning is enhanced when the environment provides the opportunity to discuss their thinking out loud, to bounce their ideas off peers, and to produce collaborative work" (Wolfe & Brandt, 1998, p. 11). Adolescents need a learning context in which personal competence is nurtured, emotions are positively stimulated, and social interaction is carefully structured.

The following box synthesizes current ideas for fostering the positive social and emotional support espoused by many scholars, including Diamond and Hopson (1998), Jensen (2000), and Goleman (1995).

Building Social and Emotional Support

1. Personalize Learning Opportunities.

Differentiate curriculum for varying abilities and interests.

Permit choice on topics, projects, and resources.

Assess understanding through multiple avenues.

Design authentic and developmentally challenging experiences.

Allow for creativity and originality.

Integrate music, art, and drama to promote individual expression.

Give adolescents opportunities to "shine."

2. Build Relationships.

Provide opportunities for peer interaction.

Structure collaborative tasks and monitor group dynamics.

Teach interpersonal skills (e.g., team and consensus building).

Provide opportunity for community connections and social action.

Connect with students' families and cultural communities.

3. Promote Inner Management.

Build in metacognitive time (e.g., reflection, discussion, response writing, self-evaluation).

Foster empathy (e.g., perspective taking, debate, role playing).

Encourage moral development (e.g., decision making, discussion, inquiry projects).

Treat mistakes as learning experiences and emphasize personal progress.

Provide opportunities for learning responsibility and ownership.

Involve classroom management planning and conflict negotiation.

Downplay extrinsic motivation and promote the value of learning.

4. Create Emotional Security.

Promote a climate of caring, respect, inclusiveness, and acceptance.

Create an atmosphere of expectancy, challenge, and limited stress.

Listen to students and help them believe in the power of their ideas.

Encourage efforts to understand and to be understood.

Your Ideas

Your Ideas

Celebrate classroom cultures and discourage prejudice.

Incorporate humor and playfulness.

5. Teach Well.

Capture curiosity through a challenging curriculum (e.g., concepts, issues, problems).

Help adolescents to see the practicality of what they are learning.

Expect adolescents to be active participants, not passive listeners.

Foster thoughtful learning and understanding.

Expand the "walls" of the classroom through technology and external resources.

DESIGNING RESPONSIVE LEARNING ENVIRONMENTS

Bransford et al. (2000) suggest that responsive learning environments include four critical components: (1) the learner, (2) knowledge, (3) the internal and extended community, and (4) assessment. An environment that is learner-centered, for example, pays close attention to the knowledge, skills, beliefs, and experiences that students bring to the classroom setting. This approach acknowledges the complex interaction of the learner, learning, and the learning environment.

McCombs and Whisler (1997) define the learner-centered perspective as one that combines a focus on the individual learner who varies in heredity, experience, talent, interest, belief system, and capability, with the "best available knowledge about learning" (p. 9). In learner-centered classrooms, teachers work to discover what students already know and think relative to the new learning at hand, and they try to identify what assumptions and misconceptions students might carry. Teachers understand that individual learners construct their own meanings based on the beliefs, knowledge, and understandings they bring to the classroom. Learner-centered instruction is thus sensitive to the students' cultures, language, homes, families, and communities (Bransford et al., 1999, 2000).

As discussed in Chapter 1, the brain is a pattern seeker that attempts to cluster and organize incoming information into previously formed synaptic structures (Caine & Caine, 1997; Caine, Caine, McClintic, & Klimek, 2005; Jensen, 2000). The active and dynamic nature of the brain enables adolescents to construct and reconstruct knowledge as they interact within their learning environment. Paying attention to students' prior knowledge, experiences, and cultural and family background, a tenet of a learner-centered environment, is important for another brain-related reason: The adolescent brain is simultaneously receptive and selective. It filters out information it considers irrelevant or that it cannot connect with existing, related neural structures.

Your Ideas

SCHOOLING MINDS NOT MEMORIES

Knowledge appears to be highly prized in schools, but, in many instances, it is not the kind that helps adolescents relate to and understand their world, and it is generally not the kind that endures. Perkins (1991) expresses concern that many teachers use what he calls a "chocolate box" model of learning. They keep trying to add pieces of differently flavored chocolates into the "candy box of the mind," but do not teach for deeper understanding. He whimsically refers to "inert" information that cannot be recalled or used meaningfully, as the "couch potato" equivalent of knowledge: "It's there, but it doesn't move around or do anything" (Perkins, 1991, p. 22).

In his book *Knowledge as Design*, Perkins (1986) writes that too much of what is taught in schools is "disconnected knowledge," information that has no context, critical perspective, or application. Historical dates and facts are learned, for example, without connection to the milestone events that shape history. Analogies are not often drawn to present-day occurrences, and varying perspectives are not examined. Without a link to thinking, facts are like "threads without a tapestry"; they remain meaningless and abstract, and are not flexible and functional in adolescents' lives (Perkins, 1986, p. 22). Focused more on schooling the memory than schooling the mind, this so-called learning is frequently antithetical to knowledge retention and understanding.

Other educators express similar concerns about "naïve" and "ritualistic" knowledge in students (Bransford et al., 1999, 2000; Brooks & Brooks, 1993; Gardner, 1999). Naïve knowledge surfaces, for example, in adolescents' misconceptions about why an object sinks or floats, or in the idea that all good poetry must rhyme, or in the prejudice that intelligence is associated with a particular race or culture. These theories are formed early in life as children try to make sense of what they see in their world, and are brought into the classroom as inaccurate beliefs (Gardner, 1991, 1999). "Ritualistic" knowledge amasses with the rote memorization of information without knowing what it means. Students might learn the textbook definition of photosynthesis, for example, or think that percentage calculation merely means to move a decimal point two places.

Teaching to the memory and not the mind is antithetical to thoughtful learning (Perkins, 1999). It is an amassing of information that merely sits in the mind's attic gathering dust. Having memorized the steps necessary for a bill to become a law, for example, does not mean that a student will be able to name them a week later or that he or she understands the political complexity that unfolds during a bill's debate on the floor of the Senate. Moreover, correctly listing these steps on a unit test does not guarantee that the adolescent will see a relationship between these steps and the ongoing legislative debate over immigration quotas or the connection between enacting a law and other parts of the legislative process. Teaching to the memory and not the mind also limits the possibility that knowledge will be transferred to other situations or used later in life.

Your Ideas

KNOWLEDGE UNDER CONSTRUCTION

Constructivism is a view of learning based on the belief that adolescents adjust prior knowledge, or mental models, to accommodate new experiences as the brain actively seeks connections with what it already knows and makes meaning (Brooks & Brooks, 1993). This view supports the purposeful in the design of instruction that relates to adolescents' prior learning and experiences and that emphasizes hands-on problem solving. Teaching strategies promote student responses and encourage students to analyze, interpret, and predict information. These strategies include open-ended questions that promote extensive dialogue among students.

Perkins (1999) describes constructivism as a philosophy that promotes thoughtful learning in the classroom. He notes three basic learning premises that undergird the constructivist instructional approach:

1. Knowledge and understanding are actively acquired. Depending on the situation, students might experiment, discuss, assume a role, debate, or investigate.
    - In history class, students could describe an event during the French Revolution by writing a letter from the viewpoint of a French aristocrat to someone in another country.
    - In language arts class, students might relate a poem to an event in their lives.
    - In science, students could gather samples from an estuary to test salinity composition and speculate about sea life and habitation.
    - In math, students might learn statistics by analyzing beverage consumption data to determine the best market location for a new soft drink industry.
2. Knowledge and understanding are socially constructed in dialogue with others. The role of questioning and making thinking "visible" through response helps teachers determine adolescents' prior knowledge and ongoing understanding.
3. Knowledge and understanding are created and recreated. Adolescents are unlikely to develop understanding with one example or one experiment. Learning needs to be reinforced and applied in a variety of ways.

How can teachers facilitate and guide productive knowledge construction? How can the "couch potato" syndrome be shaken, inaccurate assumptions corrected, or complex principles, definitions, and procedures better understood? The ACT Model "Knowledge Under Construction: The Mousetrap Catapult" provides an example. Students "construct" a better understanding of physics principles related to gravity, trajectory, velocity, and projectile motion through inquiry, experimentation, and reflective discussion. Since many adolescents have misconceptions about natural phenomena related to these principles, this experience helps to dispel these naïve assumptions. The metacognitive extension gives a structured time for students to reflect upon and process their learning, and to apply (and hopefully transfer) the principles to situations in real life. Ultimately, adolescents gain more accurate knowledge that leads to genuine understanding.

Knowledge Under Construction: The Mousetrap Catapult

Many adolescents have naïve or incorrect beliefs about natural phenomena related to certain principles of physics, including the concepts of gravity, trajectory, velocity, and projectile motion. Teachers can challenge these misconceptions through inquiry, experimentation, and reflective discussion. This instructional approach helps adolescents to construct a more accurate knowledge base that can enable genuine understanding.

Content Understanding

To help adolescents understand the principles of gravity, velocity, projectile motion, and Newton's laws. Skills of scientific inquiry are developed.

Student Learning Outcomes

- Students will construct an understanding of the motion of projectiles and the forces of gravity and acceleration by creating a mousetrap catapult.
- Students will practice skills of scientific inquiry by hypothesizing, experimenting, calibrating, and testing mousetrap catapults in a competition.
- Students will apply the principles of projectile motion to historical and real-life experiences through online research and discussion.

Key Concepts

Velocity, force, energy, spring, gravity, trajectory, energy source (potential and kinetic), trigger, ballistics, range, Newton's laws, acceleration

Strategies for Inquiry

An Inquiry-Based Competition: The early Greeks and Romans used catapults to hurl projectiles (big rocks) over large distances with great accuracy using an energy storing device. Your team's challenge is to design and construct a catapult using a mousetrap as a trigger mechanism that shoots a Ping-Pong ball eight feet into an elevated sandpit target.

Guided Interaction

- Teachers introduce the challenge and stimulate students to brainstorm ideas about how a design might work. Tools allowed are a mousetrap, glue, Popsicle sticks, plastic spoons, rubber bands, and other common materials.

- Teachers review or introduce concepts and terms, including Newton's laws, velocity, force, energy, spring, gravity, trajectory, energy source (potential and kinetic), trigger, ballistics, and range.
- Teachers review or introduce formulas to calculate the motion of projectiles and forces of gravity and acceleration.
- Teachers show sketches that provide a visual of the trajectory (see the Institute of Industrial Engineers' "Mousetrap Catapult Design Competition" pamphlet available from the American Society of Mechanical Engineers Web site: http://files.asme.org/ASMEORG/Events/Contests/Ideas/2636.pdf).
- Teachers encourage students to research catapult designs in history. The following sites are useful:

http://www.newton.mec.edu/Brown/Te/CATAPULTS/Catapult_history.html
http://www.angelfire.com/geek/CatapultChiks/ancientcatapults
http://en.wikipedia.org/wiki/Catapult

- Teachers monitor and assist students as they solve problems and create designs.
- Teachers mentor as students work with materials and design the catapult structures.
- Teachers provide significant time for experimentation, calibration, and testing.
- Teachers prepare for the competition by putting a sandpit on top of a two-to three-foot table approximately eight feet from the launch site.

Metacognitive Development and Assessment

The competition provides an authentic assessment for the successful design and construction of the mousetrap catapults. Extension questions about the task and ample time for reflection promote metacognitive development.

- How did your team decide which materials to use to construct the catapult?
- How did you calculate the trajectory?
- How would your calculations have changed had the sandpit been placed twice the distance or higher?
- How did the opportunity to work together as a team help your success in the competition?
- What is the value of experimentation in scientific inquiry?

Transfer is promoted through questions that help adolescents apply the concepts to other real-life situations.

- What are instances in which the catapult is used today? (Some answers are, for example, to launch aircraft from the deck of an aircraft carrier or in theme park roller coasters.)

For extension, students design other challenges (or variations of this competition) that use the concepts of projectile motion for classmates to solve "hands-on" or through computer simulation.

This unit is based on ideas from the Mousetrap Catapult Design Competition (http://files.asme.org/ASMEORG/Events/Contests/Ideas/2636.pdf).

For other ideas for design competition projects, see the Web site of the American Society of Mechanical Engineers (http://www.asme.org/Events/Contests/Ideas/).

Cross-Disciplinary Applications

- Students could open a small traveler's bag that contains such items as a newspaper announcing the end of World War II, a Chicago map, a tube of red lipstick, two chocolate bars, a hair net, a small diary, and a Hemingway novel. They could be asked to construct an understanding of the culture (values, interests, lifestyle) and times of the person through the clues and ensuing investigation.
- Following a nature walk in the fall during which seeds are collected, students can be asked to consider why the seeds "wait" until spring to germinate. They could speculate on what happens to seeds during the course of winter and hypothesize regarding the most favorable conditions for germination. These hypotheses can then be tested through classroom simulations, including variation of temperature or the effects of fire, water, acid (as in animals' stomachs), or "crunching" (as under human feet).
- Students could design hot air balloons from panels of glued tissue paper, speculate about attainable height and conditions for flight, and test assumptions by launching the creations using a stovepipe heater fueled by pine cones.

In the future, adolescents will need to examine large bodies of information and, according to Gardner (1999), "determine what is worth knowing" (p. 53). They should know how to think critically. They will not develop this intellectual capacity, however, by memorizing disconnected information or by parroting definitions meaninglessly. Adolescents learn through thinking, but they need to be taught to think for understanding.

BUILDING LEARNING COMMUNITIES

Adolescent learning can take place in pairs or small clusters, through individual or group activity, within the classroom setting, or through extended connections. Students in chemistry might be partnered for a lab experiment, for example, or sculpting stations positioned around an art room. Students in science class may be "dialoguing" online with youth in Scandinavia about local efforts to regulate acid rain destruction, or they may be learning about digital imaging with undergraduates at a local college. A community of learners is one that is engaged in intentional and meaningful activity in a climate of support, acceptance, and high expectancy.

Many researchers in brain-compatible learning write about the brain's social dimension in its continual effort to connect new knowledge with past experiences (Caine & Caine, 1997; Caine, Caine, McClintic, & Klimek, 2005; Siegal, 1999).

Your Ideas

The social interactions among students in a learner-centered classroom community enhance the flow of energy and information into the brain, where it is processed actively by the mind. Learning is further enhanced when social interaction and shared knowledge extends to a local or global community (Bransford et al., 1999, 2000; Lambert & McCombs, 1998, Perkins, 1999). Problem or project-based learning, service learning, WebQuests, and other technology-enhanced instruction provide opportunities for adolescents to communicate ideas and learn in a collaborative context with disciplinary experts. Through interpersonal connections, adolescents can share "brain energy" and enhance the cognitive potential of their thinking and learning.

Creating a community of learners in the classroom is additionally about making personal connections and building relationships (Beamon, 2001). Adolescent social and emotional development is enhanced when teachers provide opportunities for interpersonal networking and relationship building. Learning experiences that require cooperation, collaboration, and consensus and realistic problems that enable connections and extensions beyond the classroom foster a healthy sense of community. A few examples illustrate.

- Middle school students decide to get involved in the local humane society's effort to take care of orphaned animals. They wash the animals, build shelters, and assist in placing the animals in adoptive homes.
- High school students are paired with mentors at a local university. They meet in small advisory groups of ten to twelve to plan exhibitions and projects (Littky & Allen, 1999).
- Language arts students keep portfolios and assume responsibility for leading parent conferences.

Learning communities teach through their structure and opportunity for interaction (Sizer & Sizer, 1999). An effective learning community involves the active and dynamic sharing of ideas, knowledge, and strategy, and it is shaped by caring and support. While there is no guarantee that adolescents will transfer their learning and skills into new, related, or real-life situations, scholars such as Bransford et al. (1999, 2000) and Perkins (1992) agree that the teachers' role as decision maker is key. Prime consideration lies in helping adolescents develop the capacity for flexible problem solving and a metacognitive awareness of the thinking strategies they might use in other learning situations.

THE CONTEXT IS AUTHENTIC AND RELEVANT

This chapter began by sharply contrasting two math classes. In the first, students copy a teacher-devised problem from the overhead and use a specific formula to find the appropriate answer. In the second, pairs of math students design geometry problems based on real surroundings for peers to solve. In which instance are the students likely to remember what they have learned? Which students will be more likely to notice evidence of mathematics in the real world?

The answer is obvious. In the second example, adolescents are challenged to apply what they know about a geometric concept through an original problem. They make personal decisions about relevant problem topics, and they

Your Ideas

share their ideas. When the context of the learning experience is meaningful and responsive to adolescents as learners, they are more apt to connect, remember, and apply it to other areas of learning.

Teachers may recall a time when students, after dutifully memorizing formulas and facts, were confounded by a changed context, such as a word problem or a different application situation. The likelihood is slim that students can or will apply the content and thinking appropriately in another context, particularly if the experience lacks relevance or the teacher does not help establish a connection (Perkins, 1992). Adolescents who discuss the events of the Holocaust, for example, may not readily see any parallel to the genocide apparent in our current world. Those who learn the Pythagorean theorem may not recognize its applicability in drafting class or its necessity in the calculation of the length of a slanted roof. Likewise, students may attribute a perfect foul shot to the skill of a ball player without any thought of the principles of physics that make it possible.

Another reason for authenticity and relevance is that learning is influenced by the surrounding context, or situation. Cognitive psychologists use the term "situated cognition" to refer to the phenomenon that knowledge and skills may be "contextualized" within a particular learning experience (Greeno, 1998; Resnick, 1991). The context for adolescent learning includes the content of the lesson, the instructional activity, and the opportunities for interaction and involvement. One might consider the following illustrations:

- Enact a model United Nations to better understand the real-world concepts of negotiation and interdependence.
- Run a class business to gain relevant knowledge of the principles of consumer mathematics.
- Simulate a town meeting and discuss the impact of a proposed thoroughfare near the school in order to begin to take civic responsibility more seriously.
- Adopt a local creek, monitor variables (such as odor, clarity, temperature, and velocity), and observe the activity of plants and "critters" to gain hands-on knowledge of natural habitat and ecological harmony.
- Design multimedia book reports for use in the school media center to gain a "working" understanding of the elements of style, theme, plot, and characterization.

When the context is "real enough," adolescents are more likely to make pertinent connections with other areas of learning or with comparable situations in everyday life. A context that is shaped chiefly by information intake, minimal application, and nominal intellectual exchange, however, limits adolescent understanding and potential for transfer.

THE ROLE OF THE EXTENDED COMMUNITY

The concept of a learning community involves purposeful interaction among students and meaningful interplay between them and others who are more skilled or knowledgeable (Bransford et al., 1999, 2000). As discussed earlier, Vygotsky (1962) recognized that meaningful exchange within a social context helps

Your Ideas

students to sharpen skills for higher order thinking. He proposed that cognitive development is facilitated and enhanced through students' interactions with more advanced or capable others. His observations affirm the teacher's ongoing task to model, probe, and guide student thinking and learning. The term "scaffolding" is used to describe the various techniques teachers can use to assist students' efforts to master new content or manners of thinking (Ormond, 2000).

Vygotsky's (1978) concept of *zone of proximal development* is an instructionally pertinent idea within a learning community. This zone refers to the distance between a student's actual development capacity for independent problem solving and what he or she might attain under adult guidance or in collaboration with more advanced peers (Bransford et al., 1999, 2000). What adolescents can perform with assistance on one day, for example, may be developmentally achievable independently on another. With more sophisticated guided challenges, adolescents can become increasingly competent in problem solving and content understanding.

Vygotsky's ideas justify the need for adolescents to interact with others in the extended community. These connections enrich adolescent learning by adding pertinent information based on real-life experiences and expertise. Outside "experts" also provide helpful feedback regarding finished products or final performances. When teachers and significant others help adolescents think through the steps of a task, pose questions, articulate their reasoning, and reflect upon how improvements could be made, critical metacognitive skills are fostered. This relationship, frequently referred to as *cognitive apprenticeship*, is more explicitly illustrated in Chapter 4.

LEARNING IN THE CLASSROOM

Teachers in any discipline can structure learning experiences that build communities of learners. Cooperative activities, such as paired thinking in the art class or team problem building, as in the math example, allow adolescents to interact within the social milieu of the classroom. Group investigation and inquiry tasks promote peer collaboration and extend the social context to experts beyond. Interaction can be symbolic, as adolescents reflect and write about their thoughts in journals, search for helpful information on the Web, and use virtual reality, or interaction can be with real people. These opportunities put adolescents in contact with the valuable resources in the learning environment and help promote the belief that learning is indeed a socially shared phenomenon.

In the ACT Model "Art Has a Story to Tell," a community of learners is created through collaborative strategies that include a Socratic seminar and small group research. The teacher's goal is to help students understand that they can observe much about an artist or culture through critical observation and interpretive analysis. Assumptions, though useful to guide thinking, need to be tested for accuracy through information acquisition and analysis. The teacher has structured the learning experience to enable the adolescents to share ideas with pairs, with the larger group, and with inquiry teams. These students further interact with pertinent online sources in order to check the accuracy of their assumptions. To complete the task, they collaboratively draw conclusions from their findings and return to the larger discussion.

Art Has a Story to Tell

Adolescents who share ideas and work collaboratively on a task that they perceive is meaningful feel a sense of collective purpose and individual contribution. Under a teacher's careful planning and facilitation, a community of learners forms. This learning community extends beyond the classroom to include others who provide pertinent resources, skills, knowledge, and expertise.

Content Understanding

To help adolescents use critical analysis skills in the visual arts to gain an understanding of artistic style within a historical and cultural context.

Key Concepts

Interpretive analysis, critical thinking, artistic style, cultural and historical context, perspective, Socratic seminar

Learning Outcomes

- Students will use the skills of critical and interpretive analysis by participating in a Socratic seminar about selected art forms.
- Students will gain an understanding of the impact of cultural and historical context by making and testing assumptions about artistic style and conveyed message.
- By engaging in structured group discussion and research, students will appreciate the strategy of shared collaboration to construct knowledge.

ESSENTIAL QUESTIONS

What does a piece of art tell us about a person, a period of time, or a culture?

How can critical analysis help us understand an artist's perspective?

Strategies for Inquiry: A Challenge Question

What does a piece of art tell us about a person, a period of time, or a culture?

- Students jot down personal thoughts about the question, pair to exchange ideas, and share aloud with the class. These are recorded on the board under "What We Know." Responses may vary from references to artists' eccentric personalities to a reflection of nature.

- Teachers exhibit a piece of artwork, such as an oil-painted Egyptian papyrus, and inquire further: What assumption might you make about this work of art? Student responses may include the use of vivid colors, the importance of religious ceremony, and the symbolism of plants and animals.

Guided Interaction: A Socratic Seminar

- Several art objects and prints are placed at various locations around the room. These could include a reproduction of a Degas dancer placed on a small table; wall prints by artists such as Monet, Kandinsky, Klimt, and Picasso; a clay replica of a Xian soldier; an Italian blown-glass sculpture; a hand-painted Chinese medicine bottle; a watercolor by a Kenyan youth; or another artistic work related to a culture or time period. Large sticky notes, markers and pens, and envelopes lie beside each with enclosed identifying information.
- The teacher explains that students will participate in a Socratic seminar to analyze and interpret works of art from various cultures and historical periods. The ground rules follow:
  - Everyone participates by contributing ideas and listening actively.
  - All ideas are accepted provided the contributor can give rationale or support.
- Students are divided into small seminar teams of four or five and presented with the instructions to visit three stations of their choice and discuss and record on chart paper their responses to specified interpretive questions. If a previous group has visited the station, students discuss the questions left by others and use the sticky notes to add ideas to those of their peers.

Questions for Socratic Seminar

- What mood is the artist trying to capture?
- What details (color, technique, contrast) help convey this mood?
- How would you characterize the artist's style?
  - Support your response.
- What questions would you like to ask the artist?
- What statement or message is the artist making?
  - Discuss for 10 minutes. Summarize your interpretations on paper.

- Students also open the envelopes to confirm the artist's name, period, or culture.

Test Your Assumptions!

- Inquiry teams select one time period to research further. Using the clues provided in the envelope, they locate information on the Internet about the art piece and share findings with the class.

Metacognitive Development and Assessment

- Following the group inquiries, teachers return to the original question. Students' new ideas are recorded on the board under the category of "What We've Learned," and students are asked to compare the two sets of responses.

- Adolescents formulate conclusions about the advantages and disadvantages of making assumptions. They think of other times when assumption testing would be useful. They also respond individually in their art reflection journals on what they have learned about art's story and assumption testing.
- Students discuss the value of collaborative inquiry in the sharing and constructing of knowledge.
- As an assessment, students choose an artist or art period and emulate the style of the art or artist in an original piece of artwork.

Cross-Disciplinary Applications

- In social studies, adolescents examine a collection of editorial cartoons on a topic, such as nuclear disarmament or gun control, and assess the various artists' political perspectives on the issues.
- In science, students could speculate and determine with rationale which other planet in the solar system could support life comparable to that on Earth.
- In mathematics, students could work together to plan the best location for a "chunnel" between the Chinese mainland and the island of Hong Kong.

A community of learners is created when adolescents and teachers share ideas as they work together to expand what they know and improve how they think. A sense of relationship is built among the students through purposeful involvement in a high-level task or problem. The situation itself is realistic and allows the use of resources beyond the immediate classroom, so students can gather information and test personal ideas. Adolescents have an opportunity to inquire actively, to examine instances when their thinking might be short-sighted or superficial, and to reflect upon the importance of well-informed conclusions. The climate is one of sharing, support, and respect.

USING ASSESSMENT AS A COGNITIVE ADVANTAGE

The fourth component of a learning-centered classroom environment, as suggested by Bransford et al. (1999, 2000), is assessment. Assessment provides opportunities for adolescents to know where they stand in relation to what is expected. In this sense, assessment can be diagnostic, formative and ongoing, or summative and culminating. Importantly for adolescents, assessment helps build skills to help them assess personal work and the work of their peers. Assessment thus becomes a tool to help adolescents practice and hone their emerging cognitive capacity for metacognition. How do various teachers assess adolescent learning? Several have shared these ideas:

- I place large maps of the world in the school commons and assign students problems that require them to use longitude and latitude knowledge. I want to find out if they understand geographic location.

Your Ideas

- My students simulate a wax museum of important historical figures. Each "model" is required to represent five characteristics of the person. They also write a monologue and design a banner that displays various genres of writing that their figure would have produced.
- To show understanding of weight and equations, my class builds a math bridge.
- To demonstrate their understanding of a certain period in twentieth-century history, my students develop a timeline, write interview questions about the period, visit an assisted living facility to interview people who lived during that time, and share the information with classmates.
- To show they understand the concept of survival, my students make backpacks for survival in a chosen biome.
- To assess their understanding of literary perspective, I ask my students to write letters from the viewpoint of a character to someone in real life.
- To show understanding of geometry concepts, my class describes in writing how to derive a formula for the number of blocks in a pyramid.
- My class designs a carnival game as a culminating project for a unit on probability.

Other ideas include the assessment of environmental concepts through a travel brochure, of the justice system by a trial simulation, of the scientific process through a laboratory investigation, and of concepts in economics through the design of a campaign to attract business into an area. Adolescents build models of castles, role play literary events, create Web pages, perform newscasts, write historical poems, make drawings of scientific concepts, structure debates, and prepare book talks. They create postcards, magazines, newspapers, joke books, dances, computer maps, children's books, and multimedia presentations.

These assessment strategies share a few basic ideas. First, these teachers recognize that adolescents have different intellectual strengths, learn differently, and show their understanding in different ways. The examples support a variety of learning preferences. Second, these teachers apparently believe that adolescents are motivated when they are actively involved in something that makes sense to them. The strategies call for a demonstration of understanding within the context of the learning experience. Leading proponents of authentic assessment, including Wiggins and McTighe (1998), Gardner (1991, 1999), Perkins (1991, 1992), and Stiggins (1994), might refer to these assessment examples as contextualized performances of understanding. Rather than tests of facts that students have memorized, these measures assess understanding through meaningful application in a context closely connected to the learning experience itself. Adolescents need to know the content well in order to perform the task.

Perkins (1991) defines "understanding performance" as the evidence that makes apparent a student's insight into knowledge:

> Suppose, for example, that a learner can explain the law of supply and demand in his or her own words (not just recite a canned definition), can exemplify its use in fresh contexts, can make analogies to novel situations (let us say to grades in school rather than the cost of goods),

> can generalize the law, recognizing other laws or principles with the same form, and so on. We probably would be pretty impressed by such a learner's insight into the law of supply and demand. (p. 76)

Your Ideas

For assessment to be used to adolescents' cognitive advantage, it needs to be an ongoing and integral part of learning experiences. When it is connected closely with instruction, it draws adolescents' attention to what they know, believe, and understand. It also provides an opportunity to give feedback to adolescents as they progress. The ultimate goal of assessment is to help adolescents acknowledge and internalize the standards and cognitive skills for more sophisticated understanding, and to become more self-directive in their learning.

A critical factor in making assessment work to adolescents' cognitive advantage lies in establishing a shared mind-set for progress and continual personal improvement. The classroom conversation focuses less on what will be on the test and more on how a student might write more logically, contribute more fully to a discussion, or write more coherently (Wiggins & McTighe, 1998). The teacher's role is to guide and facilitate, to give continual feedback, to provide multiple opportunities for learning, and to help students acquire the skills for self-evaluation. The ACT Model "Using Assessment to Promote Learning Management" illustrates an assessment strategy designed to promote purposeful collaboration and learner autonomy. Under a teacher's guidance, adolescents form literature circles, select novels, and analyze elements of literacy themes, symbolism, characterization, and style. The teacher monitors as adolescents plan and manage a schedule for reading and interpretive discussion. Students help develop an assessment rubric for a culminating presentation, and time is provided for metacognitive debriefing.

Using Assessment to Promote Learning Management: Making Literary Style Your Own

Assessment can be used to help adolescents develop skills to manage their own learning. This application is a culminating assessment that serves as a final exam. Previous and more structured and teacher-guided activities, such as group presentations on other readings, help to establish expectations for small group interaction and interpretive analysis. This experience assesses understanding of specific literary elements, such as theme, style, symbolism, and characterization, and allows for individual choice and creative expression.

Content Understanding

To enable adolescents to communicate an understanding of literary elements in fiction and to demonstrate skills for interpretive analysis.

Key Concepts

Literary elements of theme, symbolism, characterization, style, interpretive analysis

ESSENTIAL QUESTION

How can interpretive analysis be used to construct an understanding of literary elements?

Learning Outcomes

- Students will convey an understanding of literary elements in fiction through a small group interpretive book analysis and creative presentation.
- Students will think metacognitively about learning assessment by sharing in the construction of a performance-based rubric.
- Students will develop metacognitive skills by engaging in active reflection about the process of collaboration and interpretive analysis.

Strategies for Inquiry: An Inquiry Group Task

Students are presented with the following instructions:

Read and discuss your group's book according to theme, symbolism, characterization, and style. Plan a creative presentation that conveys your group's interpretation of these literary elements.

Guided Interaction

- Students are divided into small literature circles of four or five based on their common preference of a novel from a recommended reading list.
- Specific days are designated as "discussion days," and students are helped to develop a schedule for reading and discussion.
- In preparation for the presentations, teachers encourage adolescents to be creative, to integrate the arts (such as dance, movement, and music), and to use technology enhancement.

Metacognitive Development and Assessment

- During discussions and planning sessions, teachers monitor and offer needed assistance but do not become an integral part of the discussion or planning.
- Assessment is in the form of a group grade for the project and individual scores for students' collaborative skills within groups. Students are involved in the formulation of evaluative criteria and help determine descriptors for various levels of the rubrics. Figure 3.2 lists a sample of rubric descriptors.
- Teachers provide a "debriefing" time following presentations when adolescents think back over the process of the book analysis and reflect on their group's decision-making and interpretive strategies.

Figure 3.2 Rubric Descriptors for Group Projects

Criteria	Outstanding	Meets Expectations	Needs Improvement
Literary elements (theme, symbolism, characterization, style)	Insightful interpretation	Adequate, correct interpretation	Misconceptions noted in analysis
Use of enhancements (music, art, dance, technology)	Creative, appropriate	Supporting use	Minimal use
Possible criteria for social skills assessment: • Participation • Contribution of new ideas • Prompting others to question			

Some tips for creating excellent rubrics follow.

- Select criteria that are both teachable and measurable. A debate's rubric criteria, for example, might include "presentation of argument," "information sources," "verbal delivery of speech," or "involvement in counterquestioning." A multimedia project might be assessed according to screen design, content knowledge, originality, and mechanics.
- Choose descriptors that communicate clearly what the criteria levels mean. Quality words should convey what is "outstanding" or "successful" or "needs improvement" on a particular assignment or performance. Descriptors such as "authentic," "detailed," "varied," and "well-documented," for example, might denote strong evidence, while unacceptable work might be "undocumented" and "superficial."
- Limit the number of criteria to be assessed and the number of levels for each. Five criteria and four levels are manageable numbers for teachers and adolescents.
- Involve students in the design or adaptation. This suggestion is critical if adolescents are to become aware of the benchmarks for personal progress.
- Don't always reinvent the wheel. Teachers are encouraged to develop rubric formats that can be modified and adapted for similar tasks. Numerous rubric models are also available.

Assessment, used strategically, helps adolescents develop the skills for self-directed learning. When students understand what they are expected to learn, they can play a major role in setting immediate and long-range goals and assessing their own progress, just as they track their scores on computer games and their performance in athletics (Wiggins & McTighe, 1998). As adolescents become more adept at self-assessment, they will be better prepared for success in the world beyond the classroom. Other assessment strategies that promote adolescent autonomy include student-led or student-involved conferences; digital and product portfolios; senior projects; various forms of publications; exhibitions or performances; and fairs that involve outside experts, business leaders, college professors, and other community members who share expertise.

LEARNING COMMUNITIES AND ADOLESCENT MOTIVATION

Adolescent motivation is a fascinating and ever-perplexing phenomenon. Adolescents are motivated by what they perceive as personally relevant, and they are aware of their own power, choice, and responsibility. What may be surprising about adolescent motivation is that these young people are naturally motivated to learn—under certain conditions, that is, and when these conditions are personally right. Motivation is individual and elusive, important to learning, yet influenced by a person's beliefs, feelings, interests, and goals (Lambert & McCombs, 1998). What is challenging about adolescent motivation, however, is that it can vary in intensity and duration among subjects, learning experiences, classrooms, and teachers. Motivation affects adolescents' willingness to learn and the amount of effort they will exert in the process (Alexander & Murphy, 1998). It can be influenced by several factors, including the following:

Your Ideas

- Knowledge in a particular content area
- Beliefs about what the teacher expects
- Adolescents' self-concept or perceived personal ability
- Anxiety and concern over grades
- Level of support in the classroom environment
- Difficulty and challenge of the task
- Social interaction
- Belief that the learning is useful, meaningful, and of consequence for others

Understanding what motivates adolescents to learn requires paying attention to the interrelated factors that naturally energize and excite them within the learning environment. Strong, Silver, and Robinson (1995) identify four essential goals that drive students' willingness to get involved and to persist in learning experiences. Each goal satisfies an underlying human need that, when met, enables students to deal effectively with the complexities and ambiguities of real life. Adolescents are motivated by (1) success, or need for mastery; (2) curiosity, or need for understanding; (3) originality, or need for self-expression; and (4) relationship, or need for involvement with others in a social context. Teachers responsive to the basic learning needs that affect adolescent motivation do the following:

- Engage adolescents through an intriguing curriculum that stimulates their curiosity
- Permit them to express personal and creative ideas
- Allow them to connect with peers and others in a broader community
- Help them recognize when their work is of high quality and of value to those around them

Adolescents have a need to know, yet are more likely to accept the academic challenge and follow it through to an acceptable completion when they feel a sense of ownership, accomplishment, and positive relationship with others in the learning environment (Deci & Ryan, 1998). Competent and autonomous adolescents who are personally and socially confident also tend to be less dependent on external contingencies such as grades, the approval of others, or the threat of negative consequences (Pintrich & Schrauben, 1992).

LEARNING COMMUNITIES ARE EMOTIONALLY SAFE

The domain of emotions, the affective side of learning, has received much current attention by cognitive psychologists, neuroscientists, and other educators in an attempt to explain the interplay between thinking, feeling, and acting (Caine & Caine, 1997; Caine, Caine, McClintic, & Klimek, 2005; Gardner, 1999;

Your Ideas

Goleman, 1995; Jensen, 2000; Sprenger, 1999). A display of emotions has been associated with levels of brain maturity, though adolescents' emotions are generally understandable reactions. Emotions can interfere with learning or they can contribute to it. Adolescents are more likely to take the risk involved in letting others know what they are thinking when they feel accepted, valued, respected, and supported individually.

Parker Palmer (1998–1999) wrote of the role fear plays in students who are "afraid of failing, of not understanding, of being drawn into issues they would rather avoid, of having their ignorance exposed or their prejudices challenged, of looking foolish in front of their peers" (p. 37). A certain level of cognitive dissonance, however, can catch adolescents' attention and open their minds to new ways of thinking. Terms such as "relaxed alertness" (Caine & Caine, 1994, 1997; Caine, Caine, McClintic, & Klimek, 2005) and "unanxious expectation" (Sizer & Sizer, 1999) have been used to describe the needed balance between challenge and anxiety in the learning environment.

Studies of the brain's activity have revealed that emotion-related physiological changes take place during the learning process (Caine & Caine, 1997; Caine, Caine, McClintic, & Klimek, 2005; Jensen, 1998; Sprenger, 1999; Sylwester, 1999). As the brain processes information, various chemicals, or neurotransmitters, rapidly "fire" information across synapses, or small spaces between nerve cells. During times of mild anxiety, the body's adrenal glands release the substance cortisol, which can provide positive mental alertness. Under more stressful conditions, however, such as when one is humiliated, ridiculed, embarrassed or startled, cortisol is released in high enough levels to interfere with neuron processing.

Under emotionally negative conditions, adolescents are less likely to reason well, to grasp concepts, to understand relationships, or to make full use of the capacities associated with higher level thinking. When students react to stress, for example, they tend to "pull back" from their optimum performance. In these instances, thinking is limited and learning is impeded. Another related finding from neurological research is that, under certain conditions, the brain will cause the body to release emotionally good chemicals that are beneficial to the thinking and learning process (Jensen, 2000; Sprenger, 1999). Positive emotions are generated by meaningful gestures of support and acceptance that help to build self-esteem and promote a positive self-concept (see below). Positive emotions can also be released through various instructional strategies that encourage social interaction, movement, creativity, and personal choice.

Promoting Positive Emotions

Actions and Activities

Exercise and movement

Constructive feedback

A smile or affirming word

A handshake or high five

Music, humor, laughter

Peer interaction

A sense of belonging and relationship

Instructional Strategies

Drama, role play, and debate

Games and simulations

Cooperative learning and team events

Personal expression and journal writing

Celebrations, storytelling, class discussion

Problem solving, projects, peer editing

Interactive technology

The role of adolescents' emotions cannot be overlooked in the plan for learning. Gardner (1999) drew attention to the positive function of emotions: "[If] one wants something to be attended to, mastered, and subsequently used, one must be sure to wrap it in a context that engages the emotions" (p. 76). When adolescents are immersed in a learning situation that stimulates their curiosity and activates their senses, they are more likely to engage emotionally.

Appropriate challenge and intrigue can create an emotional reaction in adolescents that is motivational and healthy. When neural activity is stimulated and feelings are productively engaged, complex learning connections are possible. Gardner observed that students are "more likely to learn, remember, and make subsequent use of those experiences with respect to which they had strong—and one hopes, positive—emotional reactions" (1999, p. 77). Emotions activated through sarcasm, humiliation, high levels of frustration, unrealistic expectations, embarrassment, minimal feedback, boredom, stifled expression, limited relevance, continual failure, sense of powerlessness, confusion, or lack of resources, however, have a counterproductive effect on adolescent thinking and, consequently, on their learning (Jensen, 2000; Sprenger, 1999).

LEARNING COMMUNITIES BUILD EMOTIONAL SECURITY

A climate of caring, respect, and acceptance is critical to positive adolescent social and emotional development. Educators should work hard to eliminate the stress caused by prejudice or exclusiveness, and they should challenge students by having high expectations for all.

Your Ideas

- A teacher might periodically ask students to fill out an evaluation form. Here are possible questions to include: Do I treat students with respect? Am I sensitive to students' needs? Do students feel comfortable asking questions? Are students actively interested in class work? Is enough time given for tasks? (Belton, 1996).
- A middle school teacher and students might craft a class constitution. In small groups, students can discuss ideas for an ideal society. Suggestions are presented, and the class talks about the problems faced by current society. Each student writes five rules that will help prepare for the kind of society the class envisions. These rules are categorized, a preamble is drafted, and nonpunitive interventions are detailed for those not abiding by the covenant. Rules might include listening to each other's ideas, treating all with fairness, speaking and acting in unembarrassing ways, and maintaining orderly personal habits. Consequences might include verbal and written reminders, a class meeting, and a meeting with parents or the principal (Fleming, 1996).
- Before a class debate in social studies, a teacher can remind students of several ground rules. These might include the following:
  - Listen to others' perspectives
  - Present your views with clarity
  - Support your ideas with reasoning
- On a weekly basis, a class can engage in a 20-minute seminar on various topics generated by students. Sessions might include dealing with conflict at home, peer pressure, social relationships, death, and school violence. Teachers can also use bibliotherapy, in which novels are selected for discussion based on the problems adolescents face in their personal lives.

Learning communities also promote positive social and emotional development because adolescents are allowed to learn and to show their learning in multiple ways; are given choices and opportunity for input; and are encouraged to express individual talents, to share original ideas, or to pursue areas of interest. Teachers can plan instruction that differentiates and personalizes for adolescent learners, as the following examples illustrate:

- A teacher uses a character trait strategy based on Steven Covey's book *The Seven Habits of Highly Effective People* (1989). Students are given a list of traits, including tolerant, trustworthy, problem solving, diligent, kind, courageous, peaceful, and resourceful. Both teacher and students select three they hope others would use to describe them, and discuss, write, role play, and create desk posters. Whenever students engage in inappropriate behavior, they are asked to explain how their actions are consistent (or not) with their character trait goals (Fleming, 1996).
- A middle school teacher helps students balance between "outersense" (the way they interact with others) and "innersense" (their individuality) through journaling, seminars, conferences, and personal style questionnaires. A study of the Ennegram, a 2000-year-old symbol used as a rite of passage in tribal cultures, can help them understand their identities and roles (Shelton, 1999).

- Students in a literature class choose how they do book reports. Selections include dramatic skits, book talks, poetry, or musical compositions.

Your Ideas

Perhaps most valuable in building positive social and emotional support for adolescents is good instruction. Relevant, meaningful, and broadly interactive learning experiences that stimulate adolescents' curiosity, challenge their thinking, and promote understanding enable them to develop intellectually, personally, and socially. A couple of examples follow:

- Adolescents are fascinated by the mummification process and by early views of the afterlife, and they enjoy myths and folklore. As part of an in-depth study of ancient Egyptian culture, students select and assume the role of an early figure (e.g., political leader, slave, farmer's wife, high priest, young student). They research through various sources to create a personal data sheet for the character, answering questions such as these: What is your level of education, and how is it impacted by your social status? How is what you eat affected by the economics of your family? Students should also be allowed to add personal interest questions (Tomlinson, 1999).
- With the continuing debate over the health risk of tobacco, the tobacco industry's efforts to lure youth to smoke through targeted advertisements, and the discussion at the national level about declaring tobacco a drug, a teacher poses this challenge: You have been asked by the Office of the Surgeon General to design an antismoking ad campaign geared to adolescents. Students collaborate to develop a peer survey to find out reasons for smoking. They conduct research on the accompanying health hazards and work in teams to design a marketable plan. Each team evaluates how well its members work together and how they might improve collaborative skills.

LEARNING COMMUNITIES PROMOTE INNER MANAGEMENT AND SELF-REGULATION

Linked to adolescent motivation are metacognitive skills for self-directed learning. When they can interact socially and are given responsibility, adolescents are more motivated to learn (McCombs & Whisler, 1997; Ryan, 1995; Strong et al., 1995). They become more self-managing when they are given voice and choice in classroom decisions and in their own learning experiences (Deci & Ryan, 1998). If they are not given some degree of control in the learning process, they are unlikely to develop the skills for self-regulation, and may become disinclined to learn at all (Zimmerman, 1994). To develop a sense of empowerment over personal learning management, adolescents need to take responsibility for personal viewpoints, decisions, and actions. By grappling with the perspectives of others, talking through conflict, or reflecting on personal learning progress, adolescents can begin to develop a more integrated and intrinsically motivated sense of self.

Your Ideas

Here are some examples of strategies that encourage inner management:

- A math teacher turns the teaching over to a student. The student demonstrates a problem on the chalkboard while the teacher sits in a classroom desk, models question posing, and takes notes in a learning log (Schneider, 1996).
- A teacher uses the STePS model (Structured Team Problem Solving) during class meetings to negotiate everyday conflicts, such as how to deal with cliques, stealing, or cheating. Led by a classmate, adolescents brainstorm ideas for solutions, cluster and clarify them, and create graphic visuals to show their thoughts (Metivier & Sheive, 1990; Schneider, 1996).
- Students discuss the meaning of logical consequences in terms of the four R's: *relate* logically to the behavior, be *reasonable* by focusing on the immediate event, *respect* the student's dignity, and allow the student to be *responsible* for personal actions (Evans, 1996).
- From time to time, a teacher audiotapes the classroom. Students listen to the tone of the dialogue and screen for "killer statements" by both teacher and students, such as, "That's a dumb question" (Frieberg, 1996).

LEARNING COMMUNITIES PROMOTE ADOLESCENT SELF-EFFICACY

Adolescents' social, personal, and cognitive experiences interact and affect their perceptions and learning behavior. This complex phenomenon is explained in part by current social cognitive research. Bandura (1993) describes self-efficacy as perceived beliefs about one's capability to learn in a particular area or to perform at an expected level. These beliefs affect how motivated adolescents are to try a particular task, how much effort they will put into it, and how much control they feel they have to complete the task successfully. Theorists believe that adolescents who are "efficacious" are more inclined to set personal learning goals, to determine and take advantage of available resources, to choose appropriate personal learning strategies, and to monitor their own learning progress (Zimmerman, 1994).

Social-cognitive educators urge that classroom experiences be structured in ways that help adolescents develop a stronger sense of personal competence and assume a more proactive role in their own learning management (Ames, 1992; Schunk, 1994). As adolescents strengthen affective, cognitive, and metacognitive skills, they gain the self-efficacy that is foundational for self-regulated learning. Several suggested strategies that promote self-efficacy follow:

- Enable adolescents to feel a sense of accomplishment on tasks that challenge their thinking and effort. A teacher might allow students to select a research topic of personal interest. Two students who select genetic engineering, for example, could interview a biotechnology expert at the university. They could design graphics, download a video clip of "Holly Dolly" for a multimedia presentation, and lead a class debate on the ethics of cloning.
- Teach them to set realistic learning goals and help them acquire strategies that best attain these goals. The teacher in the above example would

Your Ideas

assist as the students plan their research strategy. Guiding questions might include the following: What do you need to find out about genetic engineering? Where is the expertise, and how can it be tapped? What are the pertinent resources? What are the goals for the presentation? What assistance do you need? What can you manage on your own?

- Encourage them to attribute their success to their own ability and hard work. By permitting "guided" self-direction, teachers can help adolescents begin to manage their learning. The science students assume responsibility for carrying out the research project, yet they are mindful of when and how to seek assistance. Teachers help adolescents feel the satisfaction of personal accomplishment when they allow and acknowledge students' initiative, creativity, and achievement.
- Help them pay attention to which strategies work best for them personally in certain situations. Teachers should monitor adolescents' learning activity closely, and advise that students recognize and alter a strategy that is not effective. A time to "step back" and reflect on the process is important. Following the research presentation, for example, the students should evaluate their plan. Did the interview with the college professor extend their knowledge? What did they gain by "stretching" their technology skills? Will they seek the help of outside experts in future assignments? How does the sharing of knowledge benefit learning?

CHANGING TEACHER-STUDENT ROLES AND RELATIONSHIPS

Adolescents did not learn to ride a bike or read or even master their favorite video game by someone else doing the work. There were training wheels, picture books, and interactive tutorials, and most certainly, parents, teachers, siblings, and friends who guided, instructed, or cheered. Ultimately, however, the responsibility for solo performance and the true test of learning rested with the young person. The solo performance for adolescents will be their future use of critical and reasoned thinking, their understanding of and tolerance for global diversity, the depth of their knowledge, and their ability to think through challenging and varied circumstances. To be prepared for the future, they need to be held responsible during adolescence.

An instructional environment that enables adolescents to assume progressive responsibility for personal thinking and learning is shaped through active involvement and negotiated control. Although at times teachers must decide for students, if a teacher always determines what and how something is to be learned, or the amount of time needed, or the way learning can be demonstrated, adolescents get no practice in making decisions that manage learning. As risky as it may seem, teachers need be progressively less directive as they permit, enable, and expect adolescents to be pointedly more directive in the learning process. Learning ownership is built from the sharing of ideas, questions, and strategies early in the learning experience, and it evolves as adolescents tackle, complete, and reflect back over challenging tasks. It is based on the accumulation of experiences that guide, sometimes nudge, yet consistently and intentionally place responsibility upon the shoulders of adolescents.

Your Ideas

Sharing ownership does not mean that teachers take a back seat in the learning environment. On the contrary, whether conducting a lab experiment, working through an algebra problem, composing an essay, or researching a topic, adolescents need guidance as they develop the skills for strategic thinking and good mental management (Tishman et al., 1995). The ACT Model "Sharing the Ownership of Learning" illustrates shared ownership between a teacher and students. Teachers and students (1) set planning goals for content development, problem investigation, data analysis, and process; (2) identify steps and resources for strategic inquiry; (3) interact continually through feedback and progress checks; and (4) structure protected time for reflection at the completion of the experience.

Sharing the Ownership of Learning

Shared ownership among teachers and students enables adolescents to assume responsibility over their learning progressively. Teacher guidance, more apparent early in the interaction, decreases as adolescent self-management increases. Through this process, student metacognitive growth is promoted. The following steps can be applied to any project-based inquiry or academic challenge.

Content Understanding

- The teacher and students set goals for various stages of the learning process.

Planning Goals

What is the problem to be investigated?
Where and when should data be collected?
How should data be analyzed?
Where should progress be checked?
What are the steps needed to complete the final product or performance?

- The teacher and students discuss criteria and standards as guidelines for and evaluation of the final product. Expectations are communicated for individual contribution and group collaboration.

Strategies for Inquiry

- The teacher helps students identify the steps for strategic planning.

Planning Strategy

What questions must be answered?
Which contacts should be arranged?
What format should be used for data display?
What resources will be needed?

- The teacher helps students identify the various people affected by or involved in the issue at hand.
- Under the teacher's guidance, the class identifies any underlying procedures they need to understand. Teams of students begin to plan research strategies for data collection, such as Web searches, online visits to newspaper archives, or interviews.

Guided Interaction

- During the task, the teacher reminds students to stay mentally open to new information that might strengthen a final product.
- The teacher gives feedback to student responses, pointers on their research questions, assistance with avenues for information, and guidance as they interpret findings, shape conclusions, and prepare for the final product.
- The teacher reminds students of their goals and asks them to check their work periodically.

Metacognitive Development and Assessment

- When a simulation or experience is over, the teacher provides a pocket of time for students to reflect on the quality of the end product with regard to set standards, and on the effectiveness of the strategies used during the entire process.

A Time for Reflection

At what stages were your ideas validated?

When was your reasoning logical?

In what ways was your analysis thorough?

How did you know your resolutions were sound?

Cross-Disciplinary Applications

- In English, teachers and students monitor the planning and evaluation of a research project on an author who lived in a specific historical period. A presentation of the author's style and historical context is the end product.
- A team of science and mathematics teachers and students collaborate to design a nature trail and navigation guide based on the metric system.

A CULTURE OF THOUGHTFULNESS

Your Ideas

Perkins (1992) uses the phrase "culture of thoughtfulness" to describe a learning setting in which teachers model, expect, and make time for thought, and push for deeper understanding. A decade earlier, in her classic *The Good High School*, Harvard educator Sara Lawrence Lightfoot (1983) uses the term "intellectual play" to describe classrooms in which adolescents' personal, cognitive, and social learning needs are met. In classrooms that are communities of learners, adolescents speak and explore, teachers guide, and resources compel. The atmosphere is comfortable and nonthreatening, and the learning experiences are creative, challenging, and interactive. Student relationships are promoted, their ideas are valued, and knowledge is built collaboratively. Their emotions must be intentionally engaged, their intellects meaningfully challenged, and their relationships built within a respectful, interactive, and authentic context.

Similarly, Parker Palmer (1998) uses the words "creative tension" to describe the environment of a classroom when skillful teachers purposefully shape a space for learning (pp. 74–77). A space for adolescent learning requires this same kind of preparation. In true learning communities, teachers encourage students to explain their thinking, to use their imaginations, and to articulate their ideas. They insist that students pay attention to their thinking and how it is expressed. They provide the opportunity for students to use extended resources, to make personal choices, to assume responsibility, to reflect on their thinking and learning, and to practice important interpersonal and cognitive skills. They also expect adolescents to expend the intellectual energy needed to do an assignment well, and they challenge them to acquire a deeper understanding of content and of their own thinking capabilities.

A skilled and caring teacher acknowledges and accommodates the interacting affective, cognitive, and social factors that influence adolescent learning—and makes instructional decisions accordingly. This teacher enables students to practice valuable skills that help them interact meaningfully with people and information beyond the specific learning experience. In these learning communities of acceptance, tolerance, and meaningful challenge, adolescents become more flexible, empathetic, knowledgeable, responsible, and self-motivated learners and people.

ACTing

on the Adolescent-Centered Learning Principles Discussed in Chapter 3

Principle	*How I can put it into practice*
❑ Structure a learning environment that is conducive to adolescent thinking and learning by being responsive to students' personal, intellectual, and social needs.	
❑ Build relationships within a respectful, interactive, and authentic context.	
❑ Create a community of learning where adolescents engage in meaningful collaboration and knowledge construction.	
❑ Motivate adolescents to take more responsibility within the learning experience.	
❑ Intentionally engage feelings and emotions.	
❑ Challenge adolescent minds with an interactive and personally affirming instructional environment that is supportive and nonthreatening.	
❑ Hold students accountable for good work and continual improvement.	

CHAPTER

4

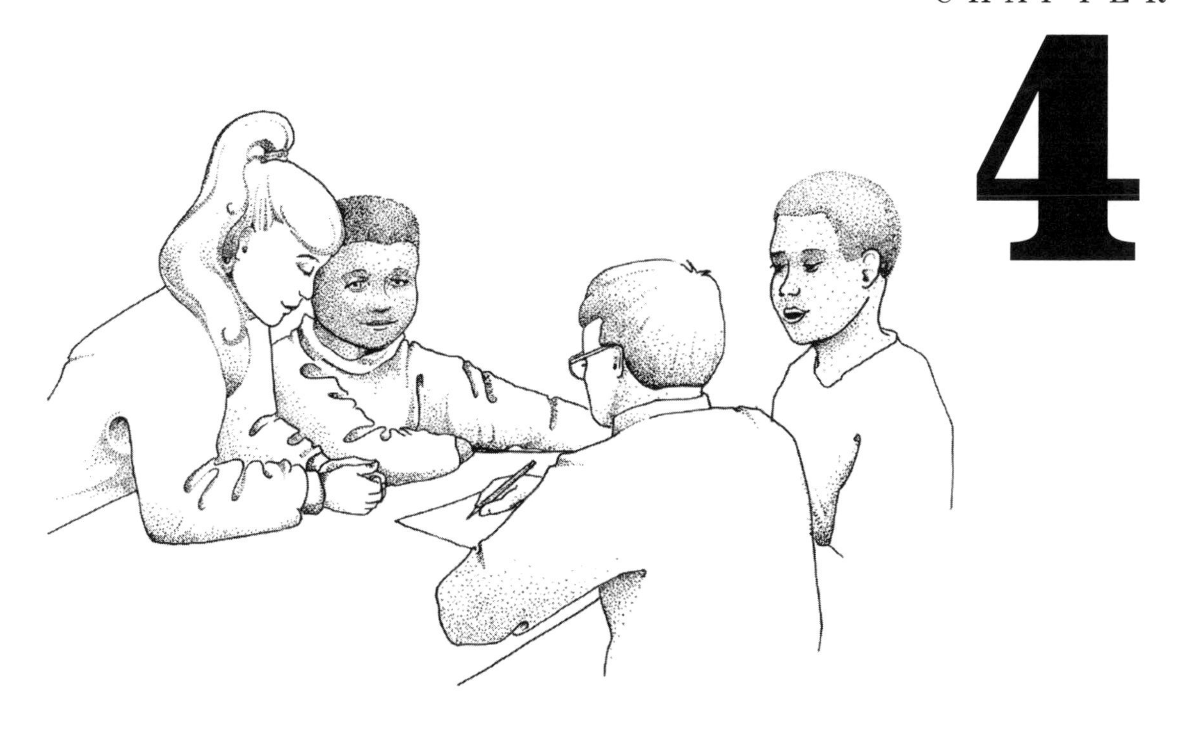

Teaching for Thinking and Understanding

PROMOTING THINKING DEVELOPMENT

For adolescents to become better thinkers, they must be immersed in settings where thinking drives the understanding of knowledge. In their book *The Thinking Classroom,* Shari Tishman, David Perkins, and Eileen Jay describe a thinking culture as one in which the language, values, expectations, and habits support an "enterprise of good thinking" (1995, p. 22). They identify several dimensions of classroom life conducive to thinking development. They emphasize initially that teachers and students should be familiar with and use vocabulary and terms that convey the thinking process or goal. The following examples illustrate.

- A science teacher uses the terms "hypothesize," "test assumptions," "experiment," "analyze findings," and "draw conclusions."
- A social studies teacher asks a student to think from an alternate perspective.

Your Ideas

- A language arts teacher uses such words as "characterize," "infer," "interpret," "justify," and "explain" during a drama and poetry discussion.
- An art teacher uses the terms "observe," "critique," "appraise," "investigate," and "compare."

When teachers speak the language of thinking, write the terms on charts in the room, demonstrate what they mean, and help adolescents recognize when they are using the skill appropriately and well, students become better thinkers. Moreover, students need to develop mental models of what higher level thinking is and sounds like for the skills to be internalized. They need, for example, to hear and use thinking language within the context of ongoing learning experiences. Table 4.1 suggests some of the thinking terminology that

Table 4.1 The Language of Thinking

Literary Meaning	*Mathematical Reasoning*	*Scientific Inquiry*	*Historical Analysis*	*Artistic Expression*
Infer	Subdivide	Classify Speculate/ Research	Investigate	Review/Scrutinize
Discern	Solve	Suggest/Suppose	Corroborate	Select
Hypothesize	Prove	Surmise/Theorize	Reflect/Establish	Recreate
Interpret/ Contend	Detect/Scrutinize	Reason	Convince/Dissent	Understand
Dissent/Consider	Weigh/Conjecture	Prove	Attest	Recognize/Perceive
Conclude/Question	Dissect	Probe	Affirm	Realize/Appreciate
Ponder	Derive/Ascertain	Propose/Postulate	Explore	Muse
Predict	Calculate/Assess	Analyze/Dispute	Inquire/Suppose	Observe/Evaluate
Opine/Summarize	Comprehend	Examine/Construe	Remember/Rebut	Relate
Perceive	Deduce	Assess	Maintain/Submit	Discriminate
Critique	Demonstrate	Claim	Resolve/Recollect	Differentiate
Relate	Estimate	Confirm/Establish	Study/Restructure	Recommend
Restate	Determine	Justify	Interpret	Describe
Review	State	Execute	Compare	Exemplify
Imply	Categorize	Implement	Generate	Produce
Contrast	Rate	Summarize		
Recognize	Explain	Plan		
Recall	Check			

can be used within and across disciplines as first enunciated by Bloom (1956) and later revised by Anderson and Krathwohl (2001). Thinking classrooms are places where adolescents and teachers place high value on thinking well (Beamon, 1997, 2001).

Your Ideas

Chapter 5 gives examples of specific disciplinary thinking language and offers several instructional suggestions that promote inquiry and problem solving within the disciplines. (See Table 5.1.) The following tips for promoting adolescent thinking and higher order knowledge development are useful for teachers in any content area (Gardner, 1991, 1999; Perkins, 1992; Tishman et al., 1995).

- Give adolescents enough time to shape questions, conduct investigations, or solve problems.
- Explain and discuss problem solving, inquiry, and other thinking strategies.
- Provide continual feedback, both corrective and supportive, so adolescents can recognize a standard for thinking appropriately within a discipline.
- Draw from adolescents their own conceptions about conducting inquiry or approaching problems.
- Promote frequent interaction so adolescents can share ideas, articulate thinking, and reflect on what they are doing and why.
- Use authentic examples, such as real historical research, scientific discoveries, mathematical problems, and significant literary and artistic works.
- Enable adolescents to build understanding collaboratively with disciplinary "experts" who have a workable understanding of the skills and content.

GETTING THE RIGHT MIND-SET

Helping adolescents acquire the mind-set for higher level thinking is an ongoing challenge. They have the cognitive ability to take an alternate perspective on an issue, for example, yet they are not generally inclined, or "disposed," to do so unless externally prompted. A social studies teacher wants students to acknowledge the reasoning behind a viewpoint that differs from their own. An issue-laden question—Should the U.S. government ban immigration?—is offered for discussion. Adolescents' responses typically reflect either the pro side, based on the rationale of economics, job security, and the problems with work visas, or the con side, reflecting America's image to the world as a free and safe haven for the downtrodden. The teacher changes tactics and asks two students to argue for an opposite perspective. The purpose is not to make the students change their minds but rather to consider how another might think in the situation.

Another strategy to encourage perspective taking is illustrated in the inquiry-based scenario in the ACT Model "Encouraging a Mind-Set for

Your Ideas

Thinking." Adolescents gather and synthesize information from varying perspectives on the current social issue of immigration. Through the experience, they become aware that different circumstances shape personal beliefs. They also develop a stronger disposition to consider the context for others' viewpoints in a fair-minded manner.

Encouraging a Mind-Set for Thinking: Immigration Then and Now

Often adolescents are not "disposed" to tolerate viewpoints that differ from their own. In a situation where they are required to gather and synthesize information that represents varying perspectives, they become more aware of the different experiences that shape personal beliefs. They also develop the disposition to consider in a fair-minded way the context for others' ideas.

Content Understanding

To help adolescents develop a personal perspective on current social issues within the broader cultural and historical context. The specific issue of focus is immigration.

Studies Standards

- The purpose and authority of government and how its powers are acquired, used, and justified.
- The interdependence, conflict, and cooperation among groups, societies, and nations.
- The complexity of issues related to historical change and continuity.
- Civic ideals and practice related to rights and responsibilities of citizens.

Key Concepts

Immigration, chronology, causality, change, interdependence, time, continuity, change, political power and authority, citizenship, civic responsibility

Learning Outcomes

- Students will develop a personal perspective on current social issues by examining the controversy over immigration in the United States.

ESSENTIAL QUESTIONS

Who immigrates?

Why do people immigrate?

Have the reasons for immigration changed over time? How and how not?

What is the experience of coming to a new country like for new immigrants?

How does immigration affect local communities?

What are the social, emotional, and economic costs and benefits of immigration for a host country?

Strategies for Inquiry

An Inquiry Challenge: More than 11 million undocumented immigrants are living in the United States and more are arriving daily. Public opinion is divided over the strain of immigration on health and education services versus the benefit of immigrants filling low-wage jobs in key sectors of the nation's economy. Congress is similarly divided on the issues of border control and improved pathways for illegal immigrants living in America to gain U.S. citizenship.

On May 1, 2006, thousands of immigrants closed businesses, boycotted work, and flooded into the streets of major American cities as a statement of their valued presence in the economic, social, and cultural tapestry of the country. Caught in the heated political debate over immigration reform, these protesters expressed concern that the security of living in the United States without legal status has come under threat.

In response to the continuing unrest and concern across the nation, government officials have called for a national summit to discuss, and hopefully settle, the problem. You have been asked to serve on a team of youth delegates. Your task is to develop a well-informed presentation that includes the various perspectives of people impacted by the immigration dilemma.

Guided Interaction

- Teams of students are formed to gather information from a variety of historical and current viewpoints.
- Strategies for data collection include interviews with local immigrants who have or have not gained citizenship, interviews with nonimmigrants, letters to members of Congress and other government officials, newspaper articles on immigration-related events, and media coverage. Stories that tell of the struggles and perceptions of immigrant families are located through newspaper and Internet archives.
- Students compare reasons for immigration to America in earlier centuries with the current one: Have motives changed? Are the challenges and conditions related to relocation more or less strenuous? Do the benefits of living in the new country outweigh the hardships?
- Students also determine the varying sides of issues related to the social, political, and economic impact of immigrants on local communities and on America as a country to understand the current political controversy. Viewpoints can be analyzed using graphic organizer tools (www.graphic.org/goindex.html/).
- Students view commonly held biases by viewing myths about immigrants (see www.justiceforimmigrants.org/).
- Students collaborate to develop researched ideas for the summit simulation. Individual perspectives are shared and shaped with choice and creativity allowed. Visuals, technology enhancements, role play, or other means can be used to present findings.

Metacognitive Development and Assessment

- Responsibility is placed on the adolescents to explore resources, acquire and analyze information, and synthesize findings that help shape personal perspectives. At various checkpoints, the teacher requires teams to assess progress and productivity and to revise strategy if needed.
- The culminating performance-based product is the summit presentation. Evaluation criteria might include
  - Acknowledgment of varying perspectives on the issue
  - Logical synthesis of data collected
  - Valid support for ultimate group perspective
  - Appropriate use of enhancements (visuals, handouts, technologies)
- Individual and peer evaluations can also assess group contribution and collaboration skills. A rubric can be developed (see Figure 4.1).
- Reflection time needs to follow the simulation for the assessment of problem-solving strategies used during the inquiry and their application to other real-world challenges.

Useful Web Sites

National Public Radio (NPR): The Immigration Debate

http://www.npr.org/templates/story/story.php?storyId=5310549&sourceCode=gaw

See how Americans view immigration through numerous perspectives.

Teacher Scholastic: Immigration

http://teacher.scholastic.com/activities/immigration/index.htm

Teacher and student resources, including a glossary of terms and research starters for learning about immigration. Features a tour of Ellis Island and stories about and interviews with past and current immigrants.

The American Immigration Center

http://www.us-immigration.com

Resources for gaining U.S. citizenship.

Ellis Island

http://www.ellisisland.org

Information on the Ellis Island Immigration Museum and the American Family Immigration History Center. A search engine finds names and countries of origin from the Immigrant Wall of Honor. Sponsored by the Statue of Liberty–Ellis Island Foundation, Inc.

Map Collections Home Page

http://memory.loc.gov/ammem/gmdhtml

Online map exhibit featuring Americana cartographic treasures at the Library of Congress. Organized into sections on cities, conservation and environment, exploration, immigration and settlement, military battles, transportation, and general area maps.

Immigration Issues

http://www.vote-smart.org

Project Vote Smart provides an array of documents, links, and opinions on immigration. A highly informative educational site.

National Museum of American History

http://americanhistory.si.edu

A great Web site to visit whether planning a trip or just taking a virtual tour. Gives descriptions of the museum, its holdings and exhibitions, programs, and activities. Provides online exhibits and links to other Smithsonian museums.

Figure 4.1 Group Collaboration Evaluation

Name of Group Member

____

Participated, contributed ideas for team discussions and decisions

1 ------------------------ 2 ------------------------ 3 ------------------------ 4 ------------------------ 5

Fulfilled responsibility for "fair share" of workload

1 ------------------------ 2 ------------------------ 3 ------------------------ 4 ------------------------ 5

Maintained a positive attitude

1 ------------------------ 2 ------------------------ 3 ------------------------ 4 ------------------------ 5

Was a team player

1 ------------------------ 2 ------------------------ 3 ------------------------ 4 ------------------------ 5

Cross-Disciplinary Applications

- In science, students grapple with a problem scenario that addresses the conflict between federal regulation of diminishing wetlands and corporate developers.
- In English, students research the rationale behind a local parental objection to the reading of a particular adolescent novel.
- In mathematics, adolescents critique varying methods for solving a problem.

Your Ideas

The willingness to entertain a viewpoint different from one's own is an example of a disposition that supports open-minded thinking (Barell, 1995). Robert Ennis (1987), highly regarded for his work in critical thinking and its assessment, emphasizes that thinking dispositions are foundational to good thinking ability and need to be cultivated intentionally by teachers. The following text box gives several research-based thinking dispositions. Other educators combine both disposition and ability when they describe the intellectual traits of good thinkers (Perkins, 1992; Tishman et al., 1995). Dispositions play a critical role in the affective dimension of the learning environment and influence the kind of thinking habits adolescents will potentially develop and use in their own lives (Paul, 1998).

Dispositions for Thinking and Learning

Disposed to

- Question and pose problems
- Seek accuracy of information
- Stay informed and consider the broader situation
- Use credible sources
- Take a position when evidence warrants
- Suspend judgment of others' ideas
- Be fair-minded, tolerant, and empathetic
- Be flexible, careful, and orderly
- Be diligent in the face of ambiguity
- Devote enough time to do a challenging task well
- Seek and evaluate reasons
- Sustain intellectual curiosity
- Be planful and strategic
- Seek clarity and understanding
- Be metacognitive, reflective, and self-evaluative

Dispositions are "teachable" over time through favorable and ongoing experiences within the learning environment (Tishman et al., 1995). Structured debate, role play, seminar, and simulation, for example, help adolescents develop tolerance for others' ideas. Inquiry-based problems that stir curiosity prompt them to wonder, question, probe, and explore information from various

Your Ideas

angles. Opportunities to reflect upon and evaluate what they have said or prepared make them increasingly aware of important intellectual standards, such as logical reasoning, clarity, accuracy, and precision.

Obviously, teachers play an important and active role in the selection of instructional strategies and in the expectations they establish for interactive behavior. When teachers model the dispositions, adolescents are more likely to emulate and internalize them. A few self-assessment questions are suggested below.

- Do I insist that students listen to each other during discussions?
- Do I have them formulate and ask each other questions?
- Do I have students revise a draft or plan a project?
- Do I ask them to rephrase an answer or elaborate on and substantiate an idea?
- Do I model appropriate mental behaviors, such as explaining aloud the steps in my own reasoning?
- Do I verbally alter my own viewpoint in light of new evidence?
- Do I allow students time to think through ideas or delve deeply into a task?

Key to helping adolescents acquire a mind-set for expanded thinking and learning is to make them aware of the affective skills they need to develop (Barell, 1995; Tishman et al., 1995). When teachers ask their students to reflect on what they learned about their own thinking, they provide an opportunity for students to recognize the disadvantage of being narrow-minded. Following the immigration simulation, for example, if students are asked to talk about their feelings, they begin to see advantage in a broadened perspective. In addition, they begin to realize the complexity of such issues and approach a new problem with a more flexible frame of mind.

TRUSTING THAT LESS IS MORE

Gallagher (1998) contends that the knowledge explosion makes total coverage "an illusion." He urges teachers to consider new instructional approaches that stress "how to access information when it is needed to solve significant problems" (p. 41). Other educators, including Gardner (1991, 1999), Perkins (1992), and Wiggins and McTighe (1998) are similarly cautious against the fruitless attempt to try to cover subject matter content in a traditional, didactic manner. The body of knowledge in any discipline is growing exponentially. It is also difficult to know what information is meaningful for adolescents to know. The following profile gives a snapshot of the current generation of adolescent learners:

They have known only one Germany.

The Vietnam War is almost as abstract to them as World War II.

Many were infants when the Soviet Union dissolved or the Persian War raged.

They have always known about AIDS, though they are unlikely to have had polio vaccine shots.

Cable, DVD players, compact discs, and the Internet have always been around.

They have grown up with microwave popcorn and remote controls.

Your Ideas

What is personally meaningful to adolescents helps determine what content to teach. If a teacher decides that the evolving political structure in Germany is pertinent, this content is made more relevant when compared to the more recent political struggles in China, Russia, or Iraq. Decisions about instructional delivery need to take into account the context of adolescents' social experiences. The information on the pages of textbooks cannot keep abreast of changes in the outside world, and adolescents' learning cannot be limited to what is written there.

CURRICULUM DESIGNED FOR THINKING AND LEARNING

Arguably, curricular decisions need to consider national standards, state and local guidelines, and assessment measures. Teachers, however, can work strategically within these parameters to identify and select knowledge that lends itself to understanding (Wiggins & McTighe, 1998). In their book *Understanding by Design*, they note that the curriculum development process begins with deciding what knowledge is essential and enduring to the discipline. The following four questions, based on the Wiggins and McTighe model (p. 11), offer a guide for sorting through the overabundant possibilities in a content area:

Does the idea, topic, or process have enduring value beyond the classroom?

Is the idea, topic, or process central to an understanding of the discipline?

Is this an idea, topic, or process that is frequently confusing or less obvious?

Does this idea, topic, or process have the potential to engage student interest?

Figure 4.2 is a visual representation of a teacher's thought processes during the planning of a social studies unit. The teacher's reasoning leads to some pertinent decisions about content. An essential understanding in the discipline of social studies, and one aligned with national standards, is that Perceptions Shape Historical Perspective. This "big idea" becomes the broad learning goal for the unit. The teacher then spends considerable time identifying and prioritizing the knowledge, skills, and dispositions believed to be pertinent to historical understanding, such as the recognition of multiple and varying points of view on an issue or cultural event, the ability to take an alternate perspective on the interpretation of a historical event, or the mindset for considering a viewpoint different from one's own. The next step is to plan instructional experiences that engage students' learning and deepen their understanding.

Your Ideas

Figure 4.2 Content Concepts

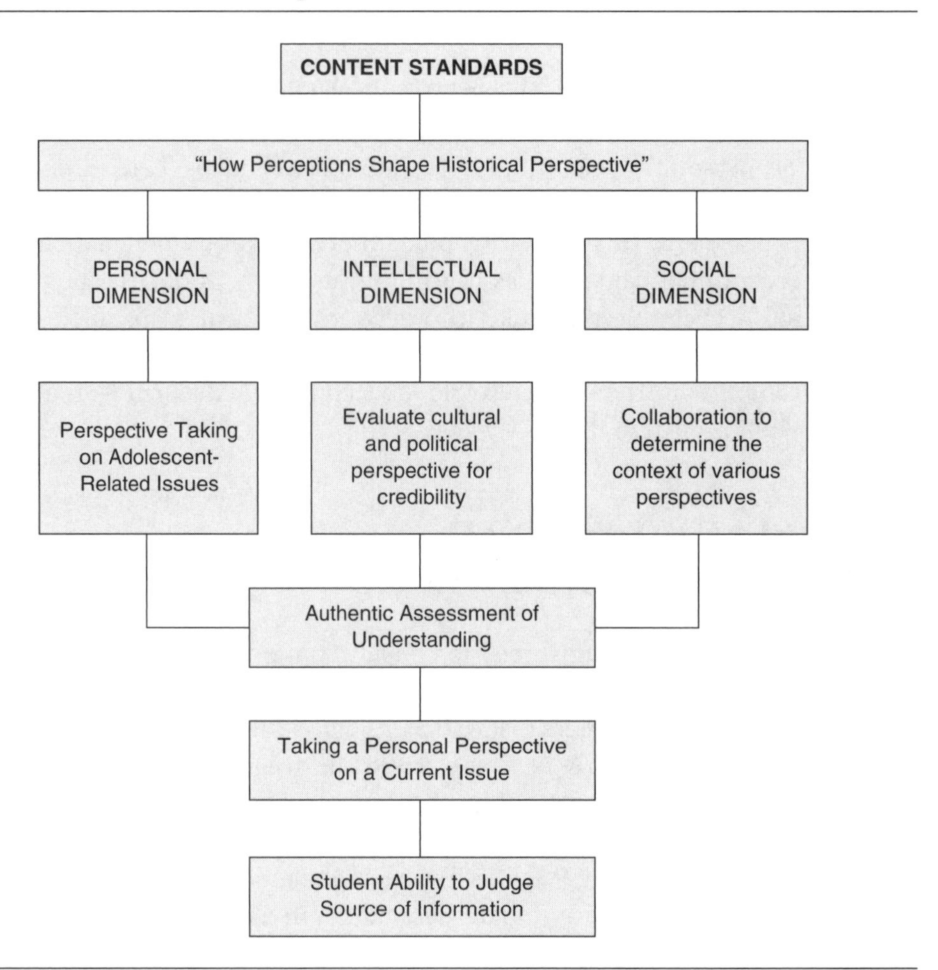

INQUIRY AND ESSENTIAL QUESTIONING

Wiggins and McTighe (1998) also distinguish between two types of questions that help students build an understanding of knowledge. These are essential questions, which are broad and more generalized, and topic- or lesson-specific questions. Essential questions deal with the more enduring ideas of a discipline. Topic-specific questions provoke thought about a particular piece of literature, work of art, scientific concept, mathematical problem, or historical event. They act as pathways to the more comprehensive essential questions (see Table 4.2).

By engaging actively and collaboratively in the process of critical inquiry, teachers help students broaden their thinking about the context for interpretation. They create an opportunity for them to express their ideas and guide as they work for insight into the complex cultural and political conditions that shape perspective. Teachers can use questioning strategically to promote adolescent thinking and understanding.

The ACT Model "Teaching for Understanding" illustrates an adolescent-centered learning experience developed according to the "understanding by design" model. Essential understandings and essential questions are identified

Your Ideas

Table 4.2 Structuring Questions to Challenge Adolescent Thinking

Essential Question	*Related Topic-Specific Questions*
How does conflict shape history?	How did the bombing of Pearl Harbor change the dynamics of World War II?
How is interdependency reflected in the environment?	What is the relationship among the strata of the rainforest?
How is symmetrical patterning apparent in nature?	What are the real-world implications of the Fibonacci sequence?
Should equity be prized at the expense of excellence?	Do you think it is fair that some of the ballet dancers in Vonnegut's (1968) "Harrison Bergeron" must wear weights on their legs?
How can nonconformity lead to creative expression?	What social, personal, and political factors influenced Dali's artistic style?

as an organizing framework for student learning. A critical analysis of the events at Tiananmen Square provides a specific historical application of the broader ideas. Task-specific questions help students think critically about the varying accounts of the 1989 coverage. Following the application, metacognitive questions expand adolescents' thinking about the role of historical and cultural context in other instances. The extension activities and culminating assessment provide additional opportunities to apply students' learning related to the organizing of essential understandings, and thus enhance the probability for transfer.

Teaching for Understanding: What's in a Perspective?

Adolescents may realize that historical accounts are based primarily on human interpretation. They frequently, however, believe that their own culture renders the true perspective and may be quick to deem alternate viewpoints as false. Perpetuated by history books and the media, this form of cultural stereotyping should be confronted. Teachers need to help students develop the critical thinking skills to determine the validity and credibility of varying perspectives. They also need to understand the social, cultural, and political contexts of these perspectives.

Content Understanding

- To help adolescents to understand that human perspectives are shaped by complex historical, cultural, social, and political factors.
- To develop the critical thinking skills to analyze and evaluate the credibility and authenticity of sources.

Learning Outcomes

- Students will determine the validity and credibility of historical and cultural perspectives by critically analyzing the varying accounts of the 1989 Tiananmen Square event.
- Students will think critically about the role of propaganda to distort the reporting of current events by examining news coverage in newspapers and on the Internet.

Key Concepts

Cultural and political context, propaganda, cultural stereotyping, cultural perspective

ESSENTIAL QUESTIONS

Why would the recorded accounts of an event in history differ?
How and why does propaganda originate? What circumstances might justify the use of propaganda?
How can the credibility of secondary sources be tested?
Are primary sources always reliable?

Inquiry Task

A critical analysis of accounts of events of Tiananmen Square, 1989

Guided Interaction

- In preparation for the task, teachers can help adolescents practice gauging perspective through informal paired debates on various issues. The cultural, religious, and personal reasons that people have alternate viewpoints on issues can be discussed. Questions can be generated by students, such as those found on the Pro-Con chart that follows. Students should be asked to support a perspective they would not ordinarily take.

Pro-Con Chart	Pros	Cons
Should marijuana be legalized?		
Should animals be put at risk by the film industry?		
Is the death penalty ever justified?		
Should athletes be required to take a drug-screening test?		

- Have students watch news coverage of the 1989 Tiananmen Square incident that occurred in Beijing, China, and discuss the historical circumstances that set a context for the event (the Cultural Revolution, Mao's reign, the pro-democracy movement). Then, read conflicting accounts of the 1989 Tiananmen Square incident. Discrepancies should be noted and personal questions formulated.

Useful Resources for Teachers and Students

Encarta Learning Zone: Tiananmen (http://encarta.msn.com/encnet/refpages/search.aspx?q=tiananmen&Submit2=Go)

Tiananmen: The Gate of Heavenly Peace contains links to articles, essays, and book excerpts on the incident (http://www.tsquare.tv/)

Foreign Policy News Clips provides news accounts from the United States (http://globetrotter.berkeley.edu/clips/1989/X111a.html)

Peking Duck is a personal site that provides a perspective from a college student who participated in the Tiananmen Square event (http://www.pekingduck.org/archives/000063.php)

- During an ensuing discussion, the teacher should probe about the historical events and conflicting political viewpoints among the Chinese people. Students can be expected to substantiate their responses with reference to source.

Task-Specific Questions

Is there an account that seems closer to the truth?
Are there similarities in any other accounts?
How can any account be justified?
Why would there be shock among Chinese officials at the protests?
How might the people's roles or ages influence the perspective?
Does the date of the reporting make any difference?

Metacognitive Development and Assessment

- Following the discussion about the Tiananmen Square accounts, the teacher should extend adolescents' thinking with reflection questions. These might include
  - Why do people see and interpret events differently?
  - How do personal emotions affect one's perspective?
  - Why is it important to consider historical and cultural context?
  - What is important to consider in the critical analysis of sources?
  - Do you think that what you read in the United States is always credible?
- Teachers promote transfer by using critical analysis skills in another context. Students examine two local newspapers and contrast the language and perspectives of regional reporters or compare a large newspaper's angle on a story with that of a small-town paper. Two book or play reviews might be read and research conducted on the reviewers. Stratified sampling surveys about political or environmental issues are sent and variations among respondents discussed. Polls across grade levels on school-related issues are planned.
- As a culminating assessment, students write a persuasive letter (or editorial) to a pertinent source (newspaper or magazine) that reflects a personal perspective on a current issue. Evaluative criteria include logical progression of reasoning, acknowledgment of alternate perspectives and their rationale, credible support for perspective, and coherence and organization.

SOURCE: John Chaffee, "Thinking Critically, 8th Edition," Copyright © 2006 by Houghton Mifflin Company.

Cross-Disciplinary Applications

- In art class, students take a painting of one artist and discuss how and why another from a different time might approach the same subject differently.
- In English class, students assume the roles of characters in different pieces of literature to discuss a modern-day issue, such as bioengineering or censorship. They would have to understand the setting context and values of the period as well as the characterization.

QUESTIONING FOR THINKING

Your Ideas

Over 2,000 years ago, Socrates used questioning masterfully to guide student thinking about important knowledge. Rather than provide the answers, his style was to ask yet another question. The purpose of Socratic discussion, according to Paul and Binker (1995b), is to help students "develop and evaluate their thinking by making it explicit." The teacher's role is to "wonder aloud," to show interest in what students think, to respect what they say, and to encourage them to "slow their thinking down and elaborate on it" (p. 335). The teacher's challenge is to guide students as they arrive at their own answers. Socratic discussion strengthens adolescents' abilities to reason logically about important knowledge.

Questioning can be used to help adolescents construct meaning from content and to think about knowledge in an extended, more refined manner (Marzano et al., 1992). By incorporating the language of thinking into questioning and by purposefully sequencing inquiry, teachers also help to strengthen adolescents' metacognitive capacities (Beamon, 1990, 1992–1993, 1997). A long-term goal of strategic questioning is that adolescents will begin to use inquiry skills independently. The following self-evaluative questions are useful to teachers as they engage adolescents in the process of inquiry, whether the focus is a novel, a historical interpretation, a problem, an experiment, or an art form (Beamon, 1993, 1997):

- Do I ask higher-level questions that cause adolescents to think and reason?
- Do my questions connect with what students know and understand?
- Do I model my own (genuine) curiosity and interest in learning?
- Do I withhold my viewpoint to encourage other ideas, yet when necessary delve into areas of misconception or narrow thinking?
- Do I expect students to present their viewpoints logically?
- Do I ask probing questions for clarification, substantiation, or extension?
- Do I set high standards for what is an acceptable response?
- Do I help students draw a connection from the immediate topic to a more relevant and abstract application?
- Do I expect students to listen respectfully to each other's views?
- Do my students feel comfortable enough to share their thinking?
- Do I allow adequate time for adolescents to think through or add to answers?

The following "SAFE" Classification Model was designed to help teachers formulate questions to challenge adolescent thinking on four cognitive levels (Beamon, 1990, 1997). Questions on the first (S) level help adolescents "set up" a content knowledge base. These query for basic comprehension, and answers are generally based on facts. Questions on the second (A) level are more analytical, however, and require adolescents to interpret contextual clues before answering. To respond to questions on the (F) level, adolescents must focus content in a direction different than originally presented. The fourth (E) level is a classification level that elicits students' evaluative thinking. Example questions illustrate possible content area applications.

Questioning to Challenge Adolescent Thinking: A "SAFE" Classification Model

Setting the Knowledge Base

Students are asked to remember facts, relate personal experiences, and make meaningful connections with new knowledge. These questions are literal, with fairly apparent answers.

What are the basic steps in this process?
What is the formula to find this function?
What are the events that led to this occurrence?
What other story was set in this location?
What in your own experience helps you relate to this character?
Who are other artists who used this style?

Analyzing the New Knowledge

These questions ask students to make inferences, to interpret information based on contextual clues, to compare or explain, and to see new relationships in the knowledge. These questions require an analysis of meaning, and answers are interpretive.

What relationship do you see among these number properties?
What can you infer about this character's motive?
How could we classify these genetic characteristics?
How does this problem-solving method compare to the other one?
How can you differentiate this perspective from the others?
Why is the historical event pivotal?

Focusing the New Knowledge

These questions encourage divergent thinking. Students are asked to make predictions, to hypothesize, to extend knowledge to a new context, or to focus it in a new direction.

Based on what you've found, what hypothesis can you formulate?
If we change this angle, what will be the effect on the perimeter?
If the story took place in another time, how might the ending change?
What is another way to view this decision?
If this composer could hear today's music, what might he say?

Evaluating the New Knowledge

These questions require students to evaluate, judge, appraise, critique, or give personal value to the new knowledge. They encourage personal reflection.

What is your perspective on the issue?
Which of the two methods worked more efficiently?
What criteria are you using to judge the value of the piece?
What argument could you present to verify your conclusion?
How can we determine the appropriateness of this decision?

Purposeful inquiry involves the strategic sequencing of cognitive questions. Teachers order questions in a way that helps adolescents connect with knowledge and that challenges them to think about it in more sophisticated ways. Through the conscious integration of cognitive questions and follow-up questions, teachers sustain a high level of inquiry and prompt adolescents to think about and improve their thinking expression. The strategic sequencing of questions during a discussion of the Tiananmen Square accounts is illustrated below.

Sequenced Questioning for Tiananmen Square Discussion

- What are your questions or observations after reading the accounts? [(**S**)*etting the knowledge base*]
- What do any of you know about the government of China or this particular protest? [(**S**)*etting the knowledge base*]
- How might your interpretation be different if you did not know that the student was in custody? [(**F**)*ocusing the knowledge in a new direction*]
- Do you see any terms or statements that seem inflammatory or that make you think the account lacks complete credibility? [(**A**)*nalysis level*]
  - What are other examples of emotional language? [**Follow-up** *for alternate ideas*]
- Why might the Chinese Chairman be compelled to justify the army's actions? [(**A**)*nalysis level*]
- Would you justify the Chairman's account? [(**E**)*valuative level*]
  Is there an account that seems closer to the truth? [(**A**)*nalysis level*]
  - What evidence can you give for your thinking? [**Follow-up** *for substantiation*]
  - Are there other reasons? [**Follow-up** *for more detail*]
  - What do you think is the basis for these discrepancies? [**Follow-up** *for rationale*]
- What have you learned about the reporting of historical events? [(**E**)*valuative level for reflection on learning*]
- What is important to consider in the critical analysis of sources? [(**E**)*valuative level for reflection on learning*]
- Do you think what you read in the United States is always credible? [(**E**)*valuative level*]

Here are some other, more general follow-up questions that sustain thinking and promote metacognitive extension.

- What is the reasoning for your answer?
- What is the basis for your conclusion?
- Is there an alternative way to look at the situation?

Your Ideas

- What evidence supports your thinking?
- What else can you (or anyone) add to your (this) response?
- What contradiction do you recognize in your reasoning?
- What might be the consequences of this decision?
- What is an example of this situation in real life?
- How does this apply in another subject area?

The purposefully sequenced questioning modeled previously is an example of Socratic style. The teacher does not dominate the discussion but rather enters at strategic points. When an interjection is made, the teacher acknowledges students' responses or summarizes their ideas but does not give an opinion. Through purposeful questions that probe, ask for rationale, or redirect, the teacher is able to maintain the momentum of the discussion as the adolescents are challenged beyond surface-level or impulsive thinking toward more fully developed ideas. The teacher skillfully guides the discussion toward more thoughtful consideration of the enduring ideas of the discipline.

TEACHING FOR UNDERSTANDING

According to Wiggins and McTighe (1998), six facets indicate true understanding of knowledge. They observe that "[u]nderstanding is always a matter of degree, typically furthered by questions and lines of inquiry that arise from reflection, discussion, and use of ideas" (p. 45). Adolescent understanding is possible when teachers go beyond the "bits and pieces" of disconnected information. Specific dates of minor historical events or isolated facts that are not linked to broader issues, trends, or themes, for example, do not spark student interest or invite critical thought. Void of energy or dimension, this information is easily forgotten because it lacks the potential to connect with anything of relevance in adolescents' current or future lives. Absorbing this kind of information becomes more of a game of Trivial Pursuit than a process of thoughtful engagement with substantive knowledge.

When Adolescents Really Understand

They Should Be Able to

1. **Explain it.** How can you explain the impact of this war on the country's economy? What accounts for this conclusion? What is implied in this action?
2. **Interpret it.** What makes sense about this play's ending? How does this style of writing reflect the political climate of the period? How does this historical event illustrate a pattern in human behavior?
3. **Apply it.** How can this knowledge of statistics be used in a different situation? In what real-world context is this economic principle applicable?

4. **Take a perspective on it.** What are the three sides of this political debate? From whose viewpoint is this article written? What are the strengths and weaknesses of this rationale?

5. **Show empathy about it.** How would you feel if you were in an immigrant's shoes? How would these changes impact the way of life for this culture? How are these decisions detrimental to these peoples' well-being?

6. **Gain self-knowledge through it.** What prejudices am I recognizing in myself? How might I formulate questions better? Where was my thinking faulty? How can I use these suggestions constructively?

Your Ideas

Teaching for understanding enables adolescents to encounter the important ideas that define and shape human existence and to realize the connecting themes and timeless patterns of the disciplines. It creates a sense of meaning and purpose in a complex data-oriented world. To attain understanding, however, adolescents must confront paradox and ambiguity, and they must deal with imbalance, mystery, and dissonance. In this process, their cognitive experiences will be enriched, and they will view themselves, knowledge, and the world differently. Teaching for understanding has the potential to transform. To promote understanding, adolescents should be actively, collaboratively, and intellectually engaged with substantive and enduring content.

When adolescents encounter the "overarching mental images" that hold subject matter together, they begin to develop an understanding of the important concepts, principles, and skills that shape the disciplines (Perkins, 1992, p. 17). This kind of knowledge is "dynamic, intellectually intriguing, and personal," and understanding it gives a "sense of power" to adolescent learners (Tomlinson, 1999, p. 31).

THINKING AND METACOGNITIVE DEVELOPMENT

Another element important to adolescent thinking development is the use of their metacognitive skills (Barell, 1995; Bransford et al., 2000; Tishman et al., 1995). Adolescents need multiple opportunities to make their thinking visible. Fogarty and Bellanca (1995b) have distinguished three phases of metacognitive practice: planning, monitoring, and evaluating (pp. 84–85). At the onset of an activity, adolescents articulate what they are trying or need to do; during a task, they stop periodically to check their progress; and, at the completion, they look back and assess how well they did. Ultimately, adolescents need to learn to organize their thinking by conscious strategy and to get in the habit of pondering how it can be improved. A few examples of instructional strategies that promote metacognitive thinking follow.

Your Ideas

Think Aloud A teacher pairs students for a "think aloud" technique for mathematical problem solving. One student assumes the role of problem solver by thinking aloud as he or she works through the problem. The second student acts as a monitor who asks questions to prompt thinking (Fogarty, 1995).

Self-Evaluation Following inquiry projects, a teacher gives each group of students an evaluation form with these questions:

- What strategies did you use to organize the investigation?
- What resources were most useful?
- What were any problems that arose?
- What factored into your decision for presentation format?
- How well did your group cooperate?
- What different strategies might you have used?

Individual Reflections Have chemistry students, for example, write individual reflections after each lab experiment critiquing the procedures used.

Stop 'n' Write Periodically During a discussion of a controversial issue in social studies, a teacher pauses for students to Stop 'n' Write their ongoing reactions on paper (Daniels & Bizar, 1998).

Three Questions As preparation for seminars, students write down three questions they have about the reading.

Learning Logs Students keep learning logs to reflect on their daily progress in understanding concepts in science or another subject (Daniels & Bizar, 1998).

TEACHERS AS COGNITIVE COACHES

Adolescents need assistance in developing and using the metacognitive skills that will help them recognize how and when their thinking improves. Only then do they begin to gauge their own progress and become more effective learners. To acquire the skills for self-regulated thinking and independent learning, adolescents need practice with being in charge. When teachers share the ownership for learning by giving students more responsibility to make decisions and choices, students gain the skills to manage and monitor their own learning direction and effectiveness.

Teaching for adolescent thinking and metacognitive development requires a changed relationship among teachers and students. The traditional image of the teacher as disseminator of knowledge and the student as passive recipient does little to promote thoughtful learning and independent thinking (Brown & Campione, 1996). How can adolescents learn to reason independently if they are always told what to believe and how to think? How can they learn to deal with the ambiguity of life if the content they face lacks complexity? How can they learn strategies if they do not practice problem solving? How can adolescents learn to formulate pertinent questions, reason logically, make thoughtful decisions, or evaluate personal thinking and its progress without guidance, assistance, and feedback?

Your Ideas

One metaphor used to describe teachers' new role is cognitive or metacognitive coach (Center for Problem-Based Learning, 1996; Gallagher, 1998; Perkins, 1991, 1992). Saloman has referred to this relationship between classroom "coach" and students as "partners in cognition" (Saloman, Perkins, & Globerson, 1991). The suggested interaction between teacher and students is illustrated in the ACT Model "A Cognitive/Metacognitive Coaching Model." The teacher guides adolescent thinking about the task through purposeful questioning, helps students to generate a K/NK board to organize their ideas, and assists as they determine strategy and course of action. The teacher also helps students prioritize findings, make decisions for the proposal, draw closure, and think about their learning. Later in the application, the teacher assists in their preparation for the proposal and allows time for reflection and evaluation on the process. Figures 4.3 and 4.4 detail possible student ideas for a K/NK board and show a task.

The teacher's role in the learning environment is strategically important. As facilitators, teachers plan and manage opportunities for adolescents to interact, make decisions, ask questions, and solve problems. They model and coach, probe and challenge, guide and monitor, motivate and encourage, expect and hold accountable, and assess and prompt. They carefully orchestrate the opportunity for adolescents to grow intellectually, socially, and personally.

COGNITIVE APPRENTICESHIP AND ADOLESCENT LEARNING

This new relationship among teachers and adolescent learners is also referred to as cognitive apprenticeship (Collins, Beranek, & Newman, 1991; Collins, Brown, & Newman, 1989). In his book *The Unschooled Mind: How Children Think and How Schools Should Teach,* Gardner (1991) describes the historical significance of an apprenticeship model. It enables young people to work closely with more advanced "experts" in the field. It helps young "novices" to continually improve their skills. This interaction further leads to a product or performance important within a society (Gardner, 1991, p. 124). In the school setting, an apprenticeship relationship among teachers, students, and others affords the advantage of helping adolescents think strategically about knowledge while they progressively strengthen cognitive skills.

A Cognitive/Metacognitive Coaching Model: A Question of Priority

Adolescents are often concerned when natural disasters affect the lives of humans and animals and the quality of their environment. Authentic problems based on real disasters, such as determining relief funding for the victims of hurricane-induced flooding, can be designed. These learning experiences promote and extend inquiry into real-world events and help adolescents broaden personal perspectives.

Content Understanding

To promote an awareness of civic responsibility and help students develop inquiry skills for real-world problem solving.

ESSENTIAL QUESTION

How do natural disasters affect the lives of people and animals and the quality of the environment?

Strategies for Inquiry

An Inquiry Challenge: The devastation from the hurricane flooding in a southeastern state has drawn national attention. The president of the United States has asked the governor to submit a proposal to the Federal Disaster Relief Agency to quality for funding up to $10 million. This plan must specify how the relief money would be used for area reconstruction and to safeguard the eastern region against future flooding disasters. You have been asked by the governor to serve on a team of investigators to develop this proposal. The plan should address the most pressing human and environmental needs in the flood-stricken area and be written in priority order.

- The teacher should guide students in the development of a "Know/Need to Know" board (see Figure 4.3). This graphic organizer will help students to (1) define the problem or task situation, (2) formulate inquiry questions, (3) identify needed information and resources, and (4) determine a course of investigative action.

Suggested inquiry questions might include . . .

What is the basic challenge of this problem?
What do we know about the situation by the information given?
What important information is missing?
What do we need to know before we can make any recommendations?
How can we learn more about the situation?
What are some initial concerns about this challenge?

Guided Interaction

- The teacher will guide as students determine a course of action to address the problem. Inquiry teams with designated tasks can be formed. Reference to the K/NK board can help students in the choice of areas for investigative focus.
- The teacher should also facilitate as students identify resources, determine strategy, generate research questions, and develop a reasonable timeline for the inquiry. A task structure analysis chart will be useful to organize strategy.
- The teacher will also need to assist as teams reconvene and collaborate to prioritize findings to make the funding recommendation.

Metacognitive Development and Assessment

- The teacher should monitor as investigative teams implement strategies and tap resources. Progress should be checked systematically through written status reports and questioning. At times, adolescents may have to rethink and change strategy.
- Students should be included in the discussion of criteria for and format of the final product.

These criteria might include the following:

Accuracy of information
Prioritization based on supporting rationale
Professional format of report
Group collaboration and individual contribution should also be evaluated.

- To promote further authenticity, local or state officials or selected public figures can assume a role in the evaluation process. A review panel might be assembled, a teleconference arranged, or the report mailed to an external source for feedback.
- Time should be provided for reflection at the close of the simulation. The problem-solving strategies and their implication for other real-world situations can be discussed.

Cross-Disciplinary Applications

- A newspaper is an excellent source for current events that can be shaped into authentic problems. The ongoing debate over money for space travel, the use of DNA for the prosecution of alleged criminals, human cloning, nuclear disarmament, animal rights concerns, and environmental protection issues are a few ideas that might appeal to the adolescent audience.

- Literature also provides a rich source of material for inquiry. As a prelude to reading Arthur Miller's *The Crucible,* for example, a teacher might pose this problem:

  It is the year 1692 in Salem, Massachusetts. The news has spread among the townspeople that a young slave girl named Tituba has confessed to witchcraft and is to be hanged at Gallow Hill. Rumors are also circulating that the girl is innocent . . .

Figure 4.3 A Know/Need to Know (K/NK) Board for Inquiry-Based Learning

What is the challenge?

The governor has commissioned a proposal for federal relief.
The plan must indicate proposed use for $10 million funding.
The proposal must prioritize the area's greatest needs.
The plan must be future-oriented.

What Do We Know?	What Do We Need to Know?	How Will We Find Out?
Eastern NC needs funding.	What are the greatest needs?	Find out details about damage.
Hurricanes have caused massive flooding.	What relief efforts have begun?	Learn about flood control.
The proposal must indicate need.	Has any money been given by other agencies?	Find out what efforts have begun.
The proposal must have a plan for use of funding.	What is the extent of the damage for area people?	Find out about interest groups.
The plan is for a limited amount.	How much has insurance helped?	Learn about the chemicals in flood runoff.
The plan must prioritize needs.	Are people still displaced?	Learn about disaster insurance.
Decisions must be made about where money is most needed.	What is the damage to area crops?	Learn the extent of crop damage.
There will not be enough for all people wanting money.	How have farmers suffered?	Learn about life in estuaries.
Everyone's needs can't be met.	What about pollution in streams?	Learn about federal funding in related disasters.
Consideration must be given to people, plant/animal life, and the natural environment.	Has pollution reached the ocean?	Learn about long-term effects of corrosion and pollution on farmland.
The governor and state are depending on us.	What will be the long-term impact on plant and animal life in estuaries?	Find out about efforts to combat pollution in streams.
This problem is HARD!	What is the impact on the environment?	Find out about COSTS!
	What interest groups are competing for funding?	Find out about other sources for federal funding.

Figure 4.4 A Task Structure Analysis for Team Investigation

	Team 1	Team 2	Team 3	Team 4	Team 5
Inquiry Task	Status of environmental damage from runoff pollution; costs for reconstruction.	Extent of damage to area farm industry (e.g., crops, livestock); costs for reconstruction.	Impact on people (homes, property, insurance); current status: displacement and assistance.	Techniques and costs of flood control efforts; other possible money sources.	Other federally funded initiatives to assist after flooding and hurricane disasters.
Resources	Newspaper archives, environmental agency, Web sites (e.g., chemical pollution, estuary life)	Local farmers, chamber of commerce, agricultural agency, newspapers	Local citizens and officials, insurance agencies	Internet (e.g., flood, conservation experts)	
Strategies	Interviews, videotaping, field notes	Phone calls, site visits, taped testimonials	Visits to relief shelters	Consultations with flood control experts (e.g., business, military)	

Cognitive apprenticeship typically includes the following features (Collins et al., 1989; Ormond, 2000):

- Modeling—students observe and listen while the teacher demonstrates and explains a task.
- Coaching—students perform the task while the teacher supports with hints or suggestions.
- Sequencing—more challenging and diverse tasks are given as proficiency is gained.
- Externalizing—students explain aloud their knowledge, thinking, and reasoning.
- Reflecting—students compare their thinking and performance with that of "experts."
- Exploring—students are helped to apply, expand, and refine the skills independently.

In cognitive apprenticeship, adolescents learn skills and acquire knowledge as they observe and practice under the guidance of a teacher, and they become successively more accomplished (Collins et al., 1989). The focus is on the mental processes used by experts in the discipline to solve complex problems or work through difficult tasks. The expert thinking thus becomes the standard that

Your Ideas

students strive to approximate. Both teachers and adolescents articulate their thinking processes, and students receive continual feedback and support (scaffolding) from the teacher. Students monitor and evaluate their own progress, make adjustments when improvement is needed, and incrementally develop competence. In the final stages, the teacher gives less assistance, referred to as fading, and students assume more responsibility.

These examples illustrate.

- A mathematics teacher guides students through the steps of a complex mathematical equation, verbalizing aloud his or her own reasoning. Students divide their papers into columns. In the left hand columns, they work additional problems, and, in the right, they record their reasoning processes. They later explain and compare their strategies with those of other students.
- A language arts teacher helps adolescents develop more sophisticated writing skills with prompt questions used by expert writers. Do I need a stronger transition between these two paragraphs? Would a different word choice communicate better what I want? Do I need to add more reasons to justify my view on the issue?

The goal of both metacognitive coaching and cognitive apprenticeship is to help adolescents acquire the knowledge and skills needed for independent thinking and learning. Instructional strategies include reciprocal teaching, procedural writing, mathematical problem solving, project-based learning, and problem-based learning (Cognition and Technology Group, 1990; Gallagher, Stepien, Sher, & Workman, 1995; Palincsar & Brown, 1984; Schoenfeld, 1985). Within this relationship, teachers foster metacognitive development by guiding and helping adolescents to think reflectively about personal learning, to monitor and improve skills, and increasingly to assume more control. The graphic in Figure 4.5 depicts this progression from dependence on the teacher's structured guidance to a more independent relationship in which adolescents rely more confidently and competently on their own power for self-regulation.

PUTTING AUTHENTICITY IN THE LEARNING TASK

Well-developed authentic learning tasks for adolescents should meet several criteria (Marzano & Kendall, 1991; McCombs, 1993). These include the following:

- **Adolescent Directed.** The experience is structured to promote student choice, acceptance of responsibility, a sense of ownership, personal control, and metacognitive awareness. A language arts teacher has teams of students design multimedia projects that featured the setting, characterization, plot, and theme of an adolescent novel. These projects are used in the media center as interactive "book talks" to entice their peers and promote schoolwide reading.

Figure 4.5 Guiding Toward Metacognitive Management

The Teacher's Role		
verbalizes thinking	guides, questions	becomes less directive (fades)
asks questions	helps with resources	connects to other situations
helps define task	monitors progress	facilitates reflection
structures groups	assists as resource	evaluates learning
helps shape strategy		
METACOGNITIVE GROWTH		
The Adolescent's Role		
watches, listens	designs inquiry	evaluates learning
verbalizes conceptions	implements strategy	reflects on process
poses questions	checks personal progress	makes learning connections
suggests strategy	reconsiders strategy	assumes future responsibility

- **Personally, Socially, and Content Relevant.** The experience is relevant to adolescents' interests and needs, and it extends to broader global issues such as human rights or environmental protection. It also carries importance within the discipline or subject area. A science class prepares for an upcoming video conference with a NASA scientist on the impact of microgravity on gene expression in order to write a position paper on government spending in space.
- **Knowledge Intensive.** The experience requires adolescents to know the subject matter thoroughly and meaningfully. It also prompts them to view knowledge from multiple perspectives and to use content across disciplines. A social studies class learns about the complexity of local government by simulating a town meeting of parents, students, teachers, officials, and business persons to debate the construction of a waterslide on property adjacent to a middle school. The students vote and project future consequences.
- **Complex and Cognitively Compelling.** The experience necessitates higher order thinking through inquiry, data collection and analysis, decision making, and reflective mental processing. Various reasoning processes are activated as adolescents question, investigate, experiment, compare, classify, substantiate, and problem solve. Math students analyze how many hamburgers were eaten in their city by gathering and comparing data from the Web sites of the National Beef Council and the U.S. Census Bureau.
- **Product Oriented.** The experience directs adolescents toward a final product or performance that is appropriate and that accommodates learning preference. These include panel discussion, a Web-based project,

Your Ideas

a videotaped documentary, a written or oral report, or a dramatic presentation. A computer graphics class collaborates with the local chamber of commerce in the design for a new logo that would capture and commemorate the county's direction for the twenty-first century.

- **Collaborative.** The task invites cooperation and collaborative engagement. A Spanish class produces language demonstration videos based on popular cultural music and clothing advertisements to share with ELL students and to strengthen their Spanish language skills.
- **Time Intensive.** The experience is generally long-term compared to more traditional instructional tasks. Through the use of electronic discussion, students conduct a study of the language use and specialized vocabulary of selected groups in the community.

Authentic learning experiences do more than merely involve adolescents in fun activities. Students work together to design products or to engage in performances that challenge them to build and think about knowledge in a context that resembles a real-life experience. The products, such as the book talks, millennium logos, and instructional videotapes in the above examples, are often contributions to the school and local community. These experiences frequently enable adolescents to consider the varying viewpoints of people involved in a realistic problem. To prepare for these tasks, students may need to gather data and discuss different perspectives on complex issues. To produce them, they need a good knowledge of content. In authentic learning experiences, adolescents are motivated and self-directed, and they gain a better understanding of the broader ideas of the discipline.

A highly effective instructional strategy for authentic learning experiences is problem-based learning (PBL). The knowledge gained through PBL extends beyond the factual to a higher conceptual level. This instructional method is the topic of the next section.

BUILDING KNOWLEDGE COLLABORATIVELY

In his book *Teaching for Thoughtfulness,* Barell (1995) proposes PBL as an instructional approach that challenges students "to engage in significant, authentic, and meaningful intellectual work" that places them in "the more active role of taking greater control of their own learning" (p. 120). He writes that students need multiple opportunities and sufficient time to think productively about major ideas, concepts, and principles. He makes the plea that ideas be the "main characters" of learning (p. 134). He cautions against the memorization of textbook explanations and abstract applications, and promotes learning experiences that confront students with complex situations that must be thought about and resolved through collaborative, knowledge-building effort. Barell explains that these situations are the ones that prime students for the complex problem solving of real life.

The problem scenarios in PBL are unstructured and designed to invite questioning and promote purposeful collaboration among adolescents, teachers, and others, including experts in the field. Students assume a role in the problem scenario and are led through a process in which they pose questions or determine "learning issues," identify what they need to know in order to address the problem, rank the learning issues in terms of importance and decide who will investigate which issue, identify needed resources and where they might be found, and gather needed information through individual and group investigation (Howard, 2006). Emphasis is placed on the students' ability to access pertinent and multiple sources and to synthesize data to address and solve the problem (Gallagher, 1998). In most cases, problem-based situations deal with real-life ethical issues and challenge adolescents to examine information from a variety of disciplinary viewpoints. The skills for critical thinking are developed through collaborative inquiry and knowledge building, and adolescents assume much responsibility over their learning.

Your Ideas

The PBL consists of several stages, as follows (Howard, 2006):

Engagement Stage: Students' interests and motivation are aroused through an intriguing scenario ("the hook") followed by questioning and discussion.

Investigation/Exploration Stage: Students acquire, organize, and analyze information gathered in response to the problem scenario.

Resolution/Refinement Stage: Students analyze options, agree upon solutions, and communicate these solutions to the appropriate audience in an authentic manner.

Debriefing Stage: Students reflect and generalize. They think metacognitively about the content and process of the PBL, and are encouraged to apply, extend, and transfer beyond the immediate problem situation.

The ACT Model "A Problem-Based Learning (PBL) Application: The Malaria Mission" provides an example (Howard, 2006). Adolescents are asked to be members of a team of professional experts, including geographers, economists, biologists, and public relations personnel, on a timely mission to Africa. Their charge (engagement) is to determine where and how vaccination trials for malaria can be conducted. They must construct convincing arguments to gain the cooperation of reluctant government officials and illiterate rural villagers. Students hypothesize about missing information, determine resources and strategies for data collection (Investigation/Exploration), and generate a solution that is presented to an appropriate audience (Resolution/Refinement). The teacher, as the metacognitive coach, guides and directs through questioning, scaffolding tools, online resources, and visual organizers; gives much responsibility and choice; and provides time for structured reflection (Debriefing).

Barell (1995) and other educators, including Stepien and Gallagher (1997), Schoenfeld (1985), and Torpe and Sage (1998), support PBL for reasons that are pertinent to students' personal, social, and intellectual development. These points summarize the value of this methodology for adolescent learners.

- Problem situations are motivational because they initially perplex, intrigue, and catch adolescents' interest.

Your Ideas

- PBL requires adolescents to gather relevant information from a variety of sources and to consider and role play multiple perspectives.
- Well-designed problems encompass important cross-curricular concepts that are historically "timeless" and currently pertinent.
- Adolescents can become more enlightened in their personal perceptions of others' viewpoints and cultural orientation and more ethical in their value formation.
- The inquiry process supports the role of the teacher as cognitive coach and the adolescent as the apprentice who gains knowledge and becomes independent.
- Adolescents use information in a meaningful way and are better able to retain the content and apply the problem-solving strategies in new situations.
- The process promotes reflection and adolescent metacognitive development.

A Problem-Based Learning (PBL) Application: The Malaria Mission

Problem-based learning (PBL) confronts adolescents with authentic problems that could realistically occur in their own experience. Students hypothesize about missing information, determine resources and strategies for data collection, and generate thoughtful solutions. Much choice and responsibility are afforded to the adolescents, although the teacher plays a strategic role as facilitator and guide during the inquiry process.

In the following PBL (Howard, 2006), adolescents are asked to be members of a team of professional experts sent to Africa to make decisions about where and how malaria vaccination trials will be conducted. The team must also make vital decisions and construct convincing arguments to gain the cooperation of African government officials who have competing interests and of people, including rural villagers, who cannot read or write. The project is supported by a multimillion dollar grant from the Bill and Melinda Gates Foundation to accelerate research into malaria, a disease that has made a comeback in Africa, killing over a million people each year, most of whom are children.

Content Understanding

To have adolescents learn about the countries of Africa, the African people, the causes and treatment of malaria, and the complex interactions of science, politics, economics, cultural beliefs, and traditions. Content includes understanding of cell theory, heredity, genetics, and environmental and ecological relationships among organisms.

Learning Outcomes

- Students will develop inquiry, problem-solving, and decision-making skills by engaging in an authentic problem experience, the Malaria Mission.
- Students will acquire content knowledge about the causes and treatment of malaria through research and interviews with experts in the field.
- Students will conceptualize the complex interactions of science, politics, economics, cultural beliefs, and traditions through their selection of countries for clinical trials and their plan for the delivery of the malaria vaccine.

ESSENTIAL QUESTION

How does the complex interaction of political, economic, and cultural systems limit or enable health issues and medical advancement?

Strategies for Inquiry

ENGAGEMENT

A letter from the Director of Mission Malaria arrives…

Dear Planning Team Member!

I am pleased that you agreed to be a member of our special Vaccination Advance Planning Team. As you know, a very important part of the Malaria Mission is to conduct clinical trials of the promising new vaccine recently developed by Silas Pharmaceuticals. You will be joined by colleagues from a number of other fields, including geographers, economists, biologists, and public relations personnel, who will add their expertise to your own in planning for the vaccination program . . .

The Advance Planning Team is charged with two responsibilities:

1. To select four countries in Africa to serve as sites for clinical trials of the new vaccine
2. To develop a plan for reaching and vaccinating as many people as possible in each selected country

I look forward to meeting you when you arrive at the research center in Mozambique.
The students are off (virtually) to Mozambique!

Part I: Select the four countries in Africa to serve as sites for clinical trials of the new vaccine

Guided Interaction and Metacognitive Development

- In order to investigate the problem, have students discuss the situation and develop a Learning Issues Board as a visual organizer to record responses to these questions: What do we know? What do we need to know? How will we find out (resources)? Add a fourth column after the investigation begins: What have we learned? Keep the Learning Issues Board visible (posted on chart paper) and updated throughout the problem-solving process. Guiding questions might include the following:
  - What do we know about this problem?
  - What do we know about Africa? About malaria?
  - What do we need to know?
  - How shall we order/sequence our investigation? Are there things that need to be done before we do other things?
  - Are any pieces of information especially important?

- What questions should be answered first?
- Where might we find the answers?
- How should we divide the questions among us?

- Help students narrow the field for selection of the four countries by a communication (a "Pointer") from the Project Director indicating that eight countries are candidates and that the Special Team must select four. Guide students to think about criteria for the selection of the four countries. Questions might include the following:
  - What characteristics would make a country a good place in which to conduct this clinical trial?
  - Should the four countries we select have the same characteristics, or should they be different? Why?
  - Are some of these criteria more important than others?
- Guide students to formulate more focused questions that help them identify their assumptions, recognize relevant issues, and plan the investigation. Here are a few sample questions to begin the inquiry process:
  - Why would the Gates Foundation give all that money to fight malaria in Africa?
  - Malaria is not a problem here in the United States. Why is it such a problem there?
  - What are we being asked to do in this problem?
  - Where is Mozambique? Why would we be going there?
- Continue to monitor as students identify resources, form investigative groups, and determine data collection and management strategies. Guiding questions include the following:
  - What would experts advise? If possible, arrange for professionals in the area to serve as resources to suggest relevant criteria to determine for the countries under consideration. Students could contact them by phone or e-mail or they could visit the class.
  - How can we record and organize all of the information we will need to consider in our decision? Have students create a database to organize information about the countries being considered. Guide as students select criteria for the databases. Categories might include geography, people, government, economy, communication, transportation, malaria distribution, and issues or potential problems.
  - How can we distribute all the research work that must be done to enable us to make good judgments? Place students in "country" teams with each gathering data about the assigned country to enter into the database. Students can also be assigned roles within the teams to gather data from a particular perspective. The geographers, for example, would gather information and begin to think like real geographers.

INVESTIGATION/EXPLORATION

- Have student teams explore selected Web sites to gather data to enter into the database on the four candidate countries.

- Facilitate as students narrow the selection to four countries that will take part in the clinical trials and prepare a rationale for the project staff.

RESOLUTION

- Provide a Decision Matrix as a graphic organizer to help students narrow their thinking and make their selection.
- Monitor as they formulate their justification.

Part II: Develop a plan for reaching and vaccinating as many people as possible in each selected country

Once the decision is made regarding which four countries will be targeted for malaria vaccination trials, students (as special team members) develop a plan for reaching as many people as possible in each selected country so that a major proportion of the population can be vaccinated. Students are instructed to select one country to serve as an advance test. The PBL continues as students "loop" back through the Investigation/Exploration and Resolution stages. They determine a method of distribution; identify the organizations, government agencies, or political leaders that have influence or power relevant to this problem; identify particular historical events that may have had an impact on the country's political, economic, and social institutions; and identify cultural factors (traditions, beliefs, values) that have a significant impact on health issues in African countries. They determine also what different kinds of information they would need to provide for women, children, the educated, the uneducated, members of different ethnic groups or religions, and people in different regions of the country.

DEBRIEFING

Assessment and Metacognitive Extension

The time has come to map out your strategy for a trial vaccination program. You have received a memo from the Project Director stating that you should be prepared to share the following with the Project Staff:

The PBL performance assessment is the presentation of a plan for a trial vaccination program. The presentation includes the following:

- What they will say to government agencies and organizations to gain support and assistance
- The educational materials they will use in the campaign to get as many people as possible to come to the vaccination centers and be vaccinated
- The location of the vaccination centers, transportation routes they will use to get themselves and materials to the sites, and the communication systems they will use to notify the people of the time and place for the vaccinations

Metacognitive Extension Questions

Sample Questions for Reflection on the Essential Question: "How does the complex interaction of political, economic, and cultural systems limit or enable health issues and medical advancement?"

- What interactions among systems did we find as we participated in this problem situation?
- Were some of the interactions limiting? Were some enabling? How?
- How did our understanding of these interactions help us make our decision and devise our vaccination strategy?
- How has an understanding of the interaction of systems helped us to solve this problem?
- How might this understanding of interactions help us to solve other problems?

Sample Reflection on Decision Making and Problem Solving

- What are the advantages of our country selection? The disadvantages?
- What influenced us most in our decision?
- What values or ethical issues influenced our decision?

Sample Reflections on Product Development

- What are the advantages of our vaccination plan? The disadvantages?
- What led us to choose that particular approach? Are there other things we should have considered?
- Is it important to respect tradition and culture, even in issues of health and well-being?
- How did the audience affect how we presented our plan?

The fully developed PBL, The Malaria Mission, can be accessed at http://org.elon.edu/t2project/article0003/index.htm

The site contains a Professional Information Center with research-based scaffolding tools and inquiry strategies, tools for differentiation, visual organizers and content enhancement tools, online resources, assessment tools, sample interviews with content experts, and professional literature about problem-based learning. The Student Investigation Center contains all materials needed for the investigation.

Another excellent interdisciplinary PBL for adolescents can be found at the Project T^2 site, entitled "The Alhambra Restoration" (http://org.elon.edu/t2project/article0001/index.htm).

SOURCE: Shared with permission from Judith Howard, Director of Project T^2 at Elon University, NC (http://org.elon.edu/t2project/index.htm).

GROUP WORK REALLY CAN WORK

Much emphasis has been placed throughout the book on the impact of shared cognition, distributed intelligence, and collaborative communities of learners, yet as any teacher of adolescents knows, *putting teenagers together in a group is risky*. As social as adolescents naturally are, they do not as naturally have the social and personal skills to work together in a group toward a common academic goal. The research, however, is clear. For students at any age, cooperative learning can promote positive self-concept, academic achievement, critical thinking, peer relationship, social behavior, and motivation to learn (Johnson,

Your Ideas

1979; Johnson et al., 1981; Johnson & Johnson, 1983). Interactive group work, implemented effectively, can benefit adolescents socially, personally, and intellectually.

A plethora of strategies, structures, and models are currently available to guide teachers as they plan for collaborative learning (Bellanca & Fogarty, 2001; Johnson & Johnson, 1983; Kagan, 1990; Sharan & Sharan, 1976; Slavin, 1980). Teachers accordingly need to be selective as to when, why, and how they incorporate peer grouping into instruction. In simple terms, group work needs to be purposeful.

Sharan and Sharan's (1976) Group Investigation Model might be used, for example, if a teacher wants to promote group inquiry into broad questions, such as "Is there a relationship between global warming and natural disasters?" and "How has the computer impacted the business market economy?" Through a similar method, Kagan's (1990) jigsaw structure, adolescents share the responsibility for a specific section of the information under study. Other structured inquiry models include problem- and project-based learning. In each of these models, adolescents follow a series of steps and are assigned specific responsibilities. Assessment is usually both individual and collaborative through a final group product.

Simpler cooperative learning structures, such as think-pair-share or numbered heads together (Kagan, 1990), are used flexibly for different purposes within daily instruction. At the beginning of a lesson, for example, students recall what they know about a topic or concept, and share with a partner. Pairs of students join other sets of two to compare hypotheses or procedures (Bellanca & Fogarty, 2001). For the "numbered heads together structure," each student in a small group has a number. Periodically during a lesson, the teacher asks the small group to discuss a new concept; however, specific questions are asked using a random number call. A student in one group, who has been assigned the number three, is asked to respond, for example, and his or her "number three" counterpart in another group is asked to elaborate, explain, or give an alternate answer. The following box gives several ideas for purposeful collaborative activity based on the work of Daniels and Bizer (1998) and Bellanca and Fogarty (2001).

For collaborative grouping, simple or formal, to work well, "solid procedures for keeping groups productive" must be in place (Daniels & Bizar, 1998, p. 60). Since it is challenging for a teacher to manage and guide multiple groups meeting simultaneously, the assigned tasks must have enough "inherent structure to operate autonomously" so that students are engaged and on task.

Additionally, adolescents need to be taught the skills for interpersonal interaction and the specific strategies for productive collaboration. They also need to know if, when, and how well they demonstrate the expected behaviors in order to improve. A few guiding questions are useful as teachers make decisions about group work (Marcus & McDonald, 1990):

1. **Where is the challenge?** To feel a sense of concerted purpose, adolescents need to be engaged in significant activity that stimulates their thinking, such as a problem to solve, a decision to make, a debate to construct, or a project to create. They also need help with skills, including decision making, problem solving, persuasion, or consensus building.

Your Ideas

2. **Where is the interdependence?** Adolescents need to be involved in a joint effort that requires the interaction of all members. Are they expected to achieve a goal or product, such as a decision, solution, project, or presentation? Is the group involvement purposeful and dependent on teamwork and shared cooperation?

3. **Where is the accountability?** In cooperative activities, adolescents need to feel individually responsible for personal contribution. Is there an assigned role, a personal response, an individual quiz, a contract, or a self- or group evaluation form?

4. **Where is the interpersonal development?** Group interaction depends on and should extend adolescents' social skills. Dispositions, including respect for others' opinions, consensus building, contribution of ideas, or perspective seeking, should be targeted and evaluated.

5. **Where is the reflection?** Accompanying group interaction should be a time to think back over and "debrief" about the process, to self-evaluate, and to assess the contributions of members of the group, socially and academically. The final product should be evaluated according to expected criteria.

Group work can be meaningful for adolescent learning if it is planned well and if teachers have instilled in students the skills and dispositions for purposeful collaboration. Working together effectively is not easy. Instruction, practice, and feedback are prerequisites, and the teacher's interactive role is essential. Structure and accountability must be apparent through specific guidelines for tasks, communicated expectations for behavior and demonstration, and organized procedures for evaluation and reflection. Adolescents enjoy the opportunity to work together to learn, yet they need to know when they are meeting expected learning standards, both academic and behavioral. Ongoing assessment that supplies constructive feedback can help adolescents direct the activity of their learning productively and manage their actions toward one another positively.

Using Group Work Purposefully

When Discussion Is Needed

- **Literature Circles**—Student-led discussion groups meet regularly to talk about books or other literary works.
- **Classroom Workshops**—From literacy to mathematics, students go through a set schedule of minilessons, work time interaction, feedback, and sharing.
- **Focus Groups**—Each group is given a facet of a problem or an element of a piece of literature. Topics can also be selected according to interests. A set of thought questions helps to guide this seminar-modeled discussion.

Mainly for Partners

- **Dialogue Journals**—Pairs of students write and exchange "conversations" on a regular basis about content, such as a story, a scientific concept, or a historical event.
- **Paired for Action**—Students are paired and given interlocking assignments that require joint activity for experimentation, observation, or reading. Partners can also be used to clarify ideas about concepts, for "think alouds" during problem solving, for "think-pair-share" dyads, or to "punctuate" a lecture, reading, or film, as in "turn to your partner and share."

Grouped for Inquiry

- **Student Survey Teams**—Adolescents choose a social issue, such as freedom of speech, gun control, drug control, or prejudice, design and send surveys to a targeted population, analyze results, exhibit findings, and respond personally to the issue through writing and discussion.
- **Group Investigation Models**—This jigsaw method is used for more sophisticated inquiry. Each student is responsible for a part of information that must be reassembled or synthesized to complete the whole "puzzle."
- **Problem-Based Learning (PBL)**—Students solve unstructured problems or conduct complex research investigations by posing questions, gathering information, analyzing results, and often presenting findings in a creative way.
- **WebQuests**—These are structured, project-based inquiries into real-world problems with research conducted mainly through Web sites. Final products are often posted on the Web.

A NEW PEDAGOGY

Darling-Hammond, noted leader in educational reform, proposes a new paradigm for powerful teaching and thoughtful learning. In her address to an audience of educators at the Fifth Annual Teaching for Intelligence Conference (1999, San Francisco), Darling-Hammond called for an instructional approach that would better meet the learning needs of today's students. She described the traditional approach as outmoded and suggested, by contrast, a "two-way" pedagogy in which students and teachers work supportively and collaboratively to build knowledge and construct understanding.

Darling-Hammond is joined by other educators, including Gardner (1999), Perkins (1992), and Resnick (1999), who call for a new way of teaching that is more responsive to adolescents and that better prepares them socially, intellectually, and personally for a challenging future. These writers urge teachers to be more strategic in their instructional efforts to promote thinking and understanding in classrooms. The following questions synthesize many ideas presented in this and previous chapters, ideas that are pertinent in teaching adolescents to be more thoughtful learners.

A New Pedagogy

- Do I build on the relevant knowledge and experiences students bring to class?
- Do I take time to find out if they have accurate and sufficient background knowledge to do an academic task?
- Do I require students to consider information from a variety of sources and disciplines?
- Is the task one that is complex enough, or is the problem interesting to my students?
- Is there an opportunity for students to use their strengths to create something that would benefit others?
- Does the experience challenge my students to use higher level thinking operations, such as hypothesis testing, inquiry, reasoning, interpretation, and synthesis?
- Do I give frequent and informative feedback to guide students as they plan and work through tasks?
- Do I allow students to share ideas with and get feedback from others, including peers and knowledgeable "experts"?
- Do my students feel "safe" to take risks or experiment with varying strategies?
- Do I provide time for students to think back over and evaluate how, what, and why they learned?
- Do I help students recognize that other learning strategies might be used in the current context or that a specific strategy might be adapted for a different context?
- Do I give students opportunities to practice and develop new levels of skill and competence?
- Am I an enthusiastic expert in my content area, and do I share this with students?

NOTHING'S SIMPLE

Young Jonas in *The Giver* (Lowry, 1993) begins to realize the complexities, the subtleties, and the magnificence of a world disclosed through knowledge. Similarly, adolescents' minds can be freed from the limitation of egocentric perspectives and naïve perceptions through understanding. Also, as with Jonas, the door to understanding opens into a world of paradox where all is not what it might appear or seem and nothing is simple. Parker Palmer (1998) writes that true insight comes with the acquired capacity "to hold paradoxes together"—to recognize and integrate the apparent contradictions that give life its complexity (p. 65). As Gardner (1999) similarly observes, "There is no need to look for the single, privileged approach to important concepts, for none exists. . . . But the purpose of education is not to provide ultimate answers; it is to enhance one's sense of understanding without dashing one's sense of mystery and wonder" (p. 185).

Your Ideas

Theodore R. and Nancy F. Sizer (1999) of the Coalition of Essential Schools summarize this challenge well:

> Schools exist to change young people. They should be different—better—for their experience there. They should know some important things, they should know how to learn additional important things, they should be in the habit of wanting to learn such important things. They should have a reasoned, but individual point of view. They should be judicious, aware of the complexity of the world. They should be thoughtful, respectful of thought and of ideas which are the furniture of thought. (p. 103)

Teaching for thinking and understanding liberates adolescents' minds in a way that inspires active and continuous intellectual inquiry and self-discovery.

ACTing

on the Adolescent-Centered Learning Principles Discussed in Chapter 4

Principle	*How I can put it into practice*
❑ Shape a classroom culture of thoughtfulness and learning.	
❑ Use instructional practices that emphasize meaningful knowledge construction, mastery of content, thinking development, and social interactions that promote intelligent behaviors in adolescents.	
❑ Foster metacognitive development by guiding and helping students to think reflectively about personal learning, to monitor and improve skills, and to increasingly assume more control.	
❑ Immerse students in meaningful, relevant, and intriguing experiences that challenge their thinking, engage their emotions, and charge them with accountability.	
❑ Develop and use instructional approaches that promote adolescent understanding through active inquiry, purposeful collaboration, and supportive technology.	

(Continued)

ACTing

on the Adolescent-Centered Learning Principles Discussed in Chapter 4

Principle	*How I can put it into practice*
❏ Free adolescent minds from the limitations of egocentric perspectives and naïve perceptions so they can be inspired to active and continuous intellectual inquiry and self-discovery.	
❏ View assessment as ongoing and integral to learning, as an opportunity for students to demonstrate understanding.	
❏ Show students multiple pathways to examine knowledge, to construct personal meaning, and to know themselves more fully.	

CHAPTER

5

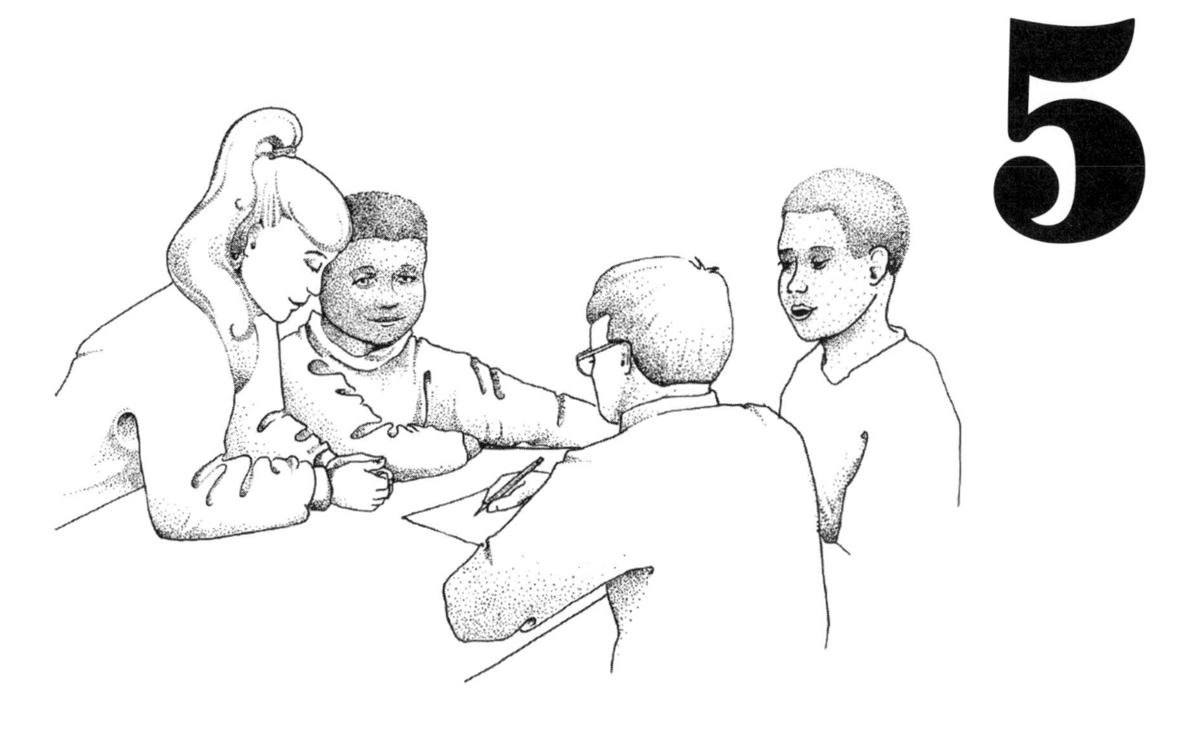

Deepening Content and Promoting Transfer

CONTENT AND INQUIRY

Adolescents need multiple pathways to examine knowledge, to construct personal meaning, and to know themselves more fully. Within each content area is a potential for relevance, extension, and impact on how adolescents view themselves, the world, and their place in it. Central to each content area is the process of inquiry. The challenge to teachers is not to deliver an inert body of knowledge but to immerse young people in a richness of content and to guide them as they actively grapple, explore, collaborate, and learn. Ultimately, these students will have to integrate the experiences of schooling into a personal philosophy of living and interacting.

Adolescent thinking, learning, and understanding are promoted in classrooms where the focus is on higher level knowledge development, problem solving, and inquiry (Tishman et al., 1995). Resnick (1999) has emphasized that learning is

Your Ideas

knowledge-dependent, while others, including Bransford et al. (2000), Gardner (1999), Paul (1998), Perkins (1992), and Wiggins and McTighe (1998), have stressed that conceptual understanding comes when students think critically and collaboratively about higher order knowledge.

Each content area has certain foundational principles and skills that should be learned, such as mathematical formulas and basic operations, scientific principles and methods of inquiry, historical timelines, or literary language. Each area also has enduring questions that inspire inquiry, strategies that direct problem solving, and a specific way of thinking about knowledge. Learning experiences that help adolescents think more as disciplinary experts can help them understand the higher order knowledge at the core of a discipline (Bransford et al., 1999, 2000).

Table 5.1 gives examples of specific disciplinary thinking and offers a few instructional suggestions that promote student inquiry and problem solving.

The following sections explore the unique domains of several disciplinary areas in terms of their encompassing ideas and their patterns of thinking. The instructional examples are designed specifically to facilitate adolescent learning and to promote students' social, personal, and intellectual development.

A different ACT is provided to illustrate adolescent learning in each of five content areas. In mathematics, the instructional emphasis is on the development of qualitative reasoning skills. In social studies, adolescents delve into critical issues that form the potential for civic action. Project-based inquiry is the format used to construct scientific understanding, and Socratic questioning challenges adolescents to consider literary viewpoints. In fine arts, students assume an active role in learning management and exhibition. The value of a solid disciplinary understanding lies in the potential for the collective impact of knowledge on adolescents' future experiences.

MATHEMATICS

The example in the ACT "Reasoning Through Mathematics" is based on a research study (Schoen, Fey, Hirsch, & Coxford, 1999) that compared the reasoning ability of adolescents taught mathematics in a traditional way with that of another group taught through guided inquiry and authentic problem solving. The members of the latter group were more inclined to assess mathematical problems holistically versus just doing the calculation, to use graphing calculators, to verbalize and reflect on their thinking processes, and to see the connection between an abstract formula and what it represented in real life.

In the ACT Model, the teacher challenges students to reason beyond the calculation by adapting the problem situation through questioning. Students are asked to make assumptions and predictions, to test hypotheses, and to write their own equations. They are guided through questioning to visualize relationships and patterns, and to think metacognitively about their own thinking and reasoning. They also apply their learning to another comparable situation in real life in an effort to promote connection and transfer.

Mathematics is more than being able to use computational skill, though knowing how to calculate is important. Competence in mathematics means being

Your Ideas

Table 5.1 Developing Higher Order Thinking

Developing Higher Order Thinking	Instructional Strategies
Historical thinking involves learning to • identify various historical perspectives • recognize that context and vantage shape interpretation • understand the relationship of past events to current events	**History** • role playing • problem-based learning • simulation • discussion • research projects
Scientific inquiry is shaped through • testing assumptions based on observations • gathering data • seeking justification • deriving conclusions	**Science** • research projects • experimentation • problem solving • online inquiry • scientific method • problem-based learning
Mathematical thinking involves • problem solving • deductive reasoning • systematic logic	**Mathematics** • word problems • learning journals • dialectic journals • problem posing • authentic data analysis
Literary thinking involves • making inferences about meaning and interpretation • checking for textual evidence • substantiating ideas • organizing for expression or argument	**Language Arts** • seminar • questioning • persuasive writing • debate • synthesis papers • presentation • perspective writing
Thinking in the fine arts involves • sensory observation • critical listening • comparative analysis • inquiry	**Fine Arts** • dramatic performance • musical composition • creative design • visual analysis • presentation • research

Your Ideas

able to use computational skills to reason, solve problems, test conjectures, and represent data in meaningful ways. With a wealth of information available on the Internet, the challenge to adolescents is not to obtain facts but to make sense of what they find. Ultimately, the goal of mathematics is to help students use the acquired skills purposefully in their own lives.

Connecting adolescent mathematical learning to what is real is easier today through technology. Statistics can be accessed from Web sites for analysis and display in graphs and spreadsheets. Digital processing creates an instant visualization of 3-D geometrical images, such as a satellite picture of the Earth for the study of pi. Mathematical instruction that involves realistic inquiry also enables adolescents to make connections across other disciplines and with real experiences (Drier et al., 1999). The following Web sites provide a variety of real-world data that can be accessed, displayed through spreadsheets, calculated, and analyzed.

Useful Web Sites for Real-World Data for Mathematics and Problem Solving

National Geophysical Data Center (http://www.ngdc.noaa.gov)

National Oceanic and Atmospheric Administration (http://www.noaa.gov)

The Center for Disease Control and Prevention (http://www.cdc.gov)

National Center for Health Statistics (http://www.cdc.gov/nchs)

Reasoning Through Mathematics: "Head Math" Beware!

Adolescents need assistance as they reason through mathematical problems. Effective mathematics instruction requires teachers to model, guide, and give appropriate feedback, or suitable scaffolding, to ensure that students reason accurately. They also need assistance in connecting mathematical abstractions to real-life applications.

Content Understanding

To help adolescents use mathematical reasoning to solve problems dealing with quadratic equations and relationships among speed, height, and scientific phenomenon.

Key Concepts

Speed, height, velocity, mathematical reasoning, graphing, acceleration, gravity

Learning Outcomes

- Students will discern the relationship among the variables of velocity, height, and speed by making assumptions and solving a real-life mathematical word problem.
- Students will transfer mathematical knowledge to other authentic instances in their own lives by considering alternate applications.

ESSENTIAL QUESTION

When is an understanding of mathematics useful in life?

Strategies for Inquiry

The Inquiry Problem: The Bulldogs' pitcher and center fielder were standing together near the pitcher's mound during pregame warm-up. The pitcher threw the baseball straight up with a velocity of 125 feet per second for the center fielder to catch. The height (h) of the ball after seconds (t) is represented by $h = -16t^2 + 125t$.

Inquiry Questions:

a. What assumption might be made about the pattern of the time-height relationship on a graph?
b. What would you predict to be the height of the baseball after four seconds?
c. Write an equation whose solution is the number of seconds after the baseball is thrown when it is 158 feet above the ground. Solve the equation, check it, and write the rationale for your strategy.

Guided Interaction

- Keep adolescents from jumping to quick solutions that merely "plug in" the formula. They need to be encouraged to visualize what the formula means. Here are some guiding questions:
  - What is the problem asking us?
  - How do you think the relationship would appear on a graph? What can you visualize?
  - If we were to plot time along the horizontal axis and height on the vertical, what might the pattern be?
  - What would the figure resemble?
- Ask students to make and check assumptions on graphing calculators. Here are other questions you might include:
  - What might be faulty about your reasoning?
  - What do you know about velocity, acceleration, and the force of gravity?
- Allow students to work parts b and c in pairs, and ask them to explain their rationale as a team.

Metacognitive Development and Assessment

- When the problems have been solved, ask these reflection questions:
  - What thinking strategies did you use to solve this problem?
  - How did trying to visualize the scenario help with your reasoning?
  - What is the disadvantage of hasty thinking?
  - How did our reasoning together help you understand the formula better?
  - How did the graphing calculators help you as a "thinking tool"?
  - What are some other real-world examples that reflect the same concept?
  - How would the formula change if the ball game took place on Mars?
- A homework assessment is an independent problem that applies mathematical reasoning to a related authentic situation, as follows:

> Some speculation exists that the Mars Lander may have missed its target due to faulty calculations. How could this have happened? How would you explain to someone how this calculation should be reasoned through for better accuracy? Write your responses in your math journals and be prepared to share.

SOCIAL STUDIES

Your Ideas

Teaching social studies effectively ultimately involves active engagement with important knowledge through guided inquiry, interactive discourse, and thoughtful reflection. The teacher's role is not to tell but to model the timeless and ongoing quest to understand people and their relationships, roles, and responsibilities as participants in a global society. Student ownership, challenge, choice, variety, technology, social interaction, community connections, real-world tasks, and authentic assessment are what make a lesson compelling and successful. Although an independent performance is expected, students collaborate about ideas and resources and assist each other with the technology applications.

In the ACT Model "Making an Issue of Social Studies: Taking Civic Action," adolescents choose topics of interest within broad essential questions generated from the social studies curriculum. They assume the role of an activist and assemble materials that support their stance on the issue in an electronic portfolio that serves as a senior project exhibition. The ACT illustrates the model of cognitive apprenticeship as students assume increasing responsibility for their own learning management.

Making an Issue of Social Studies: Taking Civic Action

When social studies is taught through important ideas and enduring questions, it becomes more meaningful to adolescents. Because social studies encompasses a variety of disciplines, including history, economics, civics, sociology, anthropology, culture, and geography, it also needs to connect across content, time, and space. Social studies understanding further involves an awareness of the values, beliefs, and attitudes that shape personal and human interaction. By developing and promoting a personal perspective under a teacher's guidance, adolescents are more likely to act independently with ethical and civic-minded responsibility.

Content Understanding

To help adolescents conceptualize that critical issues have a context often defined by varying personal beliefs and value systems, be able to engage in reflective social inquiry, understand that the consequences of their choices and actions impact themselves and others, and assume responsibility for ethical civic action as citizens in a global community.

Key Concepts

Civic responsibility, cultural diversity and assimilation, freedom and human rights, global enterprise, national security, institutional government, states' rights, power

Learning Outcomes

- Students will develop an enhanced sense of civic responsibility by engaging in focused research on a current issue of interest.
- Students will broaden personal perspectives by considering alternate sides of current societal issues.

ESSENTIAL QUESTIONS

When does world security take priority over domestic interests?

When does national power infringe on local control or individual rights?

When does progress conflict with cultural or environmental protection?

What should be the "new frontier" of the new millennium?

Strategies for Inquiry

The Task: Over the next two months, you are going to develop a position on a critical issue that faces us in the twenty-first century. Your task is to assemble a collection of materials that an activist on the issue might want to have. You will use the format of an interactive, multimedia electronic portfolio to demonstrate your understanding. Following are some modern issues that could be used in this inquiry.

individual beliefs/majority rule
national security/individual freedom
national or state/community control
global enterprise/national interests
cultural diversity/cultural assimilation
individual rights/public safety
community progress/individual liberties
worker security/employer rights

Guided Interaction

Following are some guiding questions on the various sample issues.

- When does world security take priority over domestic interests? When should it?

  Consider understanding American involvement in global concerns, such as the AIDS endemic in sub-Saharan Africa, the turmoil in the Sudan, world hunger, and natural disasters such as the flooding devastation of the tsunami in South and Southeast Asia or the hurricanes in the southern United States.

- When does national power infringe on local control or individual rights? When should it?

  Topics include censorship, prayer in schools, dress codes, cultural diversity, drug testing, cancer treatments, gun control, violence prevention, life choice, and media management.

- When does progress conflict with cultural or environmental protection? When should it?

  Think about struggles among environmentalists, private citizens, and economists, such as rainforest destruction, pollution of air and streams, logging in natural forests, endangered species, technological expansion, and global warming.

- What should be the "new frontier" of the new millennium?

  Shape perspectives on the priority for global resources, such as medicine, space, bioengineering, gene profiling, ocean harvesting, and global relationship.

Metacognitive Development and Assessment

- The portfolio provides an excellent metacognitive tool to help as students set goals, gauge progress, and stay active in their evaluation process. An exhibition day enables parents and others involved to participate, and final projects, such as CDs with video streaming or minidocumentaries and Web portals, are shared with parent organizations, community groups, and other schools. The projects are also used in adolescents' professional portfolios after graduation. See the following "Portfolio Components Checklist" for criteria that may be used in evaluation.

PORTFOLIO COMPONENTS CHECKLIST

_____ **A Creative Title**

_____ **A Table of Contents with Pagination**

_____ **A Formal Opening (200 words)**

Describe your issue and your rationale for its selection.
Provide an overview of what you plan to accomplish in this portfolio.

_____ **Research**

The critique of at least two annotated articles (online or print) supporting your position.
The critique of at least two annotated articles (online or print) challenging your position.
The script of an interview (face-to-face, phone, or online) with at least one expert on your issue.

_____ **Legal Implications**

An explanation of current local, state, and federal laws or procedures pertaining to your issue.

_____ **Promotional Pieces (Minimum of 3)**

An original slogan, bumper sticker, or political cartoon designed with graphic software.
A 20-line jingle to be shared with the class through hypermedia software.
A tri-fold pamphlet of professional quality that highlights the pros and cons of the issue.
A printed editorial for a newspaper that supports your stance.
A videotaped public service announcement that promotes your issue.

_____ **Civic Action Grant Proposal**

Formulate a project to be enacted on behalf of the issue, and write a proposal for supportive funding.
Include a cover letter written on behalf of the issue.
Prepare a three- to five-minute hypermedia presentation for the class.

_____ **A Formal Closing (500 words)**

Summarize findings, justify your position, and suggest future activities that will further your cause.

_____ **Bibliography (at least 5 sources consulted)**

_____ **Supporting Illustrations and Graphics**

SOURCE: Courtesy of Pierrie, T. (2000). Raleigh, NC: Director, Smaller Learning Communities Grant. Wake County Public Schools; and National Council for the Social Studies (NCSS) Standards & Position Statements (1997).

SCIENCE

Your Ideas

Good science instruction for adolescents means giving them time to explore, to observe, to make mistakes, to build and collect things, to calibrate instruments, to construct models, to investigate, to wrestle with the unfamiliar, and to come to "see the advantage of thinking differently" (Nelson, 1999, p. 16). How can you design a paper airplane to go the maximum distance or the fastest speed or illustrate the principles of aeronautics? More than a body of knowledge or set of answers, science is a way of thinking about the world (Adams & Hamm, 1999). This constructivist approach promotes active and collaborative inquiry as the basis for adolescent learning. Adolescents are full of wonder, and science is a good way to discover answers that lead to more questions.

Project-based learning promotes scientific understanding through collaboration and inquiry. Topics can range from space exploration, nuclear safety, and energy control to wetland ecology, environmental science, waste management, and endangered species. Adolescents attain a good knowledge of scientific principles and apply valuable problem-solving skills in an authentic context. The ACT Model "Inquiry Into Science: Heating Up!" is an inquiry-based learning experience that challenges adolescents to investigate and construct a position on issues of global warming.

Inquiry Into Science: Heating Up!

Project-based learning, particularly when enhanced by technology, can provide an excellent vehicle for inquiry into complex content. This task puts adolescents in touch with current events, findings, and perspectives related to the greenhouse effect on atmospheric conditions and climate patterns and the argument over pollution regulation and environmental conservation. Student inquiry teams research the topic and share findings through a variety of performance-based products. The National Academy of Sciences provides a real-world source for current research on global warming, a phenomenon that will, in the future, affect the quality of adolescents' lives.

Content Understanding

To help adolescents understand the changing climate conditions that sustain life and the impact of human activity upon the quality of the environment.

Key Concepts

Global warming, greenhouse gases, temperature, surface temperature, pollution, carbon dioxide, methane, atmosphere

ESSENTIAL QUESTION

What is the long-term effect of human activity on the quality of the environment?

Strategies for Inquiry

The Invitation: The Earth is heating up! On one hand, the National Academy of Sciences, after reconstructing global average surface temperatures for the past two millennia, has concluded that the Earth is the hottest it has been in 2,000 years. The federal government, on the other hand, has maintained that the threat from global warming is not severe enough to warrant new pollution controls. The Academy has been asked to report to Congress on how researchers drew conclusions about the Earth's climate over the past two centuries when modern scientific technology has only recently been available to produce detailed and accurate records. How was the Academy able to make this conclusion? Do we need to lobby for pollution control?

Guided Interaction

- Students inquire into the varying perspectives on the issue of global warming. The Web sites below are useful for researching the causes and effects of global warming. Interactive maps, videos, fact sheets, and slide shows shed light on the complexity of the topic.
- Students determine the causes and effects of global warming and make graphs or design maps of climate trends.
- Students read *Psylicon Beach* (Gross, 1998), a futuristic science fiction novel on the effects of global warming.

Useful Internet Sources for Global Warming Issues

Wikipedia: Global Warming

(http://en.wikipedia.org/wiki/Global_warming)

U.S. Environmental Protection Agency: Global Warming Archive
(http://yosemite.epa.gov/oar/globalwarming.nsf/content/indexarchive.html)

U.S. Environmental Protection Agency: Climate Change

(http://epa.gov/climatechange/index.html)

Yahoo News: Climate Change

(http://news.yahoo.com/fc/World/Climate_Change/)

This site links to court cases, videos, fact sheets, a slide show about global warming, and related news articles

An Interactive Map of Global Warming Trends

(http://www.climatehotmap.org/)

Questia Online Library: Global Warming

(http://www.questia.com/library/global-warming.jsp)

The library provides books, articles, and conflicting views on the issue.

Stop Global Warming Organization

(http://www.stopglobalwarming.org/default.asp)

Global Warming International Center

(http://www.globalwarming.net/)

Union of Concerned Scientists: Global Warming

(http://www.ucsusa.org/global_warming/)

The Discovery Channel: Global Warming

(http://dsc.discovery.com/convergence/globalwarming/globalwarming.html)

Students can ask experts about climate changes and travel the globe virtually to see global warming worldwide.

U.S. Environmental Protection Agency: Climate Change Kids Site

(http://www.epa.gov/globalwarming/kids/change.html)

Metacognitive Development and Assessment

- Ongoing assessment includes learning logs, experiments, letters, essays, creative and reflective writing, simulations, virtual site visits, forum discussion, maps and computer designs, data analyses, graphs, readings, and interviews.
- Students have many options for culminating assessment. A few ideas follow:
  - Create a ClassAct Web portal to promote the issues or to take a stand on heightened environmental protection and pollution regulation
  - Write letters to news editors and governmental officials
  - Organize a class or grade-level summit to debate the issues
  - Create a minidocumentary that includes local interviews

Metacognitive Extension Questions

- What is the value of shared inquiry in researching current problems?
- Why is it important to know both sides of an issue before making an informed decision?
- Why must scientific conclusions be based on valid and reliable data?
- What is the conflict between economic and environmental conservation?

What are the social, cognitive, and emotional benefits of inquiry-oriented science instruction for today's adolescents? They share the responsibility for thinking and doing. They are motivated to explore relevant and interesting situations and challenged to construct scientific meaning. Their thinking is stimulated and reasoning skills are honed. They interact in a social and realistic community of practice where they have the resources that support their learning. Real scientific inquiry involves human exploration and making sense from discovery that is often unanticipated.

ENGLISH/LANGUAGE ARTS

Your Ideas

Adolescents may never publish poetry or novels or short stories. They can, however, gain a sense of the power of the written word to convey feeling and an author's perspective. Teachers can help students relate to literature and learn to communicate their ideas more effectively by creating numerous opportunities for them to think from the vantage of another. Helping adolescents understand the power of words to convey feeling and perspective has a direct implication on their personal and interpersonal development. Ultimately, this knowledge can help adolescents better understand themselves and their own view of the world. Through a teacher's strategic questioning, adolescents are challenged to think about literature and to articulate their ideas. Relevant and emotionally engaging discussion can tap and help shape and broaden students' perspectives as learners.

The following ACT Model, "Seminar in Session," illustrates an instructional strategy that promotes inquiry in response to interpretive questions about issues raised by an author. Adolescents relate to the protagonist Jonah as he enters puberty and begins to question much about his life and community. Through questioning and guided interaction, the teacher helps students to think deeply about issues related to conformity and personal voice. Through metacognitive extension questions, adolescents connect and transfer the experiences to situations in their own lives.

Seminar in Session: Living in a World of Sameness

The guided discussion of a popular novel helps adolescents relate to the emotional, social, and intellectual development of a character their own age. A teacher's questions help students "step" into the fictional role and, in turn, learn more about their own feelings and ideas. The Newbery Medal novels provide a rich source for interpretive inquiry into issues that interest adolescents.

Content Understanding

To help adolescents understand the multiple meanings and interpretations of text and to use language effectively for a designated purpose and audience.

Key Concepts

Literary audience, purpose, seminar, interpretive analysis, style, prediction, conformity, human choice

Learning Outcomes

- Students will sharpen skills for literary analysis by reading *The Giver* (Lowry, 1993) and participating in a Socratic seminar.
- Students will extend the meaning of text into personal lives through inquiry-based discussion and response.

ESSENTIAL QUESTION

Is personal and intellectual choice important to being human?

Strategies for Inquiry

The main strategy is to conduct an inquiry-based seminar of the novel *The Giver,* by Lois Lowry (1993).

Key Questions for Interpretation:

- What would it be like to live in a world with no feeling or color or pain?
- How can you reconcile a society of Sameness with human choice, integrity, and intellect?

Guided Interaction

- A teacher begins the seminar with an analysis-level question, such as
  Why was Jonas perplexed when he noticed something different about Fiona's hair?
- Depending on students' responses, other questions probe, refocus, guide, or extend thinking, such as
  - Why was this so disturbing to Jonas?
  - How does knowing there is an Elsewhere make it worse to live in a society of Sameness?
  - What is the rationale for the Sameness?
  - Might intelligence have anything to do with Jonas's discontent?
- As a variation, the teacher involves the students in a Silent Seminar following the reading. Directions follow.

Silent Seminar

Purpose

The aim is to encourage all students to respond to text because it provides a "safe" unspoken method of promoting dialogue among class members. Another advantage for young adolescents is the "game" of moving yet not interacting except on paper.

Method

- Students read a selection or section of literature, silently or orally as a group.
- Students are asked to share with the class reactions and responses, ask questions, or quote passages that "grabbed their attention" while the teacher records offerings on the board or overhead.
- The class votes on the top six (or another number), which are transcribed onto separate sheets of butcher's paper around the room.
- Each student is given a marker and the "silent discussion" begins. They choose three of the posted ideas and respond in writing followed by their initials. The game part is that no one can speak or interact except to each other's comments on the charts. Responses may be in the form of other questions, proposed answers, affirmations, and disagreements. Teacher modeling may be needed.
- Play appropriate music during the activity to reduce the "noise of silence."
- When the allotted time ends, posters are removed and returned to the owner of the question or comment. This student then leads, with teacher support, a discussion of any further questions that arise from the sheet. Posters may be placed back on the wall for future reference or review as reading continues.

SOURCE: Crawford, G. (2000). *Managing the adolescent classroom*. Corwin Press: Thousand Oaks, CA.

Metacognitive Development and Assessment

- Other questions enable students to extend the meaning of a text into their own lives:
  - What is the "downside" of living in a world with no options?
  - Why might the right of choice be important to human beings?
  - What causes people pain in their lives?
  - Would you give up choice and color to not have any pain?
  - Can you think of instances in our lives when we choose to have no choice?
- As an extension, students are given a writing prompt, such as this: The Receiver continues to worry about Jonas. Write a letter back to his mentor that describes what happens in the youngster's life after the novel ends. Indicate if he is happy and why.
- Students make predictions about the sequel and then read it to test assumptions.

Dear Receiver,

I know you continue to wonder about what happened to Jonas after he left the Community. I hope this letter will help. . . .

FINE ARTS

The potential of art to connect with adolescents' lives is recognized increasingly in schools across the country. No longer limited to those with special talents, art has become a vehicle for perspective taking, problem solving, and connection with other subject areas. Art studies revolve around local painters who have written books about their technique. Art teachers have teamed with English teachers to link pieces of literature with paintings that correspond in content and style. The ACT Model "Student-Directed Learning and Exhibition" is an example of an extensive project that served as a culminating performance assessment for an upper level art class. Adolescents prepared for this major project by painting seascapes and still life and by learning through perspective drawing, mixed media, collage, pen and ink, sculpture, and print making. The teacher's feedback during these preliminary exercises helped students gain the skills and confidence for the more complex task.

Art instruction can meet the emotional, intellectual, and social needs of adolescent learners. An understanding of technique, style, and context can serve as a springboard for creativity and personal expression as students gain knowledge and an appreciation for art and its value in their lives.

Within each content area is the potential for relevance, extension, and impact on how adolescents view themselves, the world, and their place in it. Ultimately, these students will have to integrate the experiences of schooling into a personal philosophy of living and interacting. In the world of their future, the questions and problems that timelessly shape the content of the disciplines will be real, and adolescent learning will be tested. In this world, perspective, adaptability, flexible thinking, empathetic regard, personal commitment, and self-awareness will matter.

Student-Directed Learning and Exhibition: The Study of an Artist

Adolescents need guidance as they acquire the self-management skills to direct their own learning, yet ultimately they should be given the freedom and responsibility to carry out a project independently. This in-depth artist study is an example. Students choose from among Matisse, Cezanne, Dali, Warhol, Monet, Van Gogh, Vermeer, and others whose styles are distinctive. The culminating performance assessment provides an exhibition format that enables adolescents to "shine" before their peers.

Content Understanding

To enable adolescents to demonstrate an in-depth understanding of the style of a chosen artist.

Key Concepts

Artistic style, technique, expression, and medium

Learning Outcomes

- Students will acquire an understanding of artistic style by researching, interpreting, and emulating the work of a famous artist.
- Students will convey their knowledge of artistic technique through a research paper.

How is personal style reflected in art?

The Inquiry-Based Research

Choose and research an artist of your choice. Your final products must include the following:

1. A research paper about the artist and his or her unique style (the final exam grade)
2. A small copy of a specific work of the artist (to study technique and medium)
3. A large original work that emulates the artist's style in a modern context
4. A presentation before the class about the artist, using your artwork as visuals

Guided Interaction

- The teacher should establish expectations for the project and monitor as students proceed through the four phases. Frequent checkpoints and feedback are critical.

Metacognitive Development and Assessment

- Teachers should require students to keep ongoing journals about the project in order to reflect about their sketches and products.
- The final research paper should be carefully assessed for grammar, spelling, and format. A sample rubric follows.

RESEARCH PAPER RUBRIC

	Excellent (10 pts)	*Good (8–9 pts)*	*Needs Improvement (7 pts)*

Content

1. Contains an interesting and informative introduction with stated topic or paper thesis
2. Develops the thesis thoroughly; supporting information is accurate and appropriate
3. Contains a conclusion that logically summarizes ideas presented about the topic
4. Makes meaningful and relevant connections among references and personal ideas; uses professional vocabulary

Organization

1. Includes a well-developed introduction, body, and conclusion that demonstrate proper, effective paragraphing
2. Uses appropriate transitional words and phrases between sentences and paragraphs and includes a variety of sentence structures

Style

1. Uses and properly references a variety of sources
2. Demonstrates correct use of parenthetical documentation
3. Uses correct bibliographical entries and format on reference page

Usage, Mechanics, and Spelling

Errors in grammar, usage, and spelling: 0–1, excellent; 2–4, good; more than 4, needs improvement

Tips for Good Writing

- Separate major ideas into paragraphs with appropriate indentation and formatting.
- Write complete sentences and not fragments or run-ons.
- Use correct subject-verb agreement, tense, pronoun-antecedent agreement, pronoun case and reference, and avoid double negatives.
- Avoid errors in spelling, capitalization, and end and internal punctuation.

THE ONGOING QUESTION OF CONNECTION AND TRANSFER

Your Ideas

Transfer involves making a learning connection from one context to another. Mathematical skills, for example, are useful when a student is deciding how much tip to leave or calculating the savings on a pair of jeans. Learning how to organize an essay should carry over into the college classroom. The situations are similar, the path for connection is relatively straightforward, and transfer generally happens. A history teacher, however, might wonder why students do not see any parallel between the atrocities in the Sudan and Hitler's attempt to annihilate a Jewish population. The drama teacher might be surprised that students make no apparent link between the satirical content of a play and its historical context, and the language arts teacher might be surprised that students do not recognize the theme of "pride and prejudice" in their own relationships. For these more complex connections, the path is not so explicit, and it generally does not happen.

Perkins and Salomon (1989, p. 137) explained this prevailing problem accordingly: "We want students to make thoughtful interpretations of current events in light of their historical knowledge, but they have learned to remember and retrieve knowledge on cue. We can hardly expect transfer of a performance that has not been learned in the first place!"

Many teachers work hard to bridge the great "disconnect" between adolescent learning and its transfer value through the consideration of learning context. Successful teachers make the context for the new learning similar or familiar to where the transfer connections should be made. Sometimes, learning connections are not so apparently facilitated, and teachers work harder to help adolescents realize and use skills and knowledge from one context in another. Beyond a realistic context, teachers often have to "deliberately provoke" adolescents to think explicitly and metacognitively about where learning might connect, apply, or extend (Perkins & Salomon, 1989). The box below provides a few considerations concerning the ongoing challenge to teach for transfer.

Teaching for Transfer

Don't Shortchange Content

- Select broad curricular concepts, principles, and themes that are "worthy" of transfer.
- Make connections across content areas.

  A language arts teacher organizes literature around themes pertinent to adolescents' lives. For an exploration of human relationship, Bradbury's (1980) "All Summer in a Day," Frost's (1975) "The Mending Wall," and Lee's (1960) *To Kill a Mockingbird* could be used.

  In physics, students are required to read a book by a science fiction author.

Your Ideas

Consider Context

- Structure active, relevant learning experiences that promote understanding.
- Provide a wide, multiple range of comparable, analogous, and contrasting examples.

Through problem-based inquiry into historical events, adolescents better understand social and political systems and hone useful research problem-solving skills.

Civic action research projects expose students to varying perspectives on pertinent societal issues and various ways civic action is defined.

Don't Leave Anything to Chance

- Be deliberate about coaching adolescents to generalize, apply, and adapt learning.
- Provide ongoing opportunity for reflection and assessment.

A social studies teacher uses questioning to help students critique Tiananmen Square documents and to connect this understanding to an essential thinking skill: What is important to consider in the critical analysis of sources? Do you think that what you read in the United States is always credible?

Students in an art class critique their sketches by writing journals, and ultimately help to evaluate themselves through a portfolio and culminating exhibition.

Students develop the habit of asking themselves self-evaluative questions: How can I improve on this presentation? How can I write a more logical paper or better contribute to discussion?

LEARNING AND CONTEXT

The notion of transfer has been and remains complex (Bransford et al., 1999, 2000). Learning is closely connected to the context in which it happens, yet transfer is often contingent upon a good understanding of content. Conversely, since learning is contextualized, adolescents often have trouble adapting to a new situation if it varies from the original learning context. Early theories of transfer emphasized the need for similarity between learning conditions and conditions of transfer. Learning the alphabet, for example, could be transferred to word writing (vertical transfer). Learning in one school task could be transferred to a highly similar one (near transfer), and learning in content areas could be transferred to outside events (far transfer) if certain elements across each situation were identical. Furthermore, learning in one context can negatively

Your Ideas

impact performance in another, for example in solving math problems, because students transfer only a known method and are closed to alternate strategies.

Bransford et al. (2000) regard transfer as it relates to student learning. They emphasize that transfer is affected by the degree to which students initially learn with understanding, rather than memorizing facts, formulas, and procedures. A teacher, for example, helps adolescents learn and apply the formula for circumference and the concept of the Pythagorean theory through a lab in which they measure, calculate, and compare the circumference and radius of several varying circular objects. Through discussion and analysis, they may begin to understand the predictable phenomenon of *pi.* This learning is more likely to transfer to an authentic problem: where to plant a tree on the school grounds to accommodate an expanding root system.

Bransford et al. (2000) offer three other considerations related to transfer and instruction. These include (1) the need for abstract representations rather than knowledge that is overly contextualized; (2) the view of transfer as an active, dynamic process; and (3) the recognition that all new learning is built upon or transferred from previous learning. Adolescents immersed in a physics lab in which they calculate and make predictions about the speed in different intervals of a windup toy gain a better understanding of the formulas for calculating speed and acceleration and of the concept of velocity than if they had been given the formulas to solve with no context. In this example, the teacher might have to stop the lab and remind the adolescents, through a graphed illustration on the white board, the distinction between average velocity and final velocity. The teacher might further scaffold by referring students back to sections in their notebooks where the scientific concepts are defined.

A challenge thus lies in shaping a learning context that is "real enough" for the variety of adolescents in a world of change in the midst of a knowledge explosion. If learning is considered to be connected to context, it is also possible for a realistic instructional situation to be so specific that it actually limits the possibility for transfer. If adolescents are immersed in authentic learning experiences, there is limited assurance that they will know when the application to another situation is appropriate or judge when a particular approach is working.

Fogarty and Bellanca (1995a), who urge teachers to consider the skills students will need in the future, believe students should learn how to relate, how to learn, and how to choose. A "real" learning context for adolescents, then, is one in which they develop the skills for collaboration and personal connection, where they learn about their own learning and how to manage it, and where they practice the skills for knowledge acquisition, analysis, and evaluation.

Cooperative learning, inquiry, problem-solving teams, networking within the broader community through interactive technologies, mentoring, and apprenticeship programs are appropriate contexts for adolescent learning. In such interactive contexts, students are expected to conduct and interpret research, to grapple with moral and ethical issues, to practice reasoning and decision making, and to hone their skills for reflection and evaluation.

Problem-solving strategies are also important to learn for transfer, yet adolescents need to be taught to reason through whether a strategy is appropriate

Your Ideas

or how it might be modified for use in a new situation. Often, they need to "revisit" previous learning through teacher demonstration, questioning, or other scaffolding techniques. They also need to be put in "what if" situations that expose them to a variation of a problem or context, thus teaching them to use skills or apply knowledge flexibly and strategically.

THE CRITICAL ROLE OF THE TEACHER

A critical player in the transfer process is, of course, the teacher (Fogarty, 1995).

- They ask questions that push for connections: Can you identify any situations in real life when people have freedom but act as if they live in Sameness?
- They prompt: Do you recall another time in history when immigration issues caused conflict in the United States?
- They model strategy and scaffold learning: Let's use a K/NK Board to give us a visual for our ideas about the problem. Let's think about the criteria for writing effective persuasion.
- They extend and generalize: Does the technique of the surrealist painters remind you of any literary style? Can you see a use for this decision-making grid in your own life?
- They alter a situation or a problem to encourage flexible and adaptive thinking: If we crumpled the pieces of paper, what impact might it have on the velocity? Let's rewrite Frost's poem in the style of e. e. cummings?

Teachers also structure interactive opportunities that enable adolescents to experience learning in a personal, motivational, and relevant way, such as simulation, role play, seminar, debate, problem-based learning, and other realistic inquiry projects. Teaching for transfer is a complex, ongoing, and interactive process that must be intentionally orchestrated, guided, and mediated. Its goal is to help adolescents learn to use finesse and reasoning independently as they deal with a world shaped by unpredictable context. Ultimately, according to Perkins (1991), transfer is the true "measure" of teaching for understanding.

LEARNING FOR LIFE

The "brave new world" of the twenty-first century is one of international connection and unparalleled channels of rapid communication. Through technological advancements, we have transcended space, distance, and time, and the playing field is increasingly global. Powerful optical and holographic networking allows students to view Egyptian artifacts in Cairo, visit an art studio in Paris, and share ideas simultaneously with others across the world. Photons approximating the speed of light enable virtual communities and limitless exchange of information. In this new century, what people know; how they think, interact with, and treat each other; how they view the world; what they choose to do with their ideas and creativity; and how they regard themselves are critical variables.

Your Ideas

In his book *Horace's Hope: What Works for the American High School,* Sizer (1996) eloquently expresses that the "dance of youth is timeless and beautiful in its awkwardness" (p. 147). Adolescents desire to understand and to grow as human beings. This personal path is not an easy one, and they need guidance, encouragement, and the expectation that they will assess mindfully and reflect thoughtfully on their own development. The development of adolescents' creative spirits and positive attitudes carries long-term implications for the culture and the broader society.

In his book *The Abolition of Man: How Education Develops Man's Sense of Morality,* noted teacher, author, and theologian C. S. Lewis (1947) wrote that the "task of the modern educator is not to cut down jungles but to irrigate deserts" (p. 24). He urged that teachers prepare young people to think for themselves and to consider the impact of personal actions and choices. This challenge speaks to the responsibility of teachers as they ready adolescents for the experiences ahead. Adolescents' education should be characterized by activity and purpose, relevance and challenge, and meaningfulness and responsibility. It should be filled with inquiry, questioning, exploration, interaction, and purposeful collaboration. Ideas should be shared; perspectives exchanged, examined, and developed; and opportunities given to delve deeply into important knowledge and carry it forward into their own lives.

The power to prepare adolescents well for an imaginable and unimaginable future rests with teachers in middle and high school classrooms across this nation and the world. The goal is that adolescents will be ready and inclined to continue the intellectual journey, or, as Sizer (1996) writes, be willing to use their minds well "when no one is looking" (p. 56). The quality of this preparation involves a deliberate effort to help adolescents realize the value of lifelong learning and the need for responsible, responsive living. Education should be more of a broadening, rather than a narrowing. It should be about gaining wisdom. Teachers who understand adolescents and their learning needs, who realize the challenge their future will bring, and who believe in their value and potential, agree.

ACTing

on the Adolescent-Centered Learning Principles Discussed in Chapter 5

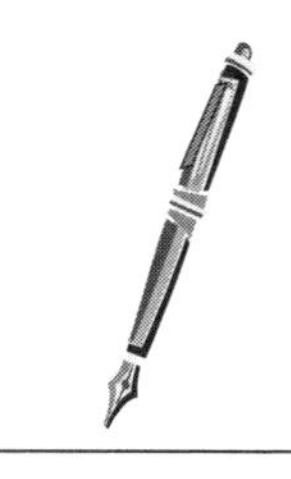

Principle	*How I can put it into practice*
❏ Use content to help adolescents strengthen their thinking skills, develop personal competence, and acquire the strategies and dispositions for self-directed learning.	
❏ Explore the broad concepts and patterns of thinking that give each discipline its substance and distinction.	
❏ Realize the importance of instructional and curricular relevance.	
❏ Develop content around integrated themes, issues, and authentic problems and projects.	
❏ Plan for social interaction and collaboration.	
❏ Foster cognitive, interpersonal, and experiential connections.	
❏ Teach for transfer deliberately through authentic context, flexible adaptation, guided reflection, and purposeful extension.	

References

Adams, D., & Hamm, M. (1999). Science: The truth is not out there. *Kappa Delta Pi Record, 35*(4), 176–179.

Adams, S., & Burns, M. (1999). *Connecting student learning and technology*. Austin, TX: Southwest Educational Development Laboratory.

Alexander, P. A., & Murphy, P. K. (1998). The research base for APA's learner-centered psychological principles. In M. M. Lambert & B. L. McCombs (Eds.), *How students learn* (pp. 25–59). Washington, DC: American Psychological Association.

Alvermann, D. E. (Ed.). (2000). *Adolescents and literacies in a digital world.* New York: Peter Lang.

Ames, C. (1992). Achievement goals and the classroom motivational climate. In D. H. Schunk & J. L. Meece (Eds.), *Student perceptions in the classroom* (pp. 327–348). Hillsdale, NJ: Lawrence Erlbaum.

Anderson, L.W., & Krathwohl, D. R. (Eds.). (2001). *A taxonomy for learning, teaching, and assessing: A revision of Bloom's taxonomy of educational objectives.* New York: Longman.

Aronson, J. (2004, November). The threat of stereotype. *Educational Leadership, 63*(3), 14–18.

Bandura, A. (1993). Perceived self-efficacy in cognitive development and functioning. *Educational Psychologist, 28*(2), 117–148.

Banks, J. (2001). *Cultural diversity and education: Foundations, curriculum, and teaching* (4th ed.). Boston: Allyn & Bacon.

Banks, J. B., & Banks, C. A. M. (2001). *Handbook of research on multicultural education.* New York: Macmillan.

Barell, J. (1995). *Teaching for thoughtfulness: Classroom strategies to enhance intellectual development* (2nd ed.). White Plains, NY: Longman.

Barell, J. (2007). *Problem based learning: An inquiry approach* (2nd ed.). Thousand Oaks, CA: Corwin Press.

Beamon, G. W. (1990). *Classroom climate and teacher questioning strategies: Relationship to student cognitive development.* Unpublished doctoral dissertation, University of North Carolina at Greensboro.

Beamon, G. W. (1992–1993). Making classrooms "safe" for thinking: Influence of classroom climate and teaching questioning strategies on level of student cognitive development. *National Forum of Teacher Education Journal, 2*(1), 4–14.

Beamon, G. W. (1993). Is your classroom "SAFE" for thinking? Introducing an observation instrument to assess classroom climate and teacher questioning strategies. *Journal of Middle Level Research, 17*(1), 4–14.

Beamon, G. W. (1997). *Sparking the thinking of students, ages 10–14: Strategies for teachers.* Thousand Oaks, CA: Corwin Press.

Beamon, G. W. (1999, October). *Using assessment to your (and their) cognitive advantage.* Paper presented at the annual conference of the National Middle School Association, Orlando, Florida.

Beamon, G. W. (2001). *Teaching with adolescent learning in mind.* Thousand Oaks, CA: Corwin Press.

Begley, S. (2000, May 8). Mind expansion: Inside the teenage brain. *Newsweek,* p. 68.

Bellanca, J., & Fogarty, R. (2001). *Blueprints for achievement in the cooperative classroom* (3rd ed.). Thousand Oaks, CA: Corwin Press.

Belton, L. (1996). What our teachers should know and be able to do: A student's voice. *Educational Leadership, 54*(1), 66–68.

Beyer, B. (1987). *Practical strategies for the teaching of thinking.* Boston: Allyn & Bacon.

Bloom, B. S. (Ed.). (1956). *Taxonomy of educational objectives, handbook 1: Cognitive domain.* New York: David McKay.

Blum, R. (2005, April). A case for school connectedness. *Educational Leadership, 62*(7), 16–21.

Bradbury, R. (1980). All summer in a day. In R. Bradbury, *The stories of Ray Bradbury* (pp. 532–536). New York: Alfred A. Knopf.

Brandt, R. (1998). *Powerful learning.* Alexandria, VA: Association for Supervision and Curriculum Development.

Bransford, J. D., Brown, A. L., & Cocking, R. R. (1999). *How people learn: Brain, mind, experience, and school.* Washington: National Academy Press.

Bransford, J. D., Brown, A. L., & Cocking, R. R. (2000). *How people learn: Brain, mind, experience, and school* (Expanded ed.). Washington, DC: National Academy Press. Retrieved June 29, 2006, from http://www.nap.edu/openbook/0309070368/html/

Brashares, A. (2005). *Girls in pants: The third summer of the sisterhood.* New York: Delacorte Press.

Brooks, J. G., & Brooks, M. G. (1993). *In search of understanding: The case for constructivist classrooms.* Alexandria, VA: Association for Supervision and Curriculum Development.

Brown, A. L., & Campione, J. C. (1996). Psychological theory and the design of innovative learning environments: On procedures, principles, and systems. In L. Shauble & R. Glaser (Eds.), *Innovations in learning: New environments for education* (pp. 289–325). Mahwah, NJ: Lawrence Erlbaum.

Burns, M. (2005–2006, December/January). Tools for the mind. *Educational Leadership, 63*(4), 48–53.

Caine, R. N., & Caine, G. (1994). Making connections: Teaching and the human brain (Rev. ed.). Menlo Park, CA: Addison-Wesley.

Caine, R. N., & Caine, G. (1997). *Understanding the power of perceptual change: The potential of brain-based teaching.* Alexandria, VA: Association for Supervision and Curriculum Development.

Caine, R. N., Caine, G., McClintic, F., & Klimek, K. (2005). *The 12 brain/mind principles in action: The fieldbook for making connections, teaching, and the human brain.* Thousand Oaks, CA: Corwin Press.

Carrier, K. A. (2005, November). Key issues for teaching English language learners in academic classrooms. *Middle School Journal, 37*(2), 4–9.

Casey, B. J., Giedd, J. N., & Thomas, K. M. (2000). Structural and functional brain development and its relation to cognitive development. *Biological Psychology, 54*, 241–257.

Center for Media Literacy. (2002–2006). *How to teach media literacy.* Retrieved June 6, 2006, from http://www.medialit.org/focus/tea_home.html

Center for Problem-Based Learning. (1996). *Professional development resource materials.* Aurora, IL: Illinois Mathematical and Science Academy.

Chaffee, J. (2003). *Thinking critically* (7th ed.). Boston: Houghton Mifflin.

Codding, J. B., & Rothman, R. (1999). Just passing through: The life of an American high school. In D. D. Marsh & J. D. Codding (Eds.), *The new American high school* (pp. 3–17). Thousand Oaks, CA: Corwin Press.

Cognition and Technology Group. (1990). Anchored instruction and its relationship to situated cognition. *Educational Researcher, 19*(6), 2–10.

Collins, A., Beranek, B., & Newman, S. E. (1991). Cognitive apprenticeship and instructional technology. In B. F. Jones & L. Idol (Eds.), *Educational values and cognitive instruction: Implications for reform* (pp. 121–139). Hillsdale, NJ: Lawrence Erlbaum.

Collins, A., Brown, J. S., & Newman, S. E. (1989). Cognitive apprenticeship: Teaching the crafts of reading, writing, and mathematics. In L. B. Resnick (Ed.), *Knowing, learning, and instruction: Essays in honor of Robert Glaser* (pp. 453–494). Hillsdale, NJ: Lawrence Erlbaum.

Costa, A. L. (1991). *The school as a home for the mind.* Thousand Oaks, CA: Corwin Press.

Covey, S. (1989). *The seven habits of highly effective people.* New York: Simon & Schuster.

Cummings, J., Bismilla, V., Chow, P., Cohen, S., Giampapa, F., Leoni, L., Sandhu, P., & Sastri, P. (2005, September). Affirming identity in multilingual classrooms. *Educational Leadership, 36*(1), 38–43.

Curtin, E. M. (2006, January). Lesson on effective teaching from middle school ESL students. *Middle School Journal, 37*(3), 38–45.

Daniels, H., & Bizar, M. (1998). *Methods that matter: Six structures for best practice classrooms*. York, ME: Stenhouse Publishers.

Danielson, C. (1996). *Enhancing professional practice: A framework for teaching*. Alexandria, VA: Association for Supervision and Curriculum Development.

Darling, D. (2005, May). Improving minority student achievement by making cultural connections. *Middle School Journal, 36*(5), 46–49.

Darling-Hammond, L. (1997). *The right to learn: A blueprint for creating schools that work*. San Francisco, CA: Jossey-Bass.

Darling-Hammond, L. (1999, April). *The essence of powerful teaching*. Paper presented at the 5th International Teaching for Intelligence Conference, San Francisco.

Davis, G. (2001). There is no four-object limit on attention. *Behavioral and Brain Sciences, 24*(1), 120.

Deci, E. L., & Ryan, R. M. (1998). Need satisfaction and the self-regulation of learning. *Learning and Individual Differences, 8*(3), 165–184.

Delgado-Gaitan, C., & Trueba, H. (1997). *Crossing cultural boundaries: Education for immigrant families in America*. New York: Falmer Press.

Delpit, L. (1995). *Other people's children: Cultural conflict in the classroom*. New York: New York Press.

DePillis, L. (2005–2006, December/January). Taking technology to Takoradi. *Educational Leadership, 63*(4), 80–81.

Dewey, J. (1933). *How we think*. Boston: D. C. Heath.

Dewey, J. (1938). *Experience and education*. New York: Macmillan.

Diamond, M. C. (1967). Extensive cortical depth measurements and neuron size increases in the cortex of environmentally enriched rats. *Journal of Comparative Neurology, 131*, 357–364.

Diamond, M. C. (1988). *Enriching heredity: The impact of the environment on the anatomy of the brain*. New York: Free Press.

Diamond, M. C., & Hopson, J. (1998). *Magic trees of the mind: How to nurture your child's intelligence, creativity, and healthy emotions from birth through adolescence*. New York: Dutton.

Drier, H. S., Dawson, K. M., & Garofalo, J. (1999). Not your typical math class. *Educational Leadership, 56*(5), 21–25.

Eliot, T. S. (1943). *Four quartets*. New York: Harcourt, Brace and World.

Eliot, T. S. (1976). The hollow men. In T. S. Eliot, *The complete poems and plays*. New York: Harcourt Brace Jovanovich.

Elkind, D. (1981). *Children and adolescents: Interpretive essays on Jean Piaget* (3rd ed.). New York: Oxford University Press.

Ennis, R. H. (1987). A taxonomy of critical thinking dispositions and abilities. In J. Baron & R. Sternberg (Eds.), *Teaching thinking skills: Theory and practice* (pp. 9–26). New York: W. H. Freeman.

Erikson, E. H. (1968). *Identity, youth, and crisis*. New York: Norton.

Evans, T. D. (1996). Encouragement: The key to reforming classrooms. *Educational Leadership, 54*(1), 81–85.

Flavell, J. H. (1985). *Cognitive development* (2nd ed.). Upper Saddle River, NJ: Prentice Hall.

Fleming, D. (1996). Preamble to a more perfect classroom. *Educational Leadership, 54*(1), 73–76.

Fogarty, R. (1995). Metacognition. In R. Fogarty (Ed.), *Best practices for the learner-centered classroom* (pp. 239–252). Arlington Heights, IL: IRI/Skylight Training and Publishing.

Fogarty, R., & Bellanca, J. (1995a). Capture the vision: Future world, future school. In R. Fogarty (Ed.), *Best practices for the learner-centered classroom* (pp. 55–72). Arlington Heights, IL: IRI/Skylight Training and Publishing.

Fogarty, R., & Bellanca, J. (1995b). Cognition in practice. In R. Fogarty (Ed.), *Best practices for the learner-centered classroom* (pp. 73–100). Arlington Heights, IL: IRI/Skylight Training and Publishing.

Fogarty, R., & Bellanca, J. (1995c). What does the ultimate cooperative classroom look like? In R. Fogarty (Ed.), *Best practices for the learner-centered classroom* (pp. 183– 203). Arlington Heights, IL: IRI/Skylight Training and Publishing.

Franklin, J. (2005, June). Mental mileage: How teachers are putting brain research to use. *Education Update, 47*(6), 1–3.

Frederick, R. (2005–2006, December/January). Tapping into students' cultural identity. *Educational Leadership, 63*(4), 69–70.

Frieberg, H. J. (1996). From tourists to citizens in the classroom. *Educational Leadership, 54*(1), 32–36.

Frost, R. (1975). The mending wall. In E. C. Lathem (Ed.), *The poetry of Robert Frost* (pp. 33–34). New York: Henry Holt and Company.

Gallagher, J. J. (1998). Preparing the gifted students as independent learners. In J. Leroux (Ed.), *Connecting with the gifted community: Selected proceedings from the 12th World Conference of the World Council for Gifted and Talented Children, Inc.* Ottawa, Canada: Faculty of Education, University of Ottawa.

Gallagher, J. J., & Gallagher, S. A. (1994). *Teaching the gifted child* (4th ed.). Boston: Allyn & Bacon.

Gallagher, S., Stepien, W., Sher, B. T., & Workman, D. (1995). Implementing problem-based learning in science classrooms. *School Science and Mathematics, 95*(3), 136–146.

Gardner, H. (1983). *Frames of mind: The theory of multiple intelligences*. New York: Basic Books.

Gardner, H. (1991). *The unschooled mind: How children think and how schools should teach*. New York: Basic Books.

Gardner, H. (1993). *Multiple intelligences: The theory in practice*. New York: Basic Books.

Gardner, H. (1999). *The disciplined mind: What all students should understand*. New York: Basic Books.

Gay, G. (2002, March/April). Preparing for culturally responsive teaching. *Journal of Teacher Education, 53*(2), 106–116.

Giannetti, C. C., & Sararese, M. (1997). *The roller-coaster years: Raising your child through maddening yet magical middle school years*. New York: Broadway Books.

Gibbs, N. (1999, October 25). A week in the life of a high school. *Time, 154*, 67–82.

Gibbs. N. (2005, August 8). Being 13. *Time, 166*(6), 40–47.

Gibson, W. (2005, July). God's little toys: Confessions of a cut and paste artist. *Wired, 13*, 118–119.

Gilligan, C. E. (1982). *In a different voice: Psychology theory and women's development*. Cambridge, MA: Harvard University Press.

Golding, W. (1962). *Lord of the flies*. New York: Coward-McCann.

Goleman, D. (1995). *Emotional intelligence*. New York: Bantam Books.

Greenfield, S. (1995). *Journey to the center of the mind*. New York: W. H. Freeman.

Greeno, J. G. (1998). The situativity of knowing, learning, and research. *American Psychologist, 53*(1), 5–26.

Gross, P. (1998). *Psylicon beach*. Scholastic Books.

Hempel, J. (2005, December 12). The MySpace Generation. *BusinessWeek Online*. Retrieved November 1, 2006, from http://www.businessweek.com/magazine/content/05_50/b3963001.htm

Howard, J. (2006). The malaria mission. *Project T2*. Retrieved June 28, 2006, from Elon University, Teachers and Technology Project Web site: http://org.elon.edu/t2project/article0003/index.htm.

Howe, N., & Strauss, W. (2000). *Millennials rising: The next great generation*. New York: Vintage Books.

Jenkins, H. (2000, April). Getting into the game. *Educational Leadership, 62*(7), 48–51.

Jensen, E. (1998). *Teaching with the brain in mind*. Alexandria, VA: Association for Supervision and Curriculum Development.

Jensen, E. (2000). *Different brain, different learners*. Thousand Oaks, CA: Corwin Press.

Johnson, D. W. (1979). *Educational psychology*. Englewood Cliffs, NJ: Prentice Hall.

Johnson, D. W., & Johnson, R. (1983). The socialization and achievement crises: Are cooperative learning experiences the solution? In L. Bickman (Ed.), *Applied social psychology annual 4* (pp. 119–164). Beverly Hills, CA: Sage.

Johnson, D. W., Maruyama, G., Johnson, R., Nelson, D., & Skön, L. (1981). Effects of cooperative, competitive, and individualistic goal structures on achievement: A meta-analysis. *Psychological Bulletin, 89*, 47–62.

Jonassen, D. H., Carr, C. S., & Yueh, H. P. (1998, March). Computers as mindtools for engaging learners in critical thinking. *TechTrends, 43*(2), 24–32.

Kagan, S. (1990). *Cooperative learning resources for teachers*. San Juan Capistrano, CA: Resources for Teachers.

Kessler, R. (2000). *The soul of education: Helping students find connection, compassion, and character at school*. Alexandria, VA: Association for Supervision and Curriculum Development.

Kolb, B. (2000). Experience and the developing brain. *Education Canada, 39*(4), 24–26.

Kolberg, L. (1981). *The philosophy of moral development: Moral stages and the idea of justice*. New York: Harper & Row.

Kolberg, L. (1983). *The psychology of moral development: Moral stages and the idea of justice* (2nd ed.). New York: Harper & Row.

LaDoux, J. (1996). *The emotional brain*. New York: Simon & Schuster.

Ladson-Billing, G. J. (1995). Toward a theory of culturally relevant pedagogy. *American Educational Research Journal, 32*, 465–491.

Lambert, N. M., & McCombs, B. L. (1998). Introduction: Learner-centered schools and classrooms as a direction for school reform. In N. M. Lambert & B. L. McCombs (Eds.), *How students learn* (pp. 1–22). Washington, DC: American Psychological Association.

Landsman, J. (2004, November). Confronting the racism of low expectations. *Educational Leadership, 62*(3), 28–32.

Larke, O. J. (1992). Effective multicultural teachers: Meeting the challenges of diverse classrooms. *Equity and Excellence, 24*(2–4), 133–138.

Lazarus, W., Wainer, A., & Lipper, L. (2005). Measuring digital opportunity for America's children: Where we stand and where we go from here. *Contentbank: A project of The Children's Partnership*. Retrieved June 28, 2006, from www.contentbank.org/DOMS.

Lee, H. (1960). *To kill a mockingbird*. New York: Warner.

Lenhart, A., Rainie, L., & Lewis, O. (2001). *Teenage life online: The rise of the instant message generation and the Internet's impact on friendships and family relations*. Washington, DC: Pew Internet and American Life Project.

Lewis, C. S. (1947). *The abolition of man: How education develops man's sense of morality*. New York: Macmillan.

Lickona, T. (1983). *Raising good children*. New York: Bantam.

Lightfoot, S. L. (1983). *The good high school*. New York: Basic Books.

Littky, D., & Allen, F. (1999). Whole-school personalization, one student at a time. *Educational Leadership, 57*(1), 24–28.

Lorain, P. (2002). *Brain development in young adolescents*. Washington, DC: National Education Association. Retrieved November 1, 2006, from http://www.nea.org/ teachexperience/msk 030110.html?mode=print

Lowry, L. (1993). *The giver*. New York: Bantam Doubleday Dell Books for Young Readers.

March, T. (2005–2006, December/January). The new WWW: Whatever, whenever, wherever. *Educational Leadership, 63*(4), 14–19.

Marcus, S. A., & McDonald, P. (1990). *Tools for the cooperative classroom*. Palatine, IL: IRI/Skylight Training and Publishing.

Marzano, R. J., Brandt, R., Hughes, C. S., Jones, B. F., Presseisen, B. Z., Rankin, S., & Suhor, C. (1988). *Dimensions of thinking: A framework for curriculum and instruction*. Alexandria, VA: Association for Supervision and Curriculum Development.

Marzano, R. J., & Kendall, J. S. (1991). *A model continuum of authentic tasks and their assessment*. Aurora, CO: Mid-Continent Regional Educational Laboratory.

Marzano, R. J., Pickering, D. E., Arrendondo, G. J., Blackburn, R. S., Brandt, R. S., & Moffett, C. (1992). *Dimensions of learning*. Alexandria, VA: Association for Supervision and Curriculum Development.

McCombs, B. L. (1993). Learner-centered psychological principles for enhancing education: Applications for school settings. In L. A. Penner, G. M. Batsche, H. M. Knoff, & D. L. Nelson (Eds.), *The challenge in mathematics and science education: Psychology's response* (pp. 287–312). Washington, DC: American Psychological Association.

McCombs, B. L., & Whisler, J. S. (1997). *The learner centered classroom and school: Strategies for enhancing student motivation and achievement*. San Francisco, CA: Jossey-Bass.

Metivier, L., & Sheive, L. (1990). *A guide to STePS: Structured team problem solving*. Baldwinsville, NY: STePS Associates.

Miller, A. (1958). *Death of a salesman*. New York: Viking Press.

National Clearinghouse for English Language Acquisition (NCELA). (2004). *In the classroom: A toolkit for effective instruction of English learners*. Retrieved June 28, 2006, from http://www.ncela.gwu.edu/practice/itc/secondary.html

Nelson, G. D. (1999). Science literacy for all in the 21st century. *Educational Leadership, 57*(2), 14–18.

Nelson, K. (2001). *Teaching in the cyberage: Linking the Internet and brain theory*. Thousand Oaks, CA: Corwin Press.

Nieto, S. (2000). *Affirming diversity: The sociopolitical context of multicultural education* (3rd ed.). New York: Longman.

Ohler, J. (2005–2006, December/January). The world of digital storytelling. *Educational Leadership, 63*(4), 44–47.

Ormond, J. E. (2000). *Educational psychology: Developing learners* (3rd ed.). Columbus, OH: Prentice Hall.

Palincsar, A. S., & Brown, A. L. (1984). Reciprocal teaching of comprehension-fostering and comprehension-monitoring activities. *Cognition and Instruction, 1*, 117–175.

Palmer, P. J. (1998). *The courage to teach: Exploring the inner landscape of a teacher's life*. San Francisco: Jossey-Bass.

Palmer, P. J. (1998–1999). Evoking the spirit in public education. *Educational Leadership, 56*(4), 6–11.

Paris, S. G., & Winograd, P. (1990). How metacognition can promote academic learning and instruction. In B. F. Jones & L. Idol (Eds.), *Dimensions of thinking and cognitive instruction* (pp. 53–92). Hillsdale, NJ: Lawrence Erlbaum.

Paul, R. (1998). *Critical thinking: Basic theory and instructional structures*. Santa Rosa, CA: Foundation for Critical Thinking.

Paul, R., & Binker, A. J. A. (1995a). Critical thinking and the social studies. In J. Willsen & A. J. A. Binker (Eds.), *Critical thinking: How to prepare students for a rapidly changing world* (pp. 475–487). Santa Rosa, CA: Foundation for Critical Thinking.

Paul, R., & Binker, A. J. A. (1995b). Socratic questioning. In J. Willsen & A. J. Binker (Eds.), *Critical thinking: How to prepare students for a rapidly changing world* (pp. 335–365). Santa Rosa, CA: Foundation for Critical Thinking.

Payne, R. (2006). *Understanding and working with children and adults in poverty*. Retrieved June 28, 2006, from Western Michigan University, Department of Teaching, Learning, and Leadership, Professor Lynn Nations Johnson Web site: http://homepages.wmich.edu/~ljohnson/Payne.pdf

Pea, R. D. (1993). Practices of distributed intelligence and designs in education. In G. Saloman (Ed.), *Distributed cognitions: Psychological and educational considerations* (pp. 47–87). New York: Cambridge University Press.

Perkins, D. N. (1986). *Knowledge as design*. Hillsdale, NJ: Lawrence Erlbaum.

Perkins, D. N. (1991). Educating for insight. *Educational Leadership, 29*(2), 4–8.

Perkins, D. N. (1992). *Smart schools: From training memories to educating minds*. New York: The Free Press.

Perkins, D. N. (1999). The many faces of constructivism. *Educational Leadership, 57*(3), 6–11.

Perkins, D. N., & Salomon, G. (1989). Teaching for transfer. In R. Brandt (Ed.), *Teaching thinking* (pp. 131–141). Alexandria, VA: Association for Supervision and Curriculum Development.

Piaget, J. (1928). *Judgment and reasoning in the child* (M. Warden, Trans.). New York: Norton.

Pintrich, P. R., & Schrauben, B. (1992). Student motivational beliefs and their cognitive engagement in classroom academic tasks. In D. H. Schunk & J. L. Meece (Eds.), *Student perceptions in the classroom* (pp. 149–183). Hillsdale, NJ: Lawrence Erlbaum.

Prensky, M. (2005–2006, December/January). Listen to the natives. *Educational Leadership, 63*(4), 9–13.

Price, L. F. (2005, April). The biology of risk taking. *Educational Leadership, 62*(7), 22– 26.

Ramachandran, V. S. (2006, January 12). Mirror neurons and the brain in the vat. *Edge, 176*. Retrieved November 1, 2006, from www.edge.org/3rd_culture/ramachandran06/ramachandran06_index.html

Renard, L. (2000, April). Teaching the DIG generation. *Educational Leadership, 62*(7), 44–47.

Resnick, L. B. (1987). *Education and learning to think.* Washington, DC: National Academy Press.

Resnick, L. B. (1991). Shared cognition: Thinking as social practice. In L. B. Resnick, J. M. Levine, & S. D. Teasley (Eds.), *Perspectives on socially shared cognition* (pp. 1–20). Washington, DC: American Psychological Association.

Resnick, L. B. (1999, April). *Learning organizations for sustainable educational reform.* Paper presented at the 5th International Teaching for Intelligence Conference, San Francisco.

Richardson, W. (2005–2006, December/January). The educator's guide to the read/write web. *Educational Leadership, 63*(4), 24–27.

Roth, K. J. (1990). Developing meaningful conceptual understanding in science. In B. F. Jones & L. Idol (Eds.), *Dimensions of thinking and cognitive instruction* (pp. 139–175). Hillsdale, NJ: Lawrence Erlbaum.

Ryan, T. M. (1995). Psychological needs and the facilitation of integrative processes. *Journal of Personality, 63*(3), 397–427.

Sagor, R. (1996). Building resiliency in students. *Educational Leadership, 54*(1), 38–43.

Saloman, G., Perkins, D., & Globerson, T. (1991). Partners in cognition: Extending human intelligences with intelligent technologies. *Educational Researcher, 20*(3), 2–9.

Schneider, B., & Stevenson, D. (1999). *The ambitious generation: America's teenagers, motivated but directionless.* New Haven: Yale University Press.

Schneider, E. (1996). Giving students a voice in the classroom. *Educational Leadership, 54*(1), 22–26.

Schoen, H. L., Fey, J. T., Hirsch, C. R., & Coxford, A. F. (1999). Issues and options in the math wars. *Phi Delta Kappa, 80*(6), 444–453.

Schoenfeld, A. H. (1985). *Mathematical problem solving.* San Diego: Academic Press.

Schunk, D. H. (1994). Self-regulation of self-efficacy and attributions in academic settings. In D. H. Schunk & B. J. Zimmerman (Eds.), *Self-regulation of learning and performance: Issues and educational applications* (pp. 75–99). Hillsdale, NJ: Lawrence Erlbaum.

Schurr, S. L. (1989). *Dynamite in the classroom.* Columbus, OH: National Middle School Association.

Sharan, S., & Sharon, Y. (1976). *Small-group teaching.* Englewood Cliffs, NJ: Educational Technology Publications.

Shelton, C. M. (1999). How innersense builds common sense. *Educational Leadership, 57*(1), 61–64.

Short, D., & Echevarria, J. (2004–2005, December/January). Teacher skills to support English language learners. *Educational Leadership, 62*(4), 8–13.

Shuell, T. J. (1993). Toward an integrated theory of teaching and learning. *Educational Psychologist, 28*(4), 291–311.

Siegal, D. J. (1999). *The developing mind: Toward a neurobiology of interpersonal experience.* New York: Guilford.

Silverman, S. (1993). Student characteristics, practice, and achievement in physical education. *Journal of Educational Research, 87*, 1.

Simpkins, M. (1999). Designing great rubrics. *Technology and Learning, 20*(1), 23–30.

Simmons, S. (1995, December). Drawing as thinking. *Think Magazine, 6*(2), 23–29.

Sizer, T. R. (1984). *Horace's compromise: The dilemma of the American high school.* Boston: Houghton Mifflin.

Sizer, T. R. (1992). *Horace's school: Redesigning the American high school.* Boston: Houghton Mifflin.

Sizer, T. R. (1996). *Horace's hope: What works for the American high school.* Boston: Houghton Mifflin.

Sizer, T. R., & Sizer, N. F. (1999). *The students are watching: Schools and the moral contract.* Boston: Beacon Press.

Slavin, R. E. (1980). *Using student team learning.* Baltimore, MD: Johns Hopkins University, Center for Social Organization of Schools.

Sousa, D. (2001). *How the brain learns: A classroom teacher's guide.* Thousand Oaks, CA: Corwin Press.

Spinks, S. (2002). Adolescent brains are works in progress: Here's why. *Inside the teenage brain.* Retrieved June 25, 2006, from http://www.pbs.org/wgbh/pages/frontline/shows/teenbrain/work/adolescent.html

Sprenger, M. (1999). *Learning and memory: The brain in action.* Alexandria, VA: Association for Supervision and Curriculum Development.

Stepien, W., & Gallagher, S. (1997). *Problem-based learning across the curriculum: An ASCD professional kit*. Alexandria, VA: Association for Supervision and Curriculum Development.

Sternberg, R. J. (1985). *Beyond IQ: A triarchic theory of human intelligence*. New York: Cambridge University Press.

Stevenson, C. (2002). *Teaching ten to fourteen year olds* (3rd ed.). Boston: Allyn & Bacon.

Stiggins, R. J. (1994). *Student-centered classroom assessment*. New York: Macmillan College Publishing.

Strauch, B. (2003). *The primal teen: What the new discoveries about the teenage brain tell us about our kids*. New York: Anchor Books.

Strong, R., Silver, H. F., & Robinson, A. (1995). What do students want (and what really motivates them)? *Educational Leadership, 53*(1), 8–12.

Swartz, R. J., & Perkins, D. N. (1989). *Teaching thinking: Issues and approaches*. Pacific Grove, CA: Midwest Publications.

Sylwester, R. (1999). *A celebration of neurons: An educator's guide to the human brain*. Alexandria, VA: Association for Supervision and Curriculum Development.

Sylwester, R. (2003). *A biological brain in a cultural classroom: Enhancing cognitive and social development through collaborative classroom management* (2nd ed.). Thousand Oaks, CA: Corwin Press.

Sylwester, R. (2004). *How to explain a brain: An educator's handbook of brain terms and cognitive processes*. Thousand Oaks, CA: Corwin Press.

Sylwester, R. (2006). Connecting brain processes to school policies and practices: A monthly column. *Brain Connection*. Retrieved June 28, 2006, from http://www.brainconnection.com/library/?main=talkhome/columnists

Thompson, P. M., Giedd, J. N., Woods, R. P., MacDonald, D., Evans, A. C., & Toga, A. W. (2000). Growth patterns in the developing brain detected by using continuum mechanical tensor maps. *Nature, 404*(6774), 190–193.

Tishman, S., Perkins, D. N., & Jay, E. S. (1995). *The thinking classroom: Learning and teaching in the culture of thinking*. Boston: Allyn & Bacon.

Tomlinson, C. A. (1999). *The differentiated classroom: Responding to the needs of all learners*. Alexandria, VA: Association for Supervision and Curriculum Development.

Tomlinson, C. A. (2005, August). Differentiating instruction: Why bother? *Middle Ground, 9*(1), 12–14.

Tomlinson, C. A., & Doubet, K. (2005, April). Reach them to teach them. *Educational Leadership, 62*(7), 9–15.

Torpe, L., & Sage, S. (1998). *Problems as possibilities: Problem-based learning for K–12 education*. Alexandria, VA: Association for Supervision and Curriculum Development.

Torpe, L., & Sage, S. (2002). *Problems as possibilities: Problem-based learning for K–12 education* (2nd ed.). Alexandria, VA: Association for Supervision and Curriculum Development.

Twain, M. (1954). *Adventures of Huckleberry Finn*. Garden City, New York: Junior Deluxe Editions.

Twist, J. (2004, June 6). Teenagers reach out via weblogs. *BBC News Online*. Retrieved November 1, 2006, from http://news.bbc.co.uk/2/hi/technology/3774389.stm

Valenza, J. K. (2005–2006, December/January). The virtual library. *Educational Leadership, 63*(4), 54–59.

Van Hoose, J., Strahan, D., & L'Esperance, M. (2001). *Young adolescent development and school practices: Promoting harmony*. Westerville, OH: National Middle School Association.

Vonnegut, K., Jr. (1968). Harrison Bergeron. In K. Vonnegut, Jr., *Welcome to the monkey house: A collection of short stories* (pp. 7–13). New York: Delacorte.

Vygotsky, L. S. (1962). *Thought and language*. Cambridge: MIT Press.

Vygotsky, L. S. (1978). *Mind in society: The development of higher psychological processes*. Cambridge, MA: Harvard University Press.

Whitman, D. (2005, May 10). The next great generation? Mysteries of the Teen Years [Special issue]. *U.S. News and World Report*, pp. 4–11.

Wiggins, G. P., & McTighe, J. (1998). *Understanding by design*. Alexandria, VA: Association for Supervision and Curriculum Development.

Wilson, L. M., & Horch, H. D. (2002, September). Implications of brain research for teaching young adolescents. *Middle School Journal, 34*(1), 57–61.

Wilson, M. (2001). The case for sensorimotor coding in working memory. *Psychonomic Bulletin & Review, 8*(1), 57.

Wolfe, P. R. (1996). *Translating brain research into classroom practice*. Alexandria, VA: Association for Supervision and Curriculum Development.

Wolfe, P. R. (2001). *Brain matters: Translating research into classroom practice*. Alexandria, VA: Association for Supervision and Curriculum Development.

Wolfe, P. R., & Brandt, R. (1998). What do we know from brain research? *Educational Leadership, 56*(3), 8–13.

Yoder, M. B. (1999, April). The student WebQuest. *Learning and Leading with Technology, 26*(7). Retrieved November 1, 2006, from http://www.iste.org/Content/NavigationMenu/Publications/LL/LLIssues/Volume_26_1998_1999_/April10/The_Student_WebQuest.htm

Zimmerman, B. J. (1994). Dimensions of academic self-regulation: A conceptual framework for education. In D. H. Schunk & B. J. Zimmerman (Eds.), *Self-regulation of learning and performance: Issues and educational applications* (pp. 3–21). Hillsdale, NJ: Lawrence Erlbaum.

Index

CORWIN
PRESS